The Family Therapist

By J. C. WYNN:

The Family Therapist
Family Therapy in Pastoral Ministry
Pastoral Ministry to Families
Families in the Church: A Protestant Survey (With Roy W. Fairchild)
How Christian Parents Face Family Problems
Christian Education for Liberation and Other Upsetting Ideas

Edited by J. C. WYNN
Sermons on Marriage and Family Life
Sex, Family and Society in Theological Focus
Sexual Ethics and Christian Responsibility

The Family Therapist

J.C. Wynn

Fleming H. Revell Company
Old Tappan, New Jersey

Quotation from ON BECOMING A PERSON, by Carl R. Rogers © 1961. Used by permission of Houghton Mifflin Co.

Quotation from HELPING COUPLES CHANGE, by Richard B. Stuart copyright © 1980. Used by permission of Guilford Press.

Quotations from FOUNDATIONS OF FAMILY THERAPY: A Conceptual Framework for Systems Change by Lynn Hoffman. Copyright © 1981 by Basic Books, Inc., Publishers.

Extracts from FAMILY THERAPY TECHNIQUES, by Salvador Minuchin and H. Charles Fishman reprinted by permission of Harvard University Press. Copyright © 1981 by the President and Fellows of Harvard College.

Library of Congress Cataloging-in-Publication Data

Wynn, John Charles, date
    The family therapist.

    Bibliography: p.
    1. Pastoral counseling.   2. Family psychotherapy.
3. Family therapists.   I. Title.
BV4012.2.W88   1987   616.89′156′0242   87-311
ISBN 0-8007-1530-6

With faith, hope, and love
for
Robert, Elisabeth, Emily, John, and Clark,
Our family's newest generation.

Acknowledgments

More than anything I have previously written, this book is the product of cooperative consultations. I owe a debt of gratitude to the family therapists who are discussed here; many of them showed considerable generosity in their responses to requests and queries. I am deeply indebted as well to students, administration, and colleagues at the multidenominational consortium of Colgate Rochester/Bexley Hall/Crozer Divinity School for the opportunity to teach and supervise the curriculum of family ministries over so many years.

To a trio of medical specialists—James M. Stewart, M.D., Arthur Moss, M.D., and James Dewees, M.D.—I am deeply grateful for their skills in coronary treatment and surgery that added the years to do this work. And to my wife, Rachel, I am profoundly thankful for her characteristic encouragement and help in the writing of this, another book; the persons to whom it is dedicated are also her grandchildren.

I thank editor William F. Hunter for permission to use the slightly altered quote "Carl Whittaker's Therapy of the Absurd"; this chapter 3 is presently in press as an article in *The Journal of Psychology and Theology*.

To three friends with expertise in psychotherapy I note a particular debt of thanks: Duncan M. Stanton, M.D., James Edd

Jones, Ph.D., and Roy W. Fairchild, Ph.D., all read portions of the typescript and offered the benefit of their valuable comments.

For the favors of technical services I thank artist Todd Rohnke, and the staff at Ambrose Swasey Library.

Many of these ideas were tried out before audiences in a dozen seminaries. Portions of this material were used in lectures or courses at Pittsburgh Theological Seminary, Princeton Seminary, Union Theological Seminary, San Francisco Theological Seminary, and Saint Bernard's Seminary. Other aspects of this material were delivered in Korea at Seoul Presbyterian Seminary and at Taejon Presbyterian Seminary, and in the Republic of South Africa at Rhodes University, Stellenbosch University, and Federal Seminary. Still other portions of these chapters were first explored in lectures at the University of Rochester, St. John Fisher College, and Alderson-Broaddus College. In all these experiences I enjoyed the compliment of the invitations, the courteous hospitality of my hosts, and the stimulating interchange with students.

J.C.W.

Contents

III
Multigenerational Family Therapists

IV
Psychodynamic Family Therapists

V
Behavioral Family Therapists

Introduction:
What the Clergy
Can Learn
From Family Therapists

When under unbearable stress, the average person turns more often to the clergy than to any other counselor. Time and again, replicated surveys rediscover that individuals or families in emotional turmoil first seek out a minister, priest, or rabbi to help them. This was the conclusion of Gerald Gurin and his colleagues in an inquiry nearly three decades ago, when they researched the nation's mental health.[1] Later a survey of 2,645 pastors verified this trend;[2] it was recently reconfirmed by Richard Kulka and his research team at the University of Michigan in 1979.[3]

What leads troubled persons so promptly to the pastor's study? Are they convinced that clergy are to be trusted? Do they ascribe to us a caring attitude? Is it because we are available and recognizable in every community (there are nearly a half million of us), or because our consultative time is free? Whatever the varied reasons that congregants and nonmembers alike seek us out, we clergy have this one characteristic in common: Our pastoral counseling has a spiritual base. That this is in contrast to secular family therapists can be seen in one sentence of a report from the Group for the Advancement of Psychiatry: "Very few therapists, regardless of their religious affiliation, ascribe a religious motivation to their conducting of family therapy."[4]

Clergy bring a different style to their work. Persons who consult them for symptomatic relief may be surprised when counseling also guides them to spiritual growth. Solving the immediate problem does not completely fulfill the task of pastoral care. That task calls for assisting persons in their spiritual development as well, for the pastor's work will go beyond the level of technical skills. As Henri Nouwen has noted, the minister is called to be skillful but not a handyman, knowledgeable but not an imposter, professional but not a manipulator.[5] The minister has the responsibility to speak the word of assurance concerning God's forgiveness in pastoral counseling as well as in divine worship. Thus the pastoral counselor assists not only in personal and family problem solving, but also in sorting out theological ethics and providing spiritual direction.

The Family Is a System

It is hardly surprising that the clergy repeatedly work with life's most intimate problems: helping persons find meaning in living; guiding them to love and be loved; coaching them in forming satisfactory relationships. These quests are close to the inmost soul of persons, to their sexual identity, to marriage, to parenting. To accomplish such work requires the counselor to be skilled in interpersonal relationships. This makes the difference between simply viewing a marital problem as a difficulty between two persons with their separate pains or seeing their relationship as a system in need of repair.

Clergy report that they are involved in pastoral counseling four to five hours each week. The bulk of this practice involves intimate family relationships. Thus the pastor's counseling load overlaps the family outreach of the church. The magnitude of this task is illustrated by Charles Stewart, who notes the ongoing needs of families within the parish:

> The congregation is made up of families at the various stages of their development. Week in and week out, these families experience accidental crises or go through various "passages": a child is born, an elderly person dies, someone is married, someone else divorces, and the families must adjust. Widows, single

parents, and divorced persons do not stand outside the ministry; they, too, need . . . support.[6]

Pastors not only see families in counseling situations but also visit families in home calling. They engage in family therapy wherever disabling relationship problems have arisen, learning to deal contextually with the family as a system, rather than as a collection of individuals. Indeed, the principle that unites all family therapists is the conviction that therapeutic change takes place exactly where the pain arose—within the family system.

Despite this unifying principle, therapists may vary considerably as to techniques they employ and theories to which they adhere, as the following chapters show; yet all share the common conviction that relationships are at least as important in people's behavior as unconscious, intrapsychic elements. It is generally assumed in the field of family therapy that a major part of the counseling task consists of lifting the "problem" label from any one member and allowing the entire family system to share that responsibility.

The pastoral counselor acting as a family therapist serves as a bridge, someone to whom the family may look for steady support and aid in getting across to one another until they can develop new patterns of communication enabling them to reach one another directly. Clergy also serve as models by demonstrating alternative moves and actions. This is done when confronting a blustering, tyrannical father, or practicing forbearance with a frenetic, manipulative mother, or exhibiting support for the frightened fourteen-year-old in her pregnancy.

We clergy have no choice about performing family counseling in our ministry; our only choice is whether we shall do so intelligently or carelessly. There is much for us to learn from professionals in the field of family therapy. Many of their methods and concepts can be adopted for our vocation. To that end, the two dozen family therapists are discussed in the chapters that follow; their usable techniques are described, and their examples are organized for reference in the Index.

Finding Your Way

For years I have been engrossed with the question of how the work of pastoral ministry can integrate the task of family therapy into practical theology. In my earlier publication, family systems theory was introduced, techniques of therapy were described, resources were detailed.[7] For this volume, two dozen leading family therapists were chosen for discussion; their distinctive styles are described to serve as usable examples for clergy.

This work is formulated for the relative newcomer to family therapy. Both seminarians and ordained clergy will find here a selection of ideas that approximate our ministerial needs. These specialists' sometimes harmonious, sometimes divergent theories are presented so that pastors might examine them, understand them, and use them in their own way. These chapters constitute an introduction to a more complete and complex corpus available directly from the family therapists. Readers who desire further information concerning any of these therapists are urged to consult their original works and attend their workshop offerings.

Each of the chapters to follow shares the same outline:
- A typical quotation from the therapist under study
- A brief biographical sketch of the therapist
- His or her style of therapy and its techniques
- Basic theoretical concepts undergirding the therapy
- Suggested applications for pastoral ministry.

The family therapists have been organized into five major categories: experiential, systemic, multigenerational, psychodynamic, and behavioral.

The first group (Satir, Whitaker, Rogers, Attneave, and Speck) is designated *experiential* not because they are from the tradition of the existential philosophers (for they are not), or even because they are all influenced by "third force" psychology, with its emphasis upon self-actualizing possibilities (as they are). Instead, they are grouped here because each works to provide families an intensive, affective experience that can thaw out their frozen tendencies and relationships.

In the second group, the *systemic* family therapists, seven leaders are described who use strategic, structural, and problem-solving theories. Their commonality is found in their use of communication therapy and their conviction that every family is a system, therefore therapy must take into account the family's systemic characteristics. Haley, Minuchin, Zuk, Weakland, Watzlawick, and the Duhls, despite their obvious individual differences, combine such systemic approaches and communication techniques in their service with families.

The *multigenerational* group hold in common their expectation that they will reach not only those members of a family who come for counseling, but their parents and children as well. Bowen, Framo, Boszormenyi-Nagy, and Paul trace the family of origin in order to find a key to the present generation. They, who also work with family systems, are especially concerned with the transmission of interactional patterns through a type of genealogy.

Psychodynamic family therapists, such as Ackerman, Bell, Wynne, and Kramer, while not unmindful of experience, communication, and system, operate out of a somewhat more apparent psychoanalytic orientation. To a man, each has based his therapeutic work upon that orientation and combined with it his own individual contribution and interpretation. Particularly interested in the projections we press onto our intimate relations and our interior, or intrapsychic, processes, they seek possibilities for self-motivated change in relationships.

Behavioral modification is the treatment of choice among the fifth group (Skinner's followers, Stuart, Kaplan, and Alexander). In their work with families and individuals, they combine behavioral therapy with their specialties, whether these be marital problems, sexual dysfunctions, or children's disorders. Their contribution is in family interactions, where reinforcement of behavior becomes a means of motivating conduct change.

It has been necessary to confine this study to family therapists of North America. There are luminaries in this field to be found in Milan, Rome, London, and Heidelberg: Maria Palazzoli-

Selvini, Maurizio Andolfi, A. C. Robin Skynner, Helm Stierlin. Likewise it is evident that there are other topics of importance in family ministries; one has only to think of family enrichment, family education, and premarital guidance, to name a few. The emphasis herein, however, is on pastoral theology and the development of ways to relieve some of the distress of church families.

It is to be hoped that this work may alert pastors to the systemic context in which individuals and families operate and may teach them the rudiments of using that context in their ministry of pastoral care. More than that an author need not ask.

I

Experiential
Family Therapists

1

Virginia Satir's
Conjoint Family Therapy

My treatment process is the same, regardless of whether the diagnosis is a psychiatric one or a social one, because I believe the two are merely different ways of labeling the dysfunctional process.

Virginia Satir

It was the first interview with the family: a visibly anxious clergyman, his nervous wife, and their sullen adolescent son, who had impregnated two teenage girls. The parents, consumed with remorse and anger, gazed glumly at the floor; the son sat isolated in the corner of the treatment room. Virginia Satir, the family therapist, took it in at a glance, looked at the boy, and then opened her interview with one astonishing sentence: "We know one thing for sure; we know that you have good seed."[1]

Donald Bloch was later to observe about that now-famous incident, "In one sentence we have positive connotation, reframing, a master power balancing—and likely enough a 'deep' interpretation of the history and dynamics of the event. . . . Satir is *sui generis*."[2]

In some ways Virginia Satir is closer to the clergy than many of the family therapists we study. With a nascent Christian humanness in her work, she can say such things as, "I am interested in

the soul. Right now I am especially interested in the spiritual part
of the human being. I decided to get into psychology because
I am committed to helping people with pain." Her treatment
of people, her compassion, her understanding, and her forgiving
demeanor place her in harmony with normative pastoral counseling.

But it is her renowned skill as a therapist that commends her
most to us. As Bernard L. Greene has observed, "She is endowed
with ability both to comprehend quickly what is going on in the
conjoint sessions and to think freely about the material in precise
psychodynamic terms."[3] Certainly no one can doubt that she is
precise. Nor would those who have seen her in action doubt her
when she states, "I enter the therapeutic situation with the expectation that change is possible and with a clear, delineated
structure for encouraging change."[4]

Who is Virginia Satir? Trained as a psychiatric social worker,
her reputation has actually grown out of her astonishing abilities
as a trainer of therapists. In that work she has served in medical
schools, schools of social work, theological seminaries, and scores
of workshops. She was once associated with the legendary Palo
Alto group that included Don Jackson, Jay Haley, Gregory Bateson, and John Weakland, who together worked out a comprehensive communication theory for family therapy. Later she became
program director at Esalen in Big Sur, where she developed a
concept of encounter groups and advanced the spread of the
human potential movement.

As a therapist, her emphasis is not on pathology, for she de-
emphasizes sickness, but on the relationships that hamper development or block maturity. Her once unorthodox ideas, now rapidly becoming standard teachings, have been of aid to couples,
parents, entire families, teachers, other therapists, and ministers.

Virginia Satir's Therapy

Satir enters a dysfunctional family as a concerned relative. No
distant, psychoanalytic stance for her, no cool objectivity with

even-voiced reflections of "Mmmm." She walks into the family system with warm interest, relating meaningfully to each person, greeting them, touching them, earnestly considering each of their contributions to the communication.

She looks forward, she reports, to three kinds of changes in each family member: a change in the perception of themselves, a change in the way each manifests thoughts and feelings, and a change in the way each reacts to the stimulus and feedback of the others.

Characteristically, Satir begins by relating to the hurt that persons in the family are feeling. In one remarkable demonstration of her technique recorded on the videotape "A Family in Crisis," Satir plunges at once into the pain that an all but immobilized family is experiencing. Then, in a sequence unique in family-therapy teaching materials, she is shown ministering to a fourteen-year-old girl who drops into an epileptic seizure during the session. Dr. Satir, still on camera, directs the care of the child and continues to deal with the family's relationship problem.

Among her wide-ranging techniques and aptitudes, she regularly works with five: modeling communication, correcting perceptions, relabeling reported emotions, reviewing family history, and rebuilding ego strength.

Modeling Communication

In the teaching of effective communication, as in anything else, showing the way by example is notably more effective than telling about it. Virginia Satir teaches people to be alert and to listen for confused and covert messages, helping them state their feelings in plain truth through examples of her own leveling in communication. This gives her counselees permission to do likewise, and encourages a clarifying openness to which a dysfunctional family would not otherwise be accustomed. She observes lines of communication, then comments about them, drawing attention to covert messages, to underlying meanings, and to recurring themes. As a therapist, she not only has this expertise in communication, but also the freedom within the family system that allows her sufficient leverage to budge that system. From being with her, families learn what straightforward communication can be and what wonders it can perform.

In communication analysis, the therapist observes how partners give and receive meaning and how they check out meaning with each other. Satir's analysis divides this transaction into four parts:

• *Persons:* Who speaks, and for whom, and who attributes credit or blame to the others

• *Congruency:* How they get their message across in language, voice tone, facial expression, or body position

• *Delineation:* How easily the person is heard and seen

• *Sequence:* For example, the wife's manifestation, her husband's response, his wife's response to his response, and then his response to her response to him.

Satir also cites three devices by which couples or families can understand what they are communicating. In the first of these, she reports fully what she hears and sees and how she understands what she sees and hears. Some therapists, according to Satir, only interpret their conclusions about what they see and hear, without also telling of their perceptions. This, she believes, contributes to what is often declared resistance by therapists.

In the second device, Satir acts as a model of communication. Thus she can ask, clarify, tell, and teach them to do likewise. "By commenting on anything and everything that seems obvious, I encourage patients to give up fears of dangerous information," she once told a group of counselors.

Her third device is to act as a resource person for her patients. Having specialized knowledge, Satir believes that she must share it in educational and collegial ways. Reflecting what patients are saying and modeling open communication for them is not enough, unless she can also pass on to them her knowledge of how they can improve their relationships.

Correcting Perceptions

Ready to correct perceptions of feeling, Satir will call attention to emotional reactions that family members have long since learned to ignore: "Can you hear the pain in her voice?" she will ask. Or, with insight that astonishes families, she will direct, "Tell him once more. We can't always understand each other when we're angry or scared." Placaters, who can never seem to say anything pointedly, may be directed to restate their message with the challenge, "Is that what you really meant to say?"

A typically dysfunctional family is unready for plain talk and unaccustomed to clear meanings, but Satir's method is to move directly into such problems. She coaches them in the ways they comment in the presence of others. She helps them express how they feel, think, and perceive themselves and others.

With such careful attention to communication, this therapist is able to aid marital partners and family members to correct their erroneous perceptions about one another. Without some such intervention, families are capable of persistent communicative blocks lasting for generations.

In dysfunctional families, the individuals continue to see one another as they expect them to be, rather than as they truly are. A family with this hapless tendency never takes into account changes for the better and never moves into improved relations until something therapeutic happens in their grim lives. As long as they are unable to comment upon their tragic situation, it goes unaided and perhaps even unnoticed. With habitually poor communication, these people rarely discover their unrealistic expectations of one another, so they are disappointed. They experience this disappointment as betrayal or rejection.

For this reason, Satir works toward correcting a family's conflictual and confused perceptions. She checks out what the speaker meant to convey in a message. She also checks out the receiver's conclusions about the intentions of the sender. Such a deliberate process aids the family in checking with one another about the giving and receiving of meanings. That simple yet unusual exercise is the goal of a communications family therapist.

Relabeling Observations

In another method of helping patients understand what they are saying to one another, Satir follows the practice of relabeling emotions that are inadequately reported. This has the virtue of picking up the reverse side of a statement and finding a positive message in a negative report. For example, anger may be interpreted as fright, or interference as caring.

Sometimes relabeling enables the therapist to remove the uncomplimentary label hung on a person and place it instead on a rule: The problem may not be so much in "uncooperative" Henry, as a person, as it is in the rule saying he must empty the trash before 8 A.M. When that kind of relabeling is executed by Satir, she aids both Henry and his parents in maintaining a higher sense of self-worth.

In Satir's opinion, unwise rules contribute to family breakdown: A rule is unwise when it does not fit in with the individual's private rules for survival, growth, and productivity. It is no surprise to learn that her therapeutic efforts are designed to change the rules, which in turn means changing the system.

An example of Satir's relabeling is found in a task she calls "separating the self from others," the ability to recognize the other's skin boundaries and acknowledge the other as a separate mechanism that runs on its own time. Without this ability, we will expect another person to become cold or thirsty or to desire sex at the same time as we do. She writes, "I take every opportunity to translate the concept of differentness, which is often used as a prelude to war, into a concept of uniqueness, which can be used as a stimulus to growth."[5]

Reviewing Family History

Satir's rationale for taking a family history with everyone present is twofold: to begin to get a disturbed family under control and to help them see that things don't just accidentally happen to them. Her instructions on this phase of counseling spell out the advantages: to relate current bad times to past good times, to connect parent-child patterns with families of origin, and to bring the present state of the family into wider perspective.[6] She reviews the married couple's early courtship days because, as she sees it, people are first interested in each other because of their

sameness, but they remain interested because of their differentness. By taking up the past and commenting upon its connection
with the present and what this nexus might mean, Satir holds out
the chance that good times can come again.

Interpreting Parent's History

A parent's talking and acting become material in the blueprint
of a child's behavior, persisting into adulthood. Some parents are
naive enough to suppose that children absorb only what the parents consciously teach. It can be a shattering experience for an
adult to be confronted with a child's behavior that matches an intolerable part of his or her own behavior. That behavior may in
time become equally shattering to someone's spouse.

Parents in the family of origin may also be unknowingly influential in a couple's role of function discrepancy. Some wives
and husbands function in a sort of mother-son or father-daughter
relationship. Thus, label and function are discrepant. This leads
to further incongruities in their marriage. As these types of behavior cannot fit, only confused messages can result. In dysfunctional
marital pairs, the partners have not achieved the shift in relationship with their parents that enables them to live as colleagues in
the world of adults. The result is that such partners often live and
operate as children, their parents still in charge of some part of
their adult lives.

Rebuilding Ego Strength

Satir teaches other therapists to provide confidence, direction,
and structure, to always build self-esteem, and to reduce threat.
The objective, transparently enough, is to bolster ego strength
among family members. The teaching goal in this therapy is maturation, and people can mature only if they have egos that are
rugged enough to cope with family relationships. Because self-esteem is essential to emotional health, the polarities of acceptance
and rejection become paramount concerns in such therapy.
How's this for dealing with the issue of self-worth in the face of
negative challenge?

So you have a tendency to be bitchy. Take it out, dress it up, and honor this tendency as part of yourself. Love it and give it a place with the rest of your feelings. You can do the same with all your tendencies. This way one tendency won't stamp out all the rest of you; it will come out and "act nice" at your bidding. And it may turn out that you summon it less and less and then, like a formal gown you have outgrown or is no longer in style, you perhaps reshape it into a play gown for your young daughter, give it away, or use it to dust with.[7]

(Quotation reprinted by permission of the author and publisher, Virginia Satir, PEOPLEMAKING, 1972, Science & Behavior Books, Inc., Palo Alto, CA)

Satir's Theoretical Concepts

Satir's attention is directed not to sick persons but to "the people system" where faulty communication occurs. Hers is a communication model for family therapy. She believes that if illness comes from inadequate methods of communication, it follows that therapy will be seen as an attempt to improve these methods. For Satir, communication refers not only to what is being said and heard, but also to the relational aspects between persons. The feedback loop in the system of communications draws upon emotions and relationships as fully as it does on words and conversation. Those interpersonal relationships involve two levels of communication. At the first and upper level, messages are direct and explicit; at the second and lower level, they are subtle and implicit. Messages are conveyed by the total context, including such unworded signals as voice, tone, tempo, facial expression, and the like.

But communication goes deeper yet, in Satir's theory. It also involves the interaction of people's very behaviors. She subscribes to a phenomenological theory of interpersonal behavior: the way that behavior or reality is perceived at the moment. Objectivity, in itself, is not the measuring rod. The person's own understanding of what is going on makes all the difference. What we know as reality is validated by the negotiation of our interactions with each other. This implies that any behavior that occurs between two people will have to be the product of both of them.

Patterns of Communication

After extensive experience in treating families with inadequate communication patterns, Satir has arrived at a memorable classification of four typical communication problems found in troubled homes. These are typified by individuals who are described as the Placater, the Blamer, the Computer, and the Detractor. These personifications are useful not only in the training of family therapists, who act out the roles in brief, impromptu skits, but are also easily comprehended by families in therapy when the therapist mentions them or after the family has read about them in some of Satir's writing, e.g., *Peoplemaking*, chapt. 5.

The Placater is the superagreeable person who volunteers to leave herself out. "Whatever you want to do is okay with me. I'm just here to make you happy," is the caricature of her position. She feels helpless and worthless, but somehow hopes that in her doormat stance she will be noticed and loved. That this hope is counterproductive is seen in its repeated failure—doormats are not very lovable. She continues to feel worthless, and she repeatedly goes through the same motions of self-defeating behavior.

The Blamer is the chronic critic who disagrees as a matter of habit: "You never can do anything right. What's wrong with you?" A faultfinder and accuser, he may actually be feeling unsuccessful and lonely. Because of his low self-esteem, he may hope to somehow feel better if he can influence someone else to feel worse. This, too, is a hope doomed to failure. Although Blamers can promote guilty feelings in others, this is accomplished without any improvement in their own low self-esteem. In an almost endless cycle, they blame, feel frustrated, then blame again in the bootless expectation of feeling superior.

The Computer, on the other hand, is superreasonable, calm, cool, and collected. He says the right words, produces the right reactions, makes the right judgments. He might say, "If you were to observe carefully, you might notice that someone here is contributing more than his share." What he means, but hardly recognizes, is that he feels vulnerable. His strategems seldom succeed. Such cool messages are too oblique for most members of the family to heed. It is easy to ignore a Computer, and most people do just that.

The Distractor is irrelevant. She will change the subject, call attention to something off to the side, or divert us from the topic at hand. If the subject is roses, the Distractor may interrupt with memories of a trip to Disneyland. If a discussion becomes confrontational, she may note that it's time to wash her hair and file her nails. The Distractor is likely to feel that nobody cares: "There's no place for me." If that is her impression, she is indulging in the wrong method to cure loneliness and isolation. Perversely, the Distractor increases her loneliness, because most people in her company become weary of this awkward approach. They will just allow her to file her nails.

Satir composes a rather droll example of how these four awkward communicators speak to the problem of one naughty boy who is negligent in the care of his room. Then she contrasts these with a straight I-message from a more direct parental voice.

(Quotation reprinted by permission of the author and publisher, Virginia Satir, PEOPLEMAKING, 1972, Science & Behavior Books., Inc., Palo Alto, CA)

>*Placating* (coming up with a hushed voice, downcast face): "I'm-uh-gosh, gee, Jim—I am sorry—you feeling OK? you know—promise me you won't get mad—no, you're doing OK, it's just—maybe you could do a little better? Just a little, maybe? Hm?"

>*Blaming:* "For Christ's sake, don't you know anything, you dumb cluck?"

>*Computing:* "We are making a survey of our family efficiency. We find that in this department, namely with you, that efficiency is beginning to go down. Would you have any comment to make?"

>*Distracting* (talking to his other son, standing by Jim): "Say, Arnold, is your room about the same as Jim's? No, nothing wrong—I was just taking a walk through the house. Tell Jim to see his mother before he goes to bed."

Then the more rational, healthier communication:

Leveling: "Jim, your room is in bad shape. You haven't made your bed since yesterday. We need to stop, take a look, and see what's wrong."[8]

Self-Esteem and Expectations

You will have noted that in each of the first four unfortunate communicative stances, the parent is struggling with a problem of self-esteem. The Placater feels worthless, the Blamer lonely, the Computer vulnerable, and the Distractor expendable. In Satir's theory, self-esteem is the major issue. It is also a major issue for many of us. How we feel about ourselves, how our self-concept was acquired, and what the family system has done to strengthen or weaken this self-concept: These factors loom large. Far too often we are inclined to put others in charge of our self-esteem, instead of taking responsibility for it ourselves. Indeed, the way we feel about ourselves affects the way we feel toward others in our own system of relationships, be it family, church, or community.

For these reasons, Satir's focus in therapy is repeatedly directed to feelings of acceptance or rejection. The rejected (in fact, the self-rejected) person can be predicted to have dysfunctional communication. As a therapist, then, she comments upon and works through any covert feelings about a person's worth that she discerns in a family's communication. And family members, who usually have never noted the effect of their interaction of words and actions, will be astonished at the revelations of this process. For them, this becomes the beginning of growth.

Often couples are so certain they know what their partner's reactions will be that they do not hear or see behaviors that fail to fit their expectations. Persons with low self-esteem will favor such a prejudiced conclusion, even in the face of new evidence that exceeds former minimal expectations. They tend to disbelieve their eyes and to give no credit for improvements. The fear of venturing into something new makes them persist in seeing acts that may no longer be there at all. Perhaps the reason for this obduracy is that old patterns of thinking, even though painful, are nevertheless familiar to them and therefore preferred. Low esteem has done its damage, and another marriage has been endangered.

Maturity

Of all Satir's working tools, as she likes to call her concepts, maturation stands out preeminent "because it is a touchstone for all the rest."[9] She defines the term in brief, practical phrases as it relates to a person. The mature person, she believes, is fully in charge of himself or herself, is able to make choices based on accurate perceptions of oneself, others, and the context, and can acknowledge responsibility for the outcome of those decisions.

Our maturity, we are hardly surprised to learn, is heavily influenced by our experience with our parents. What parents communicate to children will make a wide difference in their development. Children can receive the message that they are a disappointment—or even sick persons—from fathers and mothers. A child does not develop a healthy self-esteem unless such an understanding is validated by his parents. To attain maturity, a person must be able to eventually separate from the family, as a clearly designated individual. Pastors are familiar with adults, some of them well up in years, who are emotionally still connected umbilically to their parents. They cannot effectively break away to live on their own; they have never achieved real maturity.

Such sons or daughters are in an intolerable position if they can never be accepted as autonomous beings, but only as extensions of the parental self-system. Satir's language for this condition becomes colorful; such a person lives under "the continuing shadows of the past," or under "the parental cloak," or even with "fettered hands."

The Pastoral Counselor and the Satir Method

The pastoral counselor can learn a great deal simply by observation of Virginia Satir. For years she has trained other therapists, not so much by instruction as by being, and much of her work is transferable, even imitable. Note, for example, how she always remains present to her counselees, giving them her undivided attention. This complete concentration on people and their relationships is a powerful lesson in how to deal incisively and maintain rapport with people.

From such complete attention, one can be more accepting of counselees and their difficulties. While hers is not the unconditional positive regard of Carl R. Rogers (*see* chapt. 3), her acceptance shows a deep concern for family members and their differentness, one from the other. Satir seems very aware of what theologian Helmut Thielicke has called the "alien dignity" of persons, that is, each individual's intrinsic self-worth as a personality created by God.

With such acceptance, it is easier to communicate to counselees forgiveness for their foibles and assurance that God is a redeeming Lord who assists the fallen and the failed to stand and try once more.

In a more procedural sense, Virginia Satir points the way to careful planning and goal setting for each session of family therapy. She shows clear evidence of knowing what her objectives are and how to achieve them. She has carefully thought through her aims in family therapy:

• To aid persons individually to report congruently what they feel, hear, and think about themselves and about others

• To teach a new method of decision making within the family, so that their decisions will be made by negotiation rather than on a base of naked power

• To acknowledge personal differentness as a means of growth, so that individual uniqueness can be recognized and permitted.

Such objectives add up to an end that sounds deceptively simple, but these can make all the difference in the life of a family unable to cope. In counseling with marital pairs, Satir aims to bring about specific changes in each spouse. She plans that each will gain new perceptions of self and other (a plan that includes both cognitive and affective aspects). She leads each to a change in ways of manifesting feelings and thoughts. And she guides each spouse to altering ways of reacting to the stimulus and to the feedback that come from the other.

Virginia Satir's task is plainly defined. It's worthy enough to be adopted by others doing family therapy: "Our task is to work out ways in which everyone can get more pleasure from family life."

2

Carl Whitaker's Therapy of the Absurd

I think of [a family in chronic fighting] as a crazy situation and suggest that they sell their house and rent two apartments so that mother and son can have freedom to fight openly as any husband and wife should and that father and daughter have the freedom to live without the fighting and have a peaceful time of their own.

Carl Whitaker

Carl A. Whitaker, M.D., has developed a brand of family and individual therapy that he labels experiential, but both his colleagues and he have also referred to it as "the psychotherapy of the absurd." To be sure, its therapeutic methods contain some unconventional features that partake of the theater of the absurd, but the sharp observer will note that they are cooly calculated to produce positive results. Whitaker's long, rich experience as a psychiatrist has taught him that he can use himself in unconventional ways to elicit healthful responses.

Who is Carl Whitaker? One of the best known family therapists today, he ranks among the superstars of this field. He is emeritus professor of psychiatry at the University of Wisconsin medical school, and he conducts a private practice, as well as conducting workshops all over the nation. Now in his late sixties,

Whitaker has been at his art for a long time. He first began experimenting with family therapy as early as the 1940s in Atlanta, well before most psychotherapists had begun to practice with family groups. He was working with delinquents when he began to invite parents and other family members to join with their Identified Patient. From the first, he has been controversial and spontaneous. "Maybe it was because I worked with delinquents I gradually realized that my craziness, my childishness and even my delinquency were deeply involved in what I did."[1]

Whitaker sees his task as a strategy to increase the complexity of a family's problem, rather than restore order. The surprise is that his interventions, which induce chaos, do have therapeutic results. It is Whitaker's conviction that patients must achieve experience in therapy, rather than simply arrive at insight, as Whitaker aims to reach the deeper levels of personality. Certain that therapists cannot intellectually teach people to perceive each other differently, he first pushes them to experience themselves in new ways.

This father of seven sons and daughters is paternal and firm in his therapy; he assumes that most therapy is a symbolic parenting experience. The hundreds of pupils who come into his famed workshops have watched him in demonstrations with troubled families, to whom he relates like a burly grandfather. His nononsense demeanor with patients has evolved from long familiarity with the world of schizophrenics; he has learned how to "talk crazy" with them, how to discern their unreal, irrational worldview. This has proved a boon in working with dysfunctional families who bring in a seriously disturbed or downright sick patient.

His fame has spread through his traveling workshops, his reputation with medical students, his training tapes, and his startling style of writing.

Carl Whitaker's Therapy

To begin with, Whitaker and his cotherapists will assemble the largest system of family members they can locate, certainly all who live under the same roof, plus others. Gradually they reduce the number they meet in interview sessions, eliminating those who are peripheral to the problem after their contribution has been made in the early meetings. This way, progress is forged toward those subsystems in which the pain will be found. So insistent, however, are Whitaker and his company about the presence of the whole network that they will even construct a pseudo-family where none is available, as in the case of a university student who may be required to invite in girl friends, roommates, and others.

What a complicated mix of people this gathers! They come into therapy blaming, accusing one another, defending themselves, and challenging the family therapist. Somehow the therapist must enter that confused miniature society, which is an entire social realm, with its own peculiar rituals, roles, leadership, language, and living style. Augustus Napier notes that "the hidden rules, the subtle nuances of language, the private rituals and dances that define every family as a unique microculture may not be easy for an outsider to perceive at first glance, but they are there. The wife *knows* what the curling inflection in his voice signifies."[2]

The insistence on beginning therapy with a full house extends to grandparents as well as the nuclear family. Whitaker wrote of his commitment to gathering of the extended kin:

> My engagement with two generation families began in 1945. I decided I didn't believe in individuals. They seemed more and more like fragments of a family. Then, as time went on, I heard the ghost of grandmother knocking on the door. . . . I'm tempted to say before the first visit, "Bring three generations or don't bother to start."[3]

When this sometimes large family group convenes for its first interview, Whitaker will appoint the least interested or most antagonistic person in the family to keep in touch with him on behalf of the whole group. Often this is the father. When he is responsible for getting his sons or other family members to therapy sessions, he will likely be present himself. And if the father can command his family to come into treatment, an administrative battle is already won for the therapists. A change has been wrought at the outset, and therapy is already taking place.

Despite his authoritarian tone, Whitaker makes a distinction between controlling the therapeutic framework and controlling persons' lives. About this principle, he remains firm. People who control others are police, he opines. The therapist has a quite different task, which is to help people learn how to get control of their own lives.

He has given us a verbatim report of a telephone conversation that points up both his preference to work with the entire family and also his firmness in dealing with this preference. A woman had telephoned him for an appointment for her twenty-four-year-old son. Dr. Whitaker responded:

"I don't see patients. I just see families."
The mother responded, "Well, I'll come."
"How about your husband?"
"Well, we're getting a divorce."
I explained to her that I would not see them without the father and she said, "Okay, I'll bring him."
"Who do you live with?"
"My parents."
"Well, let's bring them."
"They aren't related to my son's problem."
"Okay. Go see someone else."
"But I want to see you."
"So bring your parents."
"Okay, I'll bring them."
"How about your husband's parents?"
"Well, they live in Montreal."
"That's okay. Just have him call me if they won't come."[4]

Ever feisty, even if in a twinkling manner, Whitaker is convinced that family therapy begins with a structural fight that the therapist must win. "I want it to be understood that I'm in charge of what happens when they get here," he tells his students. "The only thing they're in charge of is whether they will come or not."

To fill out this demand, he will give the family one set of terms, and if they balk, he will give them another set twice as difficult. In a family-therapy case, he is wont to require that the entire family come, warning them that if anyone is absent he will cancel the interview and still charge them for it. On other occasions, he is willing to work with individuals apart from their kith and kin, and in violation of his vaunted principle. If that seems absurd, well, that's the Whitaker method.

Cotherapy With Families

Individualist though he is, Whitaker operates in therapy with a colleague. He has a strong preference for working with a cotherapist, and he whimsically offers a batch of excuses for it: He needs the help, he becomes bored, or the therapy is more effective. Two therapists, he avers, are required to accomplish a clear encounter with families; successful therapy is dependent on such an arrangement.

The Family Crucible is a book-length case study of one family treated in cotherapy by Carl Whitaker and Augustus Napier. It reveals the close working relationship between two men who understand each other and respect each other's competence in therapy. That they complement each other in attitude is candidly recorded by Napier, who sees himself as the more maternal of the two, offsetting Whitaker's rather more paternal stance.

These cotherapists have worked out the problems of a team relationship. This process need cause no anxiety, and there is no reason for it to be processed outside the therapy session itself. Whitaker and Napier, in point of fact, hash out their differences in the presence of the family. One method they have perfected is to elicit the family's description of their problem and then discuss between them the dynamics of the family, who listen in on this diagnosis.

Being Purposely Absurd

In the Whitaker system, progress in family therapy consists of five stages: 1. The now-familiar attack on the family by the therapists, in order to exert initial leadership. 2. A second stage, leading the family into direct confrontation with one another and increasing the complexity of their problem. 3. A third stage, in which the family's despair mounts still higher. 4. The beginning of a creative stage wherein they adopt a therapeutic model. 5. A final stage, in which they consider how they might avoid such a problem in the future.

It is in the second and third stages that Whitaker's tactics of absurdity play their important part. He has been known to jolt families through such antics as playing a phonograph record, making a personal telephone call, reading a book, or even taking a nap during their interview.

Rather than eradicate the pathology of a family group, he may at times augment it until, as one observer says, "The symptoms self-destruct through his use of a tactic which is a kind of tongue-in-cheek put-on."[5] In working with a woman who had attempted suicide, for instance, he deromanticized her fantasies of the floral display and the weeping people at her funeral by directing her to imagine the girl friend her husband would have waiting for him.

Instead of commiserating with the desperate, he will compliment them for having desperation and reframe it as "showing concern." He plays with children in mock sternness. "You take off my left shoe," he glowers, "but never my right." He forbids them something insignificant and gets them on his side. But he deals with them firmly if their parents show no penchant for discipline. He will bite children who bite him. He will rebuke them if he feels they need it.

Having learned to speak "schizophrense" years ago in his tenure at a psychiatric hospital, Whitaker adopts the language that his schizophrenic patients speak. Adopting their terms, he reaches them through their own symbols. A rebellious and sick young man, brought in by his family, wore a flowery, inappropriate scarf. "You're telling me that you don't belong here, aren't you?" Whitaker read into the symbol. Crazy that may be, but not stupid. In his therapy Whitaker, like Carl G. Jung in his day, uses any means that appeal to him at the time: Bible passages, re-counting his own dreams, vulgarity, or parables. His mixture of exploiting the unexpected and acting as a ham performer can hardly be taught to his medical students. Like a Zen master, he says, "You can't do it by trying; but you have to try."

Upending Conventional Therapy

By inverting many of the accepted and standard procedures of social case work and traditional psychiatry, Whitaker brings to his therapy an astonishingly fresh way of working. Four examples, chosen from a rich supply, will point up the innovative nature of his family therapy.

For starters, Whitaker eschews that foundation of yesteryear's counseling, supportive therapy. Widely used though it is among the helping professions, and especially in ministry, Whitaker considers supportive therapy useless. By bold inversion he aims instead to activate the pathology in a dysfunctional family, so their anxiety mounts high enough for them to institute a process of change. His goal is never to make his patients happier. His business, instead, is to help people become more independent and able to live apart from the symbiosis of their family patterns.

Second, Whitaker bypasses the taking of a family history. Remarkably careless about the past patterns in any consecutive story, he waits for bits of historical information to simply emerge in the course of counseling. He can see much about a family's world in the ways they relate to one another, their posture in sitting, their manner of talking to one another, their tone of voice, and the assumptions and ideas they voice about life. History is hardly neglected; he just obtains his history in a different, more subtle fashion.

Third, Whitaker seems heedless about what he considers to be an aged cliché in counseling, direct communication. He prefers, in fact, an indirect approach known as metacommunication; that is, he talks through other people about how they communicate. He may ask a husband what is wrong with his wife, who is the Identified Patient. Afterwards he asks the wife what is wrong with her husband. Then, never returning to these person-centered questions of accusation again, he asks them instead, "Now, what is wrong with the marriage, the third patient here?"

In one other instance of metacommunication, he got across his message through demonstration. He brought in an assistant to handle the tape recorder, although he had no need of him, to signal to the family that the outside world and its people are also involved in their collective life.

Fourth, he discourages families in treatment from using an excess of frank I-messages at home. They are not to carry on their disputes between therapy sessions. "Bring your fights here," he admonishes. It is a gross error, he believes, for therapists to encourage patients to hash out their differences (something known in marriage and family courses as "constructive quarreling"). That kind of sharing with each other brings them back to the next session with emotional bruises.

Triangulation, that ever-constant element of families in difficulty (and also the mark of all family relationships, to some extent), is fully anticipated by Whitaker. Married couples in conflict will inevitably involve their children in their emotional stress. Describing one such couple, Whitaker reported that "although they appeared distant from each other, beneath the surface they had formed a tight, frightened togetherness." Under these circumstances, an open fight would have been hazardous to them as adults, so tension was forced to surface somewhere else—in their scapegoated child. Whitaker took the burden off the small shoulders of the child and carried it himself while that insecure couple found themselves in therapy that was more compassionate than absurd.

Whitaker's Basic Concepts

Whitaker assumes that life is a contest and acts on that assumption. Never one to shy away from stressful relationships, he emphasizes that all living involves stress, and always will. (We don't live life, he insists. It lives us.) Yet stress can be turned to positive results. Anxiety can motivate change.

Even though the body's adverse reaction to stress may make us ill at times of sudden transition in life, crises have the capacity to bring about a new level of adjustment. Whitaker believes this so strongly that he is capable of escalating the stress of families in treatment, in order to promote cure. He will then move in to take advantage of the stressful condition as a useful opening for influencing change.

It's System Against System

The family in therapy, however, is going to resist making changes. They know this, and the therapist knows it, too. It's system against system. Whitaker strongly believes there is necessary and basic conflict between the therapist and the family. By coming to the therapist, the family has admitted that their model for living has at least temporarily failed. Nevertheless, the family seldom likes the diagnosis of their condition or the therapist's opinions about where they should make changes. The therapist, therefore, must be prepared to enter the fray.

In no case will this family therapist compromise; he fully expects to prevail as the victor in any clash of wills. Unless he and his cotherapist overcome the family's preference for directing the therapy (which would leave the dysfunctional system undisturbed and unhealed), the family will not begin to experience one another differently. Therapists must exert rugged personal power to prevent being entrapped into the system of the family under treatment. They must take risks, allow themselves to become involved, and cast off professional dignity. All this Whitaker does, and teaches others to do. To enter into the world of the family is wise; to enter into their unhealthy enmeshment is unwise.

The forensic nature of this relationship between the therapist and the family appears, at first, to be harsh, but beneath it is a genuine caring for families in pain. They feel intimidated, they suffer from an enveloping symbiosis—each has become parasitic on the others. They may not consciously know it, but it is from the stuck-together family itself that they are begging freedom. They are crying for relief from their defective system and sick relationships.

It is to be expected, therefore, that one part of the family may be loudly demanding freedom and searching wildly for life, while another part is trying to quiet all this down. Whitaker believes this is the struggle of life against death. The fear of immobility (*stasis*) is a fear of nonbeing. It is widely recognized that an immobilized family is scared to death. Thus the most troublesome member of the household, the acting-out deviant, just might be the healthy one shouting out the cry of individuation: "I want to be me!"

Despite the self-styled craziness and absurdity of his methods, Whitaker treats family pathology with the utmost seriousness. With family relations so crucial to people, and with families so often threatened by outright dissolution, the healing of their wounds has his highest priority.

In spite of these basic concepts, Whitaker holds that he has no theory behind his work. In fact, he dubs his specialty "nontheoretical family therapy." Boldly he writes about how he spurns theoretical constructs, and the incredulous reader may wonder if he is writing with tongue-in-cheek again.

"Dedication to theory in family therapy work is essentially a copout, a disguise that will eventually conceal even the process of therapy. . . . It's as fallacious as the theory of unconditional positive regard, which is to say that love conquers all."[6]

Hyperbole this may be, but it forcefully registers his disdain of a rather large and prominent group of therapists who sometimes construe and debate theory at the expense of working with troubled people.

Carl Whitaker's Contributions for Clergy

Instructions to clergy doing family therapy are not to be found in the writings of Carl Whitaker, but in many instances he appears to be speaking directly to the likes of us. A collection of his advice to beginning therapists reads like a compendium of teachings for theological students. In sum, these lessons add up as follows:

- A caution against excessive administrative activity: Don't do something, just be there, he admonishes, for there are times (for example, in grief work) when presence will add up to more than words or acts.
- A warning to avoid overeagerness: Don't be too helpful, he will say, let the counselees struggle. They can do it, and they should supply their own motivation to change.
- A constant reminder for therapists to take firm leadership of the therapy sessions with families, asking their permission for nothing, but directing the arrangements.
- An insistence on involving the wider connection of relatives in therapy sessions. Whitaker believes that a failure to involve the extended family in the case can be near fatal to good results.
- An imperative never to concentrate on the family's chosen scapegoat but instead to implicate the entire system.
- A caution about taking sides with any one person or subsystem in a family, because a simple way to blow up a counseling case is to become overly identified with one particular cause or clique.
- An instruction to forego any preoccupation with good feelings and affability. Pseudomutuality is not the same as family therapy, and it prevents us from confronting anyone or any behavior openly.[7]

That some of these stern standards loom more appropriate for the pastorate than others is obvious; nonetheless, they all have some corrective to make for our ministry. The temptations to be overly active in saving persons from their failings or to overdo heartiness and good feelings are often with us. Rigorous standards that would impel us to more professional competence are all to the good. Whitaker's zany behavior may not be our own best method, but his foxy wisdom may inspire our own.

Certainly his example encourages us to use our natural assets in ministry. Because the context of pastoral counseling is within the

church and its faith, there is a certain absurdity in our sounding
like atheists when we endeavor to help people with their problems. There is a place for faith statements in counseling. There is
a place for prayer. There is a place for blessing, for confession,
and for the assurance of pardon from sin. No one session would
include all of these, but an interview in pastoral care ought not to
pass without some references to our faith that God guides lives
and lessens loads.

Carl Whitaker's practice also helps us place into perspective
the matter of our authority. While there can be no doubt that
Whitaker uses authority in a wily, effective manner, he cannot be
accused of ignorantly misusing it. The control factor in a family is
the job of the family, and not that of the pastor. The pastor who
assumes responsibility for a family and its decisions is not aiding
them toward self-reliance and may, as a result, increase their dependence. In such a case, pastors may get what they deserve
when dependent parishioners telephone them for guidance or
permission for any significant move. Our challenge is not to pull
the crutches out from under people, but to help them stand so
straight that their crutches fall away.

We are also led by the example of Carl Whitaker to work less
arduously in our counseling than we are wont to do. His admoni-
tion is not to be too helpful, lest the counselees themselves lie
down on the job and allow us to make all the effort. To put it a
different way, anytime the pastoral counselor is working harder
than the counselees, something is wrong in the process.

Too often pastors play the part of rescuers. With the old hymn
tune "Rescue the Perishing" ringing in our ears, and the paradigm of salvation conditioning our response, we tend at times to
an excessive helpfulness that is not good for our counselees.
Learning that they can be more harmed than helped by this is a
shock. But we do well to recall a recent novelist's description of a
woman who was ever helpful: "You could identify the people she
had helped by the haunted look in their eyes." Carl Whitaker's
model can help us not be harmfully helpful!

3

Carl Rogers
and
Family-Centered Therapy

The individual finds it more satisfying in the long run to live in a given family relationship on the basis of the real interpersonal feelings which exist, rather than living the relationship on the basis of a pretense.

Carl R. Rogers

Those who write about Carl Rogers invariably call attention to the Christian fundamentalism of his boyhood farm home, tracing back to it to explain his duodenal ulcer in college days, his turning away from theological education after he had barely begun, and his passionate concern for allowing persons to be themselves.

Rogers's father revered hard work, his mother, stern doctrine. Although later he could not recall even one direct command from his distant, aloof parents, all six of the children knew what was expected of them, including the fact that cards and dancing were strictly forbidden. Certainly it was not a poor home, with its slate roof, tile floors, eight bedrooms, five baths, and clay tennis court. Still, it was a deprived atmosphere for young Carl, who came to believe his family could not love him for himself, even though they might approve what he did. He felt inferior and vulnerable. He has changed a lot.

Born in 1902, Rogers grew up in the prewar Midwest of a rapidly developing America. He attended the University of Wisconsin, where activity in campus Christian life led to his attending the World Student Christian Federation in China. That experience was a turning point, where he was exposed to a different Christian perspective than he had previously known. Soon afterward he married Helen Elliot and moved to New York City, where he entered Union Theological Seminary. His parents vainly opposed all these decisions. But he dropped out of Union and entered nearby Columbia University Teachers College, where he found his vocation in psychology. He has followed that career ever since: through the Rochester (N.Y.) Guidance Center, Ohio State University, University of Chicago, University of Wisconsin, Western Behavioral Science Institute, and now the Center for the Studies of the Person at La Jolla, California.*

Carl Rogers's Therapy

Only in recent years has Rogerian theory been applied to families in treatment. His client-centered therapy had specialized in individualized problems, was later introduced into group therapy, and now to families under stress. Rogers is convinced that the interpersonal skills taught to individuals in therapy are directly transferable into the family. Like Boszormenyi-Nagy (see chapt. 12), he balances multiple contacts with family members so as to be empathic with each of them sometime during an interview session. In common with other family therapists in this study, Rogers seeks to enter into a family's life through his genuineness and concern. It is his conviction that the therapist's genuine emotional response to a family's pain can help free their frozen family relationships.

Octogenarian Rogers has lived and worked long enough to advance through a series of phases in his psychological teaching and practice. At the beginning of his career, his therapy was known as

*Carl Rogers died as this volume was going to press.

"nondirective," later on as "client centered," more recently as "person centered." There is no doubt that when applied to the family system, it becomes family-centered therapy.

Many of the same therapeutic methods that Rogers has used for years with individuals and groups are now applied in family therapy. For an effective outcome in therapy, he posits three conditions: 1. The therapist's empathic understanding of the person's feelings. 2. An unconditional positive regard for the family in treatment. 3. A congruence that makes it possible for the therapist to be genuine with the clients, "when the counselor is what the counselor is" (Rogers does talk like that).

Out of his rich collection of case histories, Rogers recalls Mrs. M., a woman who complained about her deteriorating marriage to an uncaring and distant husband. But Mrs. M. also revealed that she carried immense guilt over her premarital affairs with married men. After agonizing about her situation with Dr. Rogers, Mrs. M. decided to level with her husband and tell him why she had been so demanding and difficult. To her amazement, he proved to be understanding and forgiving. The couple thereafter became reconciled in a spirit of mutual trust. Rogers comments that Mrs. M. experienced in therapy the satisfaction of being herself, of voicing her deep feelings, and then transferred this experience from therapy to her marital relationship. She had come into congruence.

Like Mrs. M., many clients of Carl Rogers have known the anxiety that arises from personal incongruence, followed by an advance toward self-awareness, to new openness of experience and improved personal relationships. This, in terms of the experiential psychology of which Rogers is a prominent spokesman, is self-actualization.

As his person-centered therapy developed in theory and its application expanded to administration, education, business, and politics, the move into family treatment was natural. Rogers notes that person-centered therapy enhances close personal relationships, and that is where the family is. Thus applied to family therapy, this approach begins with deep trust that the family can change and grow (Rogerian theory is nothing if not optimistic). The therapist will require a sense of nonpossessive caring, warmth, and respect for the family, and will need a genuineness about personal feelings that makes for congruence in the experience.

Many family therapists emphasize the problem of resistance in families who come for counseling. Rogers does not; resistance is simply not acknowledged in this modality. Instead, the family is motivated toward growth and self-actualization. Rogers firmly is confident the human organism is weighted toward positive development and the therapist who is in tune with this tendency can facilitate it. The therapist who believes the clients, who respects their being, and who does not bring preconceived ideas into the session will assist families to gain a satisfying relationship.

Ronald F. Levant, a family-centered therapist in the Rogerian tradition, puts it this way:

> This is a therapy in which the therapist is not so much expert as coparticipant in, and facilitator of, the process of therapy. The role does not involve history taking, diagnosis, treatment planning, or the use of therapeutic techniques to induce change (whether they be paradoxical maneuvers or interpretations). Rather it involves facilitating the release and development of self-regenerative and self-enhancing powers within the family members. It also involves a direct encounter on a person-to-person basis with family members. It is a therapy that is based to a very large extent on the person of the therapist.[1]

The Course of Family-Centered Therapy

The beginning of a course in Rogerian family therapy frequently involves the entire nuclear family, but then advances into smaller subgroups such as the marital pair or, if indicated, a parent-child combination. In any case, the family-centered therapist must have empathy with every member of the family and a genuineness that they all can trust. A genuine emotional response to family pain has the positive effect of freeing clients. At the same time, the therapist also exhibits trust in allowing the family some control over what issues are to be taken up and what timing is to be followed; this is unusual among family therapists. But the practice is useful, Levant writes, in reducing guilt, anxiety, and defensiveness.

As therapy proceeds, families begin to see inconsistencies between their experiences and their self-concepts. Previously these gaps were denied, perhaps in order "to keep peace," but now individuals gradually gain trust and the freedom to be themselves. Put another way, their concept of self is reorganized toward greater congruence. No wonder: The Rogerian therapist works consistently toward that very end, exploring those incongruities, exposing feelings, exhibiting unconditional positive regard, even to very difficult persons (what modeling this is for a family!), and moving them toward a new experiencing of themselves and their relationships. If this is effective, they will begin to discover a changed concept of themselves—actually new selves in action. The objective, which is so different from that of psychodynamic family therapies, is the growth of people rather than the reduction of symptoms.

Rogerian-trained therapists are not without their own techniques. Active listening is by no means the only task they work on. They clarify the feelings of family complainants. They use a variety of nondirective leads to draw persons out. They empathically experience what the clients are experiencing, to sense their inner world. They maintain a genuine regard for the family, even if annoyed or tired (and they can say so if they are).

Convinced that change and growth in people are more likely to take place when unconditional positive regard is given them, the Rogerian therapist models how a parent might treat a child, a wife her husband, or an adolescent her siblings. *Unconditional* here has a hard, absolute meaning. It cannot mean accepting some feelings but not others; it is a total acceptance. Therapists who are sensitive to their own feelings as well as to those of others come nearer to this demanding standard.

In this process the family becomes increasingly free about expressing feelings, and these feelings refer more and more to their real selves, rather than to their masks. Inevitably they come to

understand some of the incongruities between certain experiences
and concepts of themselves. This can be a threat, but if the
therapist continues to show positive regard for the presence of
anxiety, as well as its absence, and to incongruence as well as congruence, that threat can be met. Thus the concept of self can become reorganized, and *real selves* with expanding awareness
begin to interact with one another. Families are reconciled; individuals become genuine.

The family's acceptance by the therapist has led to acceptance
of themselves and of their togetherness. The more the therapist
sees them as persons rather than as objects, the more they can do
the same. In the course of their therapy, existential learning has
been taking place, for Rogerian therapy is, if nothing else, an
educational experience. Families learn to move away from their
masks and become more honest. They move away from the burden of living according to others' expectations. What's more,
they move toward an openness to the future and an acceptance of
one another.

In one of several instructive films showing Carl Rogers during
therapy, *Three Approaches to Psychotherapy*, this progression of
realizations is depicted. Gloria, the divorced mother of Pam, is
deeply concerned over her own guilt feelings and her relationship
with the little girl. In a sterling but impromptu natural performance, Rogers turns Gloria's sights away from her child to herself, helping her understand her feelings, accept herself, and make
decisions. Acting on his assumption that the person is autonomous, capable of intelligence, and free of pathology, Rogers demonstrates that a client will respond healthily and revise her ways
of dealing with a family problem.

A Rogerian Credo

Carl Rogers has outlined his beliefs about the therapist's work
in a way that has proven useful to many others:

 • In my relationship with persons I have found that it does
 not help, in the long run, to act as though I were something
 that I am not.

- I find I am more effective when I can listen acceptantly to myself, and be myself.
- I have found it of enormous value when I can permit myself to understand another person.
- I have found it highly rewarding when I can accept another person.
- Experience is, for me, the highest authority. . . . It is to experience that I must return again and again, to discover a close approximation to truth as it is in the process of becoming in me.
- The facts are friendly . . . painful reorganizations are what is known as learning.
- What is most personal and unique in each one of us is probably the very element which would, if it were shared or expressed, speak most deeply to others.
- It has been my experience that persons have a basically positive direction. . . . I have come to feel that the more fully the individual is understood and accepted, the more he tends to drop the false fronts with which he has been meeting life, and the more he tends to move in a direction that is forward.
- Life, at its best, is a flowing, changing process in which nothing is fixed.
- I have found it enriching to open channels whereby others can communicate their feelings, their private perceptual worlds, to me. I can by my own attitudes create a safety in the relationship which makes such communication more possible.
- The more I am open to realities in me and in the other person, the less do I find myself wishing to rush in to "fix things."
- Evaluation by others is not a guide for me. The judgments of others, while they are listened to, and taken into account for what they are, can never be a guide for me.
- To withold one's self as a person and to deal with the other person as an object does not have a high probability of being helpful.[2]

In his early professional years, Rogers confesses, he was asking how he could treat, or cure, or change this or that person. Now he phrases the question differently: "How can I provide a relation-

ship which this person may use for his own personal growth?"
This is consistent with his avowed belief that to withold oneself
as a person and to deal with the other person as an object does
not have a high probability of being helpful.

Basic Rogerian Concepts

First and basic to Carl Rogers's theory is a surpassing optimism
and positive attitude toward human nature. He considers revolutionary the growing recognition that at the innermost core of
human nature—the deepest layers of personality—the base is
positive and basically socialized, forward moving, rational, and realistic.

This, of course, is antithetical to Sigmund Freud's theory of
personality, which is structured, in part with the id, an irrational, impulsive, hedonistic force that requires the guidance of the
more reasonable ego. That, however, is not the only place Rogers
has reacted against Freudian theory. He opposes its diagnostics
(which presume a pathology), its concept of the unconscious (he
instead posits a phenomenological awareness), its interest in personal historical roots (his interest is in the immediate experience).
Rogers sees his theory as a breakaway from Freudian theory, and
it is. It is, in fact, the best known of third force (humanistic) psy-
chologies, which stand so plainly in contrast to the first (psychoanalytic) and the second (behavioral) forces.

Second, Rogers is wedded to a deep respect for learning
through experience. This method, he firmly teaches, is vastly superior to simply being informed about life. The parent who states
his or her own concern to a child and yet allows the child to test
the issue through experience is going to aid the child to reach a
congruence in personality. Rogers's method of dealing with a
misbehaving and disagreeing child is as follows:

> I can understand how satisfying it feels to you to hit your
> baby brother (or to defecate when and where you please, or to
> destroy things) and I love you and am quite willing for you

to have those feelings. But I am quite willing for me to have my feelings, too, and I feel very distressed when your brother is hurt (or annoyed or sad at other behaviors), and so I do not let you hit him. Both your feelings and my feelings are important, and each of us can freely have his own.[3]

Except for the improbability of such a speech coming from an ordinary person, this is plain evidence of how rationally and educationally Rogerian methods deal with acting-out behavior. It is easy to see where Parent Effectiveness Training gets its I-messages, its active listening, and its reasonableness.

Third, Rogerian theory holds that it is the relationship that is the most important factor in the process of personal change, not the therapist's skill, the techniques, or the psychological school. It is here that an immediate transfer can be made from therapeutic theory to family living. Many experiences in the therapeutic situation are duplicable in the home; this usability of interpersonal relationships is foremost among them. Family life, as Rogers has shown, is more complex than heretofore assumed. It is living with the *process*, and not simply the *institution*, that makes change possible but requires assistance from time to time. Whether that assistance is in the form of therapy, enrichment programs, or educational courses, it can use family-centered theory in the relationships involved.

Those interpersonal relationships are of inestimable value in helping us to experience ourselves and our lives fully. Significant others, as the social psychologist would call them, have the utmost to do with helping us realize our potential.

This teaching comes from a man who once thought that nobody could love him and that he was a vulnerable, inferior person. Yet he learned that the emphasis in relationships is on the *we*, rather than a *they versus me*. He began to see that being yourself in a world that often presses you to be otherwise makes for a hard battle, and that too many people sacrifice the wisdom of their own experience to gain someone else's love.

Fourth, a key principle in Rogers's theory has been the concept of holism: the practice of viewing the person as an integrated organism. Affirming the justification of a person to be wholly what he is, and to protect that wholeness and uniqueness, has been a product of the unconditional positive regard Rogers proclaims. It carries over to family life and therapy, for the family as a whole is also the shared consciousness of parents and children and of their collective experience. In fact the existence and nature of the family depend upon the members' ideas and convictions about it.

Fifth, Rogers has a phenomenological approach to psychology that is more pronounced than others in the experiential schools. He puts great store in the subjective nature of human experience. Having vast respect for the ways people view their world and explain their views, he accepts their positions and believes their stories. He teaches others to imitate this same procedure in their family living, holding that every person exists in a phenomenological world with internal and external realms of experience. How the world looks to them is the essential key to how they experience life and how to get along with them. Understanding others consists of getting into their experience. This is basic to marital counseling, and can obviously also be applied in education, business, and politics.

On Becoming Partners

In a remarkably tolerant view of personal partnerships, married and unmarried, Rogers has set down in *Becoming Partners* his understanding of what it takes to achieve a growing, enriching relationship.[4] Not surprisingly, Rogers affirms the individuation of each person, implying that the more you realize yourself as differentiated, the better your opportunity for a strong relationship. In the process of becoming yourself, you can expect to:

• Discover yourself and your awareness of inner feelings.

• Accept yourself and begin to *own yourself,* a precious possession that is desirable to live with.

• Drop your masks and pretenses. You no longer need to be fearful of being known, for you have come to accept what you are.

• Experience values of your own, rather than being governed by another's "oughts."

The person who makes progress in these realizations can begin to be a worthy partner, neither a slave nor a slave owner, not a person to be taken for granted. Once a person has achieved such a stage, it is all but inevitable that he will encourage his partner in the same direction.

Wisely, Rogers adds a disclaimer. If such development occurs only in one person and is not realized (or is even opposed) in the other, then the distance between them will increase and, without some miracle, will separate them entirely.

Family Communication

Communication in the family is only different from communication in any other relationship in its intensity and intimacy. Rogerian theory affirms that good two-way communication makes people feel pleased, warm, and satisfied. It also can make them feel enriched and growing, convinced that the other persons have also profited. Such satisfaction comes when one can really *hear* someone else, understanding the meaning below the words. Often there is a deep human cry beneath a superficial statement.

There can be consequences to really hearing: a grateful look, a feeling of release, a need to tell more about an experience, perhaps an openness to growth and change. This is because we like to be heard. When we are bursting with insoluble problems, caught in tormented circles, inundated with despair, or filled with guilt and confusion, our horrors can be lessened if we are heard.

Rogers believes a person comes to dislike himself when he can't hear another, feeling himself to be a failure. But it may be that he doesn't hear because the truth is too threatening. Frustration results when someone tries to express something from deep within his private world and no one understands. It can be a shatteringly lonely experience for a mate or a child. On the other hand, we feel deep satisfaction when we can communicate the reality of ourselves to another. And it remains a joy to find reality in another—no mask, no defense, only the transparent self. It is enriching when one person can truly prize and appreciate another and can let that feeling flow out toward the other. A person

slowly learns that tender, positive feelings are not dangerous to
give or receive.

These, according to Rogers, are some of the implications of client-centered therapy for family life. Taking principles from the
experience of therapy and applying them to the family, he has
concluded that we find it satisfying to express strong and persistent emotional attitudes where they arise, to the person they concern, and to the depth to which they exist. This is more
satisfying, he insists, than pretending such feelings do not exist.
As we express ourselves more freely, we can lay aside some of our
defenses and truly listen to other people. Then, miracle of mira-
cles, there comes an increasing willingness for the other person to
be himself or herself!

A Pastoral Addendum

The impact of Carl Rogers's thought and leadership upon the
clergy of America has been immense. His millions of books sold,
many films and tapes, and teaching have reached all denomina-
tions and faiths, with good reason. Rogers's person-centered gospel is unabashedly inspirational. This strong faith in humanity,
this confidence in self-actualization, this affirmation of one's
being—who would not feel encouragement from such psychological good news?

In addition to that, Rogers has prepared a ready-to-use form of
therapy. More than any other, it depends upon the person of the
therapist and how he uses himself, rather than on clinical intern-
ship or the mastery of a system. Learning to listen actively, reflect
clearly, and empathize with a suffering person or family draws on
a pastor's natural aptitudes and helps him grow in his vocation, as
well. Utilizing communication skills and ordering them in harmony with Rogerian teachings enhances a person's ministry and
improves relationships in counseling, in congregational business,
and in one's own family.

Citing other advantages to this approach, Howard Clinebell
notes that it can be used by clergy with "natural counseling apti-

tudes but with limited formal training" and that it "is within the potential competencies of many parish ministers."[5]

Rogerian principles guide us to utilize our educational knowledge, because Rogerian theory is intrinsically educational. It does not claim too much to say that this is a teaching therapy. Rogerian principles imbue the therapist-pastor with a therapeutic attitude to begin with, because the values inherent in the system are so notoriously positive about affirming human potential.

Where is the pastor who has not found it necessary to aid persons who are acting in self-defeating ways, confessing to feelings of inferiority, battling with low self-esteem, or experiencing alienation? For such problems as these, the Rogerian approach to individual and family therapy is well suited. It is little wonder that many of Rogers's once revolutionary ideas have been interwoven into the practice of social workers, guidance counselors, personnel directors, teachers, and clergy.

Still, there are concerns and criticisms about the widespread application of the Rogerian method. Theologically sensitive clergy are prone to ask where sin fits in with all this approval and acceptance. Realistic observers question the lack of any sense of tragedy in most of the upbeat, person-centered literature. In all the educational emphasis of Carl Rogers and his school, they search for a discipline of the conscience or a help in making critical judgments.

There is another misgiving voiced by psychologists who have used Rogerian methods: They wonder about their effectiveness with desperate cases—the suicidal, the deeply depressed, the violent, the obsessed. Is empathic listening sufficient to accomplish anything therapeutic in time for such persons? And is the therapist to remain affirmative and accepting no matter how dangerous or threatening the disturbed client may be? The commendation of Rogerian therapy therefore is made both with gratitude and with caveat. There can be no doubt that it has vast advantages in family treatment. Through it, families can be led to better communication, more genuine acceptance of one another and of their differences, and deeper appreciation of their own assets. In some

difficult and refractory cases, another therapy or a referral may
be indicated, but that could be said for any school of therapy.
That is why we have so many of them, and why so many of us
have become eclectic in choosing differing strokes for different
folks.

4

Ross Speck and Carolyn Attneave in Network Therapy

There is no other single goal—not cure, not treatment, but to enable people to cope and to share their strengths in coping, and set them up to handle the inevitable next crisis of living.

Ross Speck and
Carolyn Attneave

Early in her counseling career, Carolyn Attneave began to organize impromptu treatment teams of clergy, physicians, teachers, scout leaders, and relatives around families in trouble. She had seen how a small town could support and guide a nine-year-old schizophrenic girl, with the storekeeper, schoolteacher, neighbors, and kinfolk all aiding the parents through their care and understanding. As a single parent herself, she located adoptive grandparents and siblings for her two children at St. Christopher's parish in Lubbock, Texas.

Even in childhood, Dr. Attneave began to notice the interrelated patterns of association and custom that humanity effects through community life. Her mother had belonged to the Delaware Indian tribe, and young Carolyn had spent long visits with her maternal family in Arizona. Later experience in social work with black communities, stratified southern families, and blind, deaf, and paraplegic adults would make her aware of the interdependent needs and strengths that surround all of us.

This background provided a natural bond when she met Ross V. Speck, who had his own convictions about how social networks operate to transcend kinship lines. Speck, reared in a small Canadian town, had known the experience of extended family and network connections, and had come to share a conviction similar to Attneave's about people helping people.

Dr. Ross V. Speck is clinical professor in the department of psychiatry and human behavior at Jefferson Medical College, Philadelphia. He serves on the national research committee of the American Association for Marriage and Family Therapy, and is a member of the American Family Therapy Association. The prolific author of more than seventy research papers and editorial advisor to two family-therapy journals, he is known as a specialist in family problems of schizophrenia, depression, and delinquency.

Dr. Attneave was trained at the Philadelphia Child Guidance Clinic and worked with the Massachusetts Department of Mental Health, where she coached nonprofessionals in community and human development. She is currently professor of psychology and Director of Indian Studies at the University of Washington, in Seattle.

The common interest Speck and Attneave share in the development of the theory and techniques of social-network intervention has occupied a major amount of their professional time since 1965.

Network Therapy

A social network includes the nuclear family and all of the kin, but it also encompasses friends and neighbors, associates at work, and significant others from church, school, and institutions who are willing to risk involvement. The assembling of a network

brings together many people who know one another, share knowledge and experience of one another's rituals, and bring to their
meeting vestiges of guilt, secrets, collusions, and memories.
When the intervention team assembles a network for therapeutic
purposes, their accumulated tensions are also inevitably assembled.

The Case of a Three-Year-Old Terror

One example of how the network plan operates is offered by
Speck and Attneave in *Family Networks*. It involves a three-year-
old boy whose frightening behavior featured the grabbing of
knives and his threats to kill anyone nearby. He was one of four
children, all under school age, living with a widowed mother. The
father had been stabbed to death with a knife in a neighborhood
quarrel in front of his family, who were watching television at the
time! Now the little boy appeared to be trying to avenge his father's death.

Of the siblings, one was mongoloid, one severely damaged
from birth defects and hyperactive, and one—only one—without
apparent problems. This troubled young family had moved out of
the neighborhood where tragedy had struck them and were now
residing in a new area, with few friends or relatives nearby.

The customary approach to such a case, Speck and Attneave
remind us, has been the "sick-and-needy-person model." That is,
treat the grief problem of the family, find a social agency to help
the mother with the children, and assign professionals to the case.
However, in this case the network procedure was brought to bear,
instead. A rapid assembling of their few friends, neighbors, some
relatives, agency personnel, church-related persons, and foster-
family types made up a group sizable enough to tackle the problem. Under the stimulation of the network program, the mother
and this assemblage of persons inaugurated some fresh and creative plans, found help for control of the miscreant boy, and aided
the lonely, grieving mother to mourn and to find more friends.
"The tribal unit," the authors assert, "accomplished all this in a
much more efficient and self-perpetuating fashion than the con-

ventional pattern of professional responsibility and patient dependence."[1]

Psychotherapists could do worse than review the ancient tribal wisdom that called on a wide network of people to cooperate in the succor of a few. As a matter of fact, this team claims some advantages to network therapy that conventional means may not afford. "When networks or tribes become stuck in reverberating pathological processes, and many do, the members can be helped better by network intervention than by the herding of individuals into clinics."[2]

From Retribalization to Exhaustion-Elation

Following a significant number of cases similar to the three-year-old terror, Speck and Attneave know now what to expect. They have ascertained that a network program proceeds through a spiral of six typical stages. The gathering of forty or fifty persons—some eager, some resistant, but all puzzled—and guiding them through a therapeutic experience calls for experienced workers who know how to work their interventions. Leadership is supplied by a conductor, with the assistance of an "intervention team."

The first of these stages is *retribalization*. This event brings together people who have not seen one another in a long time. The noise level is high, and excitement is palpable. The conductor might begin with some nonverbal exercises: jumping up and down will do, followed by a swaying step to release tension, then by a request for persons to express in one word how they feel.

The conductor presents an introductory talk about the goals and problems before the network group, and lays out the schedule for future sessions.

Second comes the inevitable *polarization*, a stage in which people naturally and without premeditation choose up sides. The conductor can use some of these subgroups to "fishbowl" a demonstration in the center of the circle, to work out role plays, or to spark discussion of the family problem that brought them all together.

Third comes the stage of *mobilization*. Energy has been developed by the polarization process; it can be focused and mobilized constructively. Now tasks can be pressed on the network. Areas of need are described. Suggestions are solicited for meeting those needs.

Fourth, a certain degree of *depression* can be expected. Facing up to the difficult tasks before them will bring not only resistance and some discouragement, but even desperation. Yet, in a group of forty or more people, there will be some energetic activists who can be counted on to attempt solutions to the problems and draw others out to join them. Now the conductor can form subgroups of a half-dozen persons each, and these can be assigned discussion topics that deal with how to meet the tasks before them. The topics could involve anything from hospitalization to finding a job for an unemployed single parent.

Fifth comes *breakthrough*. The conductor will attempt to move action from the network intervention team to the network itself. The subgroups are assigned the task of discussing solutions and returning with reports at the next meeting. The group process often gets moving at this meeting, and the subgroups may stay on hours after the intervention team has departed, to accomplish their assignment.

Sixth comes the anticipated *exhaustion-elation* in both the team and the network. A natural recovery period follows and leads to the next meeting. A cycle of these six emotional experiences (or some part of them) can be expected at each meeting.

Preparations for Networking

Network therapy for a family problem such as that of the mother with the three-year-old terror will require skillful preparation. Attneave and her colleagues make no pretense that just anyone can pull off this kind of leadership, or that every troubled family would benefit from the network procedure. Networking is not offered as a panacea, but as an alternative form of therapy. Psychodynamic therapy will benefit one kind of family, behavior modification will reach another. Individual psychotherapy, group

therapy, crisis intervention—each has its procedures in which patients, therapists, and techniques are combined and operated.

There are two indicators for network therapy: presence of the
type of stress that can be ameliorated through relationships with
other people, and the availability of a social grouping that can
comprise a network.

"The role of the conductor is somewhat like that of a good discussion leader. . . . A sense of timing, an empathy with emotional
highlights, a sense of group moods and undercurrents, and some
charismatic presence are all part of the equipment that is desirable. Along with the ability to command attention, the leader
must have the confidence that comes with considerable experience in dealing with difficult situations and knowing human
beings under stress."[3]

Teams usually include three or more leaders. They are coached
in nonverbal encounter techniques; they work with the conductor
to verify impressions, check strategies, trade roles, or let off steam.
Network sessions run from three to four hours, and the work is
strenuous, so teams must be resilient. If they are, and if the network gets into the planned organization, the family in distress is
going to be helped.

Network Theory

Networks are no novelty in human experience. They operate in
many guises. They may be found as religious revival meetings,
alumni gatherings, peace marches, and rock concerts. The network effect can be seen in much of daily life as a fundamental
characteristic of social behavior. The experts say, "The social network is a relatively invisible, but at the same time a very real,
structure in which an individual, nuclear family, or group is embedded. There are malfunctioning social networks as well as malfunctioning families and individuals. The retribalization goal of
social network intervention attempts to deal with the entire
structure by rendering the network visible and viable and by attempting to restore its function."[4] Speck and Attneave see this

form of therapy not as an atavistic referral to some patterns of the distant past, but as a way of restoring a lost vital element of relationship. The goal of network intervention, as they explain it, is to use the power of an assembled community to shake a rigid system and free up those changes the people would like to effect.

With impressive confidence in community resources that can develop creative solutions for people's predicaments, Speck and Attneave warn that the same social network that heals can also hurt:

> Most of the behaviors traditionally interpreted as symptoms of mental illness derive from the alienation of human beings from just these relationships and resources. . . . Our experience is that in some instances the entire social network causes and perpetuates pathology, scapegoating the individual and/or the family.[5]

Network therapy is designed to reconnect such alienated persons and families. If problems have arisen from broken relationships, then solutions are to be found in rebuilding relations. The network is designed to reopen the system and correct our rampant depersonalization.

Members of a network gradually begin to realize that they are part of a human cluster. It is then that the network effect starts to be felt. With no desire to oversimplify the explanation of an ingenious intervention, Attneave and her cohorts do remind us that we are naturally part of one great bundle of life. Network theory partakes of that insight.

The Pastor's Network

It will have occurred to every pastor who reads about Carolyn Attneave and Ross Speck that the parish church is a natural network. In it are to be found individuals, families, and the extended kin of in-laws and cousins. Beyond them, however, lies a network of friends and acquaintances, business associates, schoolmates, people who grew up together, fellow workers on committees, sister representatives on boards and task forces—a nearly endless network of Christians in communication with one another.

The realization that we have networks in the parish church is nonetheless a far cry from organizing them into the kind of therapeutic work described by Attneave and Speck. That work not only requires a demanding attendance record at sessions and the intentional investment of a large number of people, but also requires a trained leadership team capable of handling a difficult process. It must be added candidly that the parish network capable of this degree of devotion to a family's problem would be unusual. They would be expected to sustain their emotional support through a trying series of meetings that involve some self-revelation and cooperation across personal connections not previously explored. Though it be an indictment of sorts to point it out, the fragile fabric of many parishes is incapable of supporting such a heavy demand. It is ironic that Speck and Attneave can assemble a congregation of somehow-related persons to perform in this way, while the average pastor might dread the emergence of resistance and pettiness such network therapy could evoke in the subsequent life of the church.

To admit this, however, is not to exhaust the possibility of adapting network principles to the realities of a church still struggling toward realization of ministry. A few parishes will be capable of finding a leadership team for a family-therapy network and following through with the prescribed working sessions. Many others will be obliged to alter the schedule and trim the details a bit, but long experience proves this can be done. Parish organization is capable of numerous adjustments that can be of aid to families under stress. To cite only a few, parishes are adept at meeting problems of illness, loneliness, and acute financial need. They have also shown skill and compassion at welcoming refugee families into the community. So far they prove less adept at helping families through scandals and shame, adolescent delinquencies, divorce and single parenting, chronic disability, and chronic depression.

Parish churches do minister effectively to families in bereavement, aiding them through their grief work and subsequent adjustment. Their organizational life is also capable of reaching those who are alone through nurture groups, couples' clubs, family clusters, guilds, and circles. Deacons and others regularly assist families in financial need, by lending money, supplying food, or extending scholarship grants.

In such difficulties as these, the existing parish network is already operational. Though distinctly different from details of the Speck-Attneave program, some of these measures can meet similar needs. Moreover, many churches offer an outreach to members and families through carefully trained teams for lay ministry. Some of these teams counsel bereaved persons following the death of a loved one. Some are persons who have already experienced the specific problem that troubles a family, e.g. parenting a handicapped child or supporting a family whose breadwinner is confined to a mental hospital or incarcerated in prison. This sort of people-to-people parish program, which brings together those of similar experience for mutual encouragement, is a typical network achievement of church life.

Ever since its inception, the Christian church has resembled an extended family in which we are all brothers and sisters of one another through Christ. Our historical network is established through our theology and readied for use in compassionate ministry.

Surely the parish can do better in extending ministry to those in distress from divorce and alcoholism. We have enough persons who have suffered from these disasters and passed through the ordeal of adjustment that mutual-aid groups could be provided. Allowing for limitations of staff, skill, and resources in membership, the church can also be ready with referrals to appropriate agencies and helping professionals. Here the parish network spreads well beyond membership lines, to constituency and neighborhood. The network modality is not beyond the capability of parish churches; it simply calls for adaptation to a ministry similar to what has been the expertise of the church for centuries.

But wait. There is still another application of network therapy in church life, and that is to the clergy itself. Attneave has seen this clearly.

Social networks have also proved helpful for people in difficult or sensitive positions, such as clergy. They offer a useful way to explore the social difficulties that pastors face, allowing them to talk freely and frankly about all aspects of their social needs and roles. Discrepancies between clergymen's expectations of themselves and their perceptions of parishioners often cause tension. One or more of the conventional modes of therapy may be helpful in reducing such tension; but when the initial appraisals of the situation include the use of a family network map, it allows for an exploration of the context in terms that are nonjudgmental, yet theologically acceptable. Clergy of many faiths have also found it useful to think of the seasonal and life-cycle celebrations and rituals of their liturgies as examples of spontaneous assemblies of family networks. They report that it deepens their appreciation of the processes involved within a congregation at times of personal celebrations like weddings, bar mitzvahs, or of seasonal festivals and holy days.[6]

II

Systemic
Family Therapists

5

Jay Haley
in Strategic
Family Therapy

A therapist who is incompetent and does no more than sit in silence and scratch himself will have at least a fifty percent chance success rate with his patients.

Jay Haley

The Power Tactics of Jesus is the arresting title of one book by therapist Jay Haley. As it turns out, this wry venture into Christology has more than a little to do with family therapy. Haley discusses Jesus's use of paradox, as in calling for simultaneous conformity and change in regard to the law ("Think not that I am come to destroy the law" *versus* "Ye have heard that it was said by them of old time . . . but I say unto you . . ."). He also describes Jesus' canny use of power to corner adversaries and disciples alike, Pilate as well as Peter, in an irreverent exegesis of the Gospels.

These concerns with paradox and power are integral to Haley's methods in family therapy and central to his therapeutic philosophy. Haley's own use of paradox in therapy is a clever power play designed to gain control of a family system, thence to alter that system toward health.

Who is Jay Haley? Currently codirector of the Family Institute of Washington, D.C., he is also clinical professor of psychiatry at the University of Maryland. He formerly served on the renowned staff of the Mental Research Institute at Palo Alto, also the address of Virginia Satir, Don Jackson, and Gregory Bateson. Later he moved to direct research at the Philadelphia Child Guidance Clinic, where he worked with Salvador Minuchin and Braulio Montalvo. Their history records that these three held an informal seminar for forty minutes twice daily in their car pool, as they commuted between home and clinic, thereby working out many issues of concept and technique. As editor of *Family Process*, Haley sorted out the burgeoning literature and vocabulary of the expanding family-therapy movement, brought practitioners into contact with one another, and recorded the advances being made by separate therapists otherwise out of touch with one another.

Andrew Ferber, who coaxed an autobiographical statement from Haley for the collection *The Book of Family Therapy*, pictures him as a brilliant curmudgeon: "irritating, fascinating, always helpful, always right, and always not quite complete . . . a persistent gadfly, generous with criticism, stingy with praise, fun at the right distance, but opaque up close."[1] Now Haley is chiefly occupied with the training of teachers of family therapists and conducting traveling seminars on this topic with his wife and codirector, Cloé Madanes. Their presentations and carefully styled writing have become highly influential in the family-therapy movement.

Jay Haley's Therapy

For a therapist of Haley's demeanor and convictions, it follows somewhat naturally that he has a penchant for giving directives to his families in therapy. As a matter of fact, therapeutic directives make up a significant part of his method. These directives can be as simple as a nod that encourages a counselee to continue, a smile that affirms, a frown that checks. They can also be more explicit verbal cues: "Tell me about that," or "I had hoped you wouldn't repeat that error." Directives can be to do one thing or not do another. They can be straight; they can be paradoxical; and they can be very authoritative.

But there are certain kinds of directives that are out of place in therapy: those that would involve the therapist in making decisions for a counselee. No therapist desires the responsibility of answering questions from dependent clients along the lines of "Should I quit my job?" or "Do you think I ought to divorce my husband?" Decisions for matters such as these belong to the counselees. Nor are the Haley directives ever to be confused with good advice. To make wise advice workable requires rationality, and people who are disturbed enough to seek therapy may be temporarily short on rational thinking. Thus telling a disturbed couple to treat each other considerately is generally not useful at all.

One type of directive is a direct order, given as an assignment. Haley directs; he does not suggest. He is precise in the details of his assignments. Normally there are only two types: telling people what he wishes them to do or telling them what he does not want them to do. His imperatives and prohibitions sometimes have the purpose of fostering rebellion. In all instances, he aims to avoid debate by stating the directive firmly and without adducing any reasons: "I'm going to ask you to do something that you'll think rather silly, but I want you to do it anyway. I have my reasons, but I'd rather not go into them."

A passive, unemployed man may be directed to apply for a job in a business he would not care for at all. No matter, it's good practice for his assertiveness training. A depressed woman may be required to accomplish a series of small tasks, simply to activate her energies. The more trivial the tasks are, the more likely she is to become disgusted but also successful and less depressed.

At the following interview, the person will be asked to review the assigned task and report its accomplishment or failure. Haley exudes sternness for failures, not because someone has failed him as therapist, but because the counselee has failed.

Some of these tasks are what Haley dubs "metaphorical."

They take a roundabout route to make a major contact, rather than colliding with it head-on. For example, a family had adopted a little boy who exhibited severe anxiety in one area: He was terrified of dogs. Haley directed that the little fellow adopt a dependent little puppy. A needy, affectionate puppy was located and brought home for the lad to care for as his own adoptive charge. He soon lost nearly all his terror of dogs and also began to live with increased security and ease in the home of his adopting parents.

Paradoxical Directives

A craftier form of directive in Haley's method is the paradoxical injunction borrowed from Milton Erickson's uncommon therapy (often cited by Haley). Simply put, the paradox upsets the power balance in the family system and moves the system into some new and different direction that has long been resisted. The essence of a paradoxical directive is to prescribe the symptom: directing persons to do what they are already doing, until they weary of it.

The final step in such a paradoxical directive is itself paradoxical. In this stage the therapist feigns surprise and indicates, in one way or another, "Well, you certainly fooled me! You arrived at a solution I hadn't considered." If the therapist were to respond artlessly with, "That's just the outcome I had planned," it would blow the improvement and likely return the family to their previous crisis.

Strategic family therapy seeks to rearrange the locus of power within a family. Haley, in one memorable case, created a malfunctioning unit in a family system. A mother and a grandmother were at odds over the behavior of a bed-wetting child. The grandmother interfered with her daughter's management of the child; the mother was uncertain and upset about her own responsibilities. Hardly unexpectedly, the child continued with chronic enuresis.

Haley simply assigned exclusive responsibility for the child's discipline to the grandmother, ordering the mother to remain aloof from the relationship. When, after one week's unhappy experience as disciplinarian, the grandmother was pleading to be relieved of her onerous task, Haley, who habitually champions the parent, reversed the directive and assigned the mother exclusive care of the child. This was accompanied by a directive to the grandmother to stay out of the relationship. Grandmother seemed satisfied with that and retired from the job. Mother took over. The bed-wetting diminished and, in a rather short time, ceased altogether.

After long experience with the use of paradoxical directives, Haley has outlined the method in eight succinct stages:

- Establish a relationship with the family or counselees.
- Define the problem clearly and unambiguously.
- Set the goals distinctly and make sure they are understood.
- Offer a plan whereby the task is to be accomplished.
- Gracefully disqualify the current authority on this problem (mother, teacher, friend) and take over the power.
- State the paradoxical directive as a prescription.
- Observe the response and continue to encourage the customary, undesired behavior.
- Then avoid taking credit for the change that follows.[2]

Case histories can be assembled that illustrate the effectiveness of prescribing the symptom in scores of problems: bed-wetting, masturbation in public, conflict over child discipline, eating problems, hypochondria, and compulsive arguing, to name a few. Although paradoxical directives are not to be used with schizophrenic patients, they are highly effective with many distressed persons.

Perhaps the most famous illustration of this technique comes from Milton H. Erickson's unusual practice, which profoundly influenced Haley's work.[3] In this case, Dr. Erickson was confronted with a pair of newlyweds, both of whom were enuretic. He demanded their unquestioning and unfailing obedience, and then prescribed an unusual assignment. What they had once done by accident, they were now to do intentionally. For two weeks they were to wet the bed before getting into it each night.

At the end of this fortnight, they could enjoy one dry night and sleep in the bed without wetting it. But on the following morning of the sixteenth day, "You will arise, throw back the covers, look at the bed. Only as you see a wet bed, and only then, will you realize that there will be before you another three weeks of kneeling and wetting the bed."[4]

Every night, with great embarrassment, the couple knelt and wet the bed as directed. And on the morning of the sixteenth day, when they threw back the covers, their bed was dry. They tacitly colluded to cease obeying Dr. Erickson and went to bed that night without performing the soaking ritual. This they did for three consecutive weeks with a completely dry bed. Vincent D. Foley, commenting on this astonishing result, writes:

> Did the couple make the decision to change their behavior or did they follow the injunctions of the therapist? Did their unconscious perhaps obey the therapist? Did they realize the use of paradox? Is it really important for them to know the answers to these questions? Haley would argue that it is neither important or necessary since change could be and in fact was produced without their understanding.[5]

The Beginning Therapist's Problems

After considerable experience in training family therapists, Haley is able to categorize the tendencies of beginning therapists that thwart effective work with families. These he contrasts with the work that seasoned therapists do and novices will accomplish later. Because these same errors are likely to be repeated by pastors, they are presented in the left-hand column of the following chart, to be compared to the practices of the experienced therapist on the right.[6] (See p. 79.)

Haley's Basic Concepts

For Haley, family therapy is inextricably systemic. Not only is it altogether evident that the family itself is a system, but the

Seasoning of the Therapist

The Beginning Therapist	The Seasoned Therapist
Tends to emphasize the individual as the focus of treatment	Emphasizes the individual's inner feelings as the product of relationships
Tends to be unduly interested in background history of the family	Uses the family's past history only to understand better the present, and works with minimal information
Tends to gather information and to emphasize diagnosis and evaluation before intervening	Begins interventions at an early stage, de-emphasizing diagnosis
Tends to describe the family's problems as if they were independent of the therapist	Works with present data: observes not that they are hostile to each other, but that they have shown the therapist how hostile they can be
Tends to bring out the underlying feelings and attitudes of the family, even if destructive	Knows it is a waste of time to review a family's unsavory feelings about each other
Tends to adopt the same method of therapy for every family who comes for consultation	Knows that family therapy requires different approaches for different problems
Tends to focus on one person at a time and have that individual talk to the therapist	Orchestrates the therapeutic work to attend simultaneously to the entire family and their observable interaction
Tends to side with one faction, e.g. a victimized child	Is careful to balance any side taking so that it comes out even, or to avoid it altogether
Tends to overemphasize what is going on in the family at the time	Takes the more positive stance of highlighting therapeutic goals and results

therapeutic group also comprises a system. Husband, wife, and therapist make up a social system in which relationships are built and problems can occur. In this peculiar triad, the family therapist cannot be free of responsibility for what begins to occur in the marital dyad. In common with other communication theorists (in fact, chief among them), Haley understands the therapist to be an active participant in the family's interaction.

The Limitations of Conventional Therapy

Haley holds strong opinions. He has outspoken convictions that vary from those of other family therapists. He believes there are marked limitations to the claims made for personality change, the effectiveness of diagnostics, the value of having patients understand their therapy, the usefulness of interpretation by the therapist, and the validity of one stereotyped modality of treatment.

Too much is claimed for the power of change through therapy. He believes colleagues to be in error when they assume that theories about doublebind communication (*see* Index) or identification of the Identified Patient will change persons or alter relationships within a family. Such theories describe conditions, but do little more than that. Likewise, Haley believes psychodynamic theorists make a mistake when they think that if people understand what they are doing that is damaging themselves, they will stop, and never do it again. He holds that people do not change radically just because they have gained new insight.

Nor is the skill of diagnostics much honored by this matter-of-fact theoretician. Diagnosis, Haley contends, is overrated, puffed more for the comfort of the therapist than for any value it may bring family members. Diagnostics actually belong to an irrelevant model of counseling, the medical model, while Haley's communication model has little in common with medicine. In any case, diagnosis tends to be inappropriate for the process of therapy, and ought to be kept to a minimum. Its payoff is so modest that the effort is contraindicated.

There is little need for the family to understand the course of therapy or its rationale. Therapists have no obligation to overexplain their work. Indeed, it could be counterproductive to say to a family, "I am going to ask you to sculpt this scene because you have a hard time describing your emotions in words." Such a judgment might freeze the family in a still more inarticulate condition, and Haley would be disdainful of any therapist so awkward as to utter that sentence. He would also be critical of the widespread, though defensible, practice of ministers identifying their procedures to counselees. Such propensities, he would contend, mitigate the power of the therapist.

Interpretation is another procedure in counseling that Haley views as of little worth. In sharp contrast to some psychotherapists of the psychodynamic school, he would eschew such interpretations as this: "You must see, then, that your attitude toward your own son is a reflection of how your father evidently regarded you." Haley's reason for rejecting this kind of interpretation, even though it has long been a standard technique in some schools of counseling, is a coldly practical one: Interpretation does not bring about any change in attitude or behavior.

Haley reserves some of his scorn for those consistent, doctrinaire therapists who have just one therapeutic approach and stick with it all the time. Specific problems require special techniques in his system; no one standard therapeutic method is going to be workable in all cases. Different approaches have different advantages, he cogently contends. The perceptive therapist will draw upon an ample file of counseling techniques to treat particular problems with appropriate modes.

The Person of the Therapist

Equally sure of his beliefs about the profession of a family therapist, Haley is clear that a therapist has no choice but to exert personal power tactics for the good of the family, to serve as a model for people to emulate, and to work with the family as a whole, rather than with individuals.

The therapist is to remain in firm control for a very good reason: "If family members gain control over what happens, they will perpetuate their system and their distress."[7] No client-centered stance here, no democratic sharing of decision making, either. Rather, we witness a process of negotiation with power. It would be a mistake, however, to suppose that this power is grasped for its own sake, in some interpersonal competition. Haley's use of control is practical: Families will get better sooner if they are in consultation with a therapist who takes charge. A wise therapist will simply not allow clients to decide how therapy is to proceed.

In addition, there is no getting around the fact that the therapist serves as a model for the family, demonstrating calmness, avoiding personal entanglements, and clarifying communication. The way the therapist handles arguments, meets opposition, deflects anger, or defuses the seduction of flattery will teach families how to follow these same lines. It is all part of the educational process inherent in marriage and family counseling. In fact, by his example, Haley encourages parents to work together to protect their hierarchy and preserve the boundaries between themselves and their children.

Certain about the need for the therapist to treat the family as a whole, Haley criticizes the practice of counseling one person at a time about relational problems. He is convinced that individual treatment often fails as therapy. It is preferable to see everyone in the household as a group and to form no coalitions with any members or subgroups. He grants that some limited headway can be made through working with an individual, but it is an uphill and inefficient way to operate. He teaches that while it is possible to change persons by seeing them alone, the skill required is often too much to ask of the average therapist.

Jay Haley's Contributions for Ministry

Haley's influence in family studies is immense, and his contributions have merit for the ministry, as well. He is gifted with a scintillating style and a talent for the synthesis of ideas. His is an intensely practical approach that comes through with quite plain instructions for trainees in family therapy. Here, for example, (with my own observations in parentheses) are his "musts" from *Problem-Solving Therapy* about the temptations a therapist must resist:[8]

• Therapists must avoid ever minimizing their counselees' problems (because the problems loom large in the experience of the sufferer, regardless of how they appear to others).

• Therapists must avoid abstractions (troubled people need concrete images).

• Therapists must avoid coalitions with counselees (watch those entangling alliances with victims and scapegoats).

• Therapists must avoid debates about life and meaning (a pitfall for clergy, for whom it's a temptation).

• Therapists must avoid the assumption that all problems are identical (to pained counselees, they are unique).

• Therapists must avoid the attempt to appear wiser than they are (try instead, "Obviously you know more about your marriage than I do; I simply bring an outside opinion").

• Therapists must avoid crystallizing power struggles (avoid mentioning power; instead clarify and relabel counselee behaviors).

• Therapists must avoid irreversible positions (prevent people from stating uncompromising positions they cannot change).

Haley's writings are peppered with succinct bits of wisdom: In an interview, speak first with the least involved adult; peg your gains, in order to prevent slippage; get the problems defined as issues rather than as persons, and so forth. Haley teaches therapists to participate to the fullest in their interviews, to comment aloud on what is happening to them, to use candor and plain speech, and to stay clear from what he dubs the five B's: being passive, being inactive, being reflective, being silent, and being wary.

Haley's wit has entertained many a training conference and a host of readers. He is known for his mastery of the *bon mot*. His definition of a normal family is one in which no one has ever had therapy or been arrested. His denigration of cotherapy is famous:

"Just as many swimmers who are uneasy about drowning will associate with a life preserver, so do many therapists prefer company when they dive into a family."[9]

Haley's bent for paradoxical communication shows through not only his therapy, but also in his instructions to other therapists. Here, for example, is a list of pointers on how the therapist (or pastor) can fail:

- Insist that the presenting problem is unimportant.
- Assume that only years will effect any change.
- Arouse people's guilt.
- Ignore the counselee's real world.
- Neglect attention to the family life cycle.
- Refuse to define goals.
- Avoid evaluation.
- Ignore theory and its contribution.

Faced with that ever-typical difficulty, the chronically scrapping couple, Haley applies his own fresh strategy in a gem of luminous sense:

> As an example of a typical problem, a couple can be continually fighting. . . . The therapist can relabel or redefine their fighting effectively because they are not expressing what is really on their minds; he can suggest that their fighting is a way of gaining an emotional response from each other and they both need that response; he might say that when they begin to feel closer to each other they panic and have a fight; or he can suggest that they fight because inside themselves is the feeling that they do not deserve a happy marriage. With a new label on their fighting, and directed to go home and have a fight, the couple will find their conflict redefined in such a way that it is difficult for them to continue in their usual pattern. They are particularly tempted toward more peace at home if the therapist says they must fight, and that they must for certain reasons that they do not like. The couple can only disprove him by fighting less.[10]

In short, Haley offers ministers an armamentarium of procedures to use in their pastoral family therapy. To be sure, his paradoxical directives are too heavy for most of us to be able to manage. But his insistence on planning, on clarity, and on plain talk, to choose only a few, are of eminent use. We can't go wrong with that kind of intelligent procedure. His commitment to systems theory is summed up in one succinct observation: "As he gains experience, the therapist begins to view family therapy not as a method but as a new orientation to the arena of human problems."[11]

6

Salvador Minuchin's Structural Family Therapy

I am not an authoritarian family therapist; I am a therapist who believes in authority.

Salvador Minuchin

"My name is Sal" sounds like an innocuous way to begin a family interview, but it obscures the powerful punch that soon follows in the therapeutic work of Dr. Salvador Minuchin. A family in his care will quickly experience challenge, stress, and the need to restructure the ways they relate to one another. He has become famous for such discipline in therapy.

Who is Salvador Minuchin? Once described in a *New Yorker* profile as "the Pavarotti of family therapists,"[1] Minuchin is not only a performer; he is also an expert in his specialty. His spectacular work, as seen in live sessions before entire conventions of therapists or on videotape, have put him in a class by himself.

Minuchin and his wife, Patricia, are currently engaged as independent consultants, trainers, and supervisors in New York City. He is also a research professor of psychiatry at New York University Medical Center.

In both his previous work at the Wiltwyck School, where poor blacks were his patients, and also at the Philadelphia Child Guidance Clinic, he applied family therapy to the poverty culture.

In Philadelphia he once directed an experiment in which eight blacks and Puerto Ricans were trained as family therapists or supervisors to train still others in the ghettos and barrios. This program reached more than thirty people before the federal grant that funded the project was cancelled. But by the time the project was forced out, Minuchin had demonstrated what he had planned: Family therapy is not limited to middle-class clients, where it has its widest acceptance, but can be applied among welfare families, as well. In addition, he had confirmed his own style of therapy. Knowing that poverty-level families tend to be more active and also disdainful of delay and abstractions, he moves rapidly with them, and keeps them moving, too.

Disorganized families tend to be headed by an overwhelmed and powerless mother who has few consistent rules; their communication is often fractured, their noise level high, their misunderstandings rife. Families of the slums, being contemptuous of the system, may ignore ordinary protocol, but so does Minuchin.

Born of Jewish parents in an Argentinian village in 1921, Minuchin grew up in a shtetl-like setting that approximated an extended family. Apparently his family was not sophisticated about the Spanish language, or they might not have given their young Smerl his alternative Spanish name of Salvador (Savior), so dear to local Roman Catholic families.

He grew up to attend medical school and later served as a physician in the Israeli army. It was the Holocaust that aroused Minuchin's interest in victimized children and their family background. He came to apply this interest to families in pain and poverty; and that is how he became their champion and therapist.

Salvador Minuchin's Therapy

Minuchin begins by observing the ways family members relate to one another. This, as with much else, he does without appearing to be working at all. He greets the family, kids them along, cajoles some persons a little, strikes up conversations about unexpected subjects, all the while watching the typical transactions of family members. His purpose is to "draw a family map," making a preliminary assessment for himself. Through all this he is engaged in "joining and accommodation," as he calls it, an operation that creates a therapeutic system and establishes him as its leader.

As the therapist, Minuchin goes on to probe the family structure. He inquires about relatives, keeps alert for a parental child (one assuming the role of a little mother), listens for any indication of temporary loss (unemployment, recent hospitalization, and so forth), and observes the health of the marital subsystem to ascertain its longevity (is it the first marriage for both partners?) and its prospects for stability or divorce. He is joining and tracking the family as he accommodates to their system and accepts them at the outset, without seriously threatening their structure as yet. For the present, he clarifies statements and follows their interests.

To Minuchin, the art of family therapy

> . . . means to join a family, experiencing reality as the family members experience it, and becoming involved in the repeated interactions that form the family structure and shape the way people think and behave. It means to use that joining to become an agent of change who works within the constraints of the family system, intervening in ways that are possible only with this particular family to produce a different, more productive way of living.[2]

The objective is for family and therapist to form a partnership, with a more or less formulated common goal: to free the family symptom bearer of her symptoms, to reduce conflict and stress for the whole family, and to learn new ways of coping.[3]

In this joining phase, the therapist can be downright folksy. He uses two maneuvers related to size when working with small children: one is by height (he kneels to be at the level of a child he's talking to), and the other is through an appropriate level of language (asking the name of the child and her sister, for example).

Joining and Restructuring

In Minuchin therapy, joining the family involves more than entering their ambience and getting acquainted with their peculiarities. It also includes the process whereby he diagnoses their problems and gathers data about their characteristics. Joining is an early step toward exerting a change in the family structure. There is no getting around the need for the structural family therapist to come into the context of the family with whom he or she is working.

In one example of many, Minuchin cites a twelve-year-old asthmatic girl who had been referred to a child psychiatrist for her mounting physical and emotional problems. The psychiatrist insisted upon seeing the entire family. Almost immediately upon meeting them, he drew the family's attention to another problem, an older sister's obesity. In that, their context was enlarged, suddenly and unwillingly, to yet another Identified Patient. From that point on, work proceeded on the relationships between the parents. The child with the asthma began to get along with less medication. The therapist had accepted their already vexing concern and had even amplified it, had joined their perspective, and then helped them to restructure their experience with one another. That restructuring brought about the change.

Restructuring operations are the main work of this type of family therapy, and can be utilized only after accommodation has been made. Restructuring operations are those confrontational interventions that challenge family members and compel a change in their system. Thus, although Minuchin has joined the family system as an avuncular friend, he also maintains sufficient freedom to make interventions that are intended to upset the family organization, forcing its members to adjust to him in ways that will facilitate movement toward therapeutic goals.

Accommodation operations are used to gain entry into the family. They consist of getting acquainted, sharing mutual interests, and friendly exchanges, but Minuchin has a clear purpose behind them:

> I like to tell anecdotes about my own experiences and thinking, and to include things I have read or heard that are relevant to the particular family. I try to assimilate the family's language and to build metaphors using the family's language and myths. These methods telescope time, investing an encounter between strangers with the affect of an encounter between old acquaintances.[4]

In *Family Therapy Techniques*, he and H. Charles Fishman discuss restructuring the unresolved conflicts of parents as follows:

> The therapist might say to the parents, "When a four-year-old is taller than her mother, maybe she is sitting on the shoulders of her father," or, "A four-year-old is no match for her parents if they pull together," . . . or, "You two must be doing something wrong. I don't know what it could be, but I am sure if you think together, you will find out what it is, and moreover, you will find out the solution."
>
> If the therapist decides to concentrate on the spouse dyad and their dysfunctional transaction and in that way to separate the overinvolved mother-child dyad, he will have to handicap the child's detouring strategy. He must say to the child, "When you explain your parents' behavior, or when you support your mother or father, I am fascinated by how fast you move from being 10 years old to being 65 or 208 years old, and then running back to become 4 years old. But isn't it strange when you become your mother or father's grandmother? I will help you grow down. Bring your chair near me and be quiet while your parents deal with issues that concern them, where you don't have any reason to be, and no competence whatsoever." Or the therapist can tell one or both of the parents, "I want you to help your child to grow down by asking her to be quiet while you two discuss your issues."[5]

As an example of paradoxical therapy, Minuchin recounts the case of the Henry family, which consisted of a nineteen-year-old son and his divorced mother.

The two lived alone, extremely isolated and enmeshed. They
came to therapy originally because the youth had a psychotic
episode. Following hospitalization, he returned to college and
did fairly well. But as the young man's social life began to develop, his mother became increasingly depressed.

One day they call their therapist and the young man reports
that he is suicidal. He says he is afraid he is going to "jump out
the window." The therapist tells the mother that he sees the
son's suicidal threat as extremely serious and it is her responsibility to keep her son from harming himself. He gives the
mother the assignment of keeping an eye on her son so that he
does not jump out the window. No matter where he goes, the
mother is to watch him. They are to sleep in the same room,
and the mother is to attend class with the young man. The
mother consents, because she, too, feels the gravity of the son's
threat and is impressed by the therapist's description of his suicidal behavior as her responsibility. So the mother and son
spend more time together than they have for years. She sits in
class and goes around campus with him.

As the young man is taking sailing class, they call the therapist to ask whether the mother should also go out sailing with
him. The therapist says that indeed she must, since he might
do something suicidal like jump out of the boat. So the next
day, a rainy Saturday, mother and son go out in the sailing din-
ghy. After a few days the son calls up stating that he wants to
be freed from having his mother go everywhere with him. The
mother is similarly motivated. The therapist, however, tells the
mother that she should not allow her son to go out alone until
she is convinced that he is not suicidal. Mother and son fight
more than they have in years. The mother investigates adult
education. The young man spends a good deal of time on the
phone. Finally, the mother gets her son to assure her that he is
not suicidal. Relieved, both go back to their everyday lives,
each irked with the other and more autonomous than they
have ever been.[6]

Minuchin's therapy emphasizes structural change as the objective of family therapy. This objective is accompanied by change
within the individuals, too. Systemic change and personal change
go hand in hand. Restructure of the family system is not the

change itself, but can lead to it. In the starvation disease of anorexia nervosa, for example, Minuchin proceeds to join the family as usual, then begins to remove the problem of the child from family interaction. With the Identified Patient thus attended, Minuchin will work with restructuring family relationships simultaneously while continuing his therapy with the presenting problem of the I.P. herself.

> An individual therapist tells the patient, "Change yourself, work with yourself, so you will grow." The family therapist makes a statement of a different order. Family members can change only if there is a change in the contexts within which they live. The family therapist's message is, therefore, "Help the other person change, which will change yourself as you relate to him and will change both of you."[7]

Diagnosis Without Apology

Unlike some family therapists, Minuchin has no hesitation about using either the term or the technique of diagnosis. To him it is the process whereby the therapist accommodates to the family, accepting them and blending in with them, and begins to assess their total experience of interaction from his new vantage point.

Diagnosis is a process in which he estimates the strengths of the family's structure and their boundaries, tests their flexibility, and checks out how enmeshed or disengaged they are. He determines the developmental stage the family has reached (preschool, child-launching stage, or whatever), and he evaluates how their symptoms are used by them to maintain their family system. Through all this, Minuchin continues to assess their predominant transactional patterns and their available alternatives. He also probes their areas of support and stress. It turns into a thoroughgoing diagnosis.

Minuchin's diagnostic work, like that of many family therapists today, is combined with his interventions. His so-called accommodation to the family is mixed with challenges to their family structure and system. He customarily questions their pathology. In irritation, they attempt to explain their patterns to the therapist, only to find that their operations are far more complex than they knew and that aspects of competent and harmonious behavior also need to be acknowledged, to round out the picture.

In these cases, he utilizes standard statements of puzzled amazement to emphasize his incredulity at the family's contentions: "Isn't it wonderful how you can elicit from your child only his negative, monsterlike characteristics, while he seems to present to me only an intelligent and humorous ability to look at life?"

Escalation of Stress

Conspicuous in Minuchin's therapy is a dissonant measure known as "escalating the stress," a deliberate maneuver to unbalance the family system so it may be restructured in a healthier shape. His procedure features such shocks as verbally attacking a woman until her passive husband finally comes to her rescue and unites with her against the new threat of this therapist. Or Minuchin will goad an anorectic girl who has the starvation disease: "Tell your mother she doesn't love you enough; that's why you look like a scarecrow."

The rationale for this "mad" method of arousing and angering counselees is that it shifts the area of conflict to a new problem. By creating a no-exit crisis, Minuchin forces families to examine their relationships in an utterly new light. Families then experience movement in their problem because their perception of reality has been challenged, and they begin to see the outlines of alternative possibilities. When this is successful (and for Minuchin it is effective in a stunning number of cases), relationships are respliced in a new configuration that becomes self-confirming.

Structural Techniques in Therapy

Minuchin's techniques are legendary. He prohibits anyone from talking about another family member in session: "She is taking your voice," he will warn the person being described. He

often rearranges the seating, to break up coalitions or block interruptions. He champions underdogs, to help them change position
in the family hierarchy. When a husband is overcontrolling,
Minuchin will scold *the wife* for allowing her husband to be so
dominant.

> Instead of telling a family member to change, I tell another
> member, who has a significant complementary relationship to
> the first, to help the first to change because the first cannot do
> it alone. This tactic uses the power of the family's own system
> of mutual constraints, which makes it difficult for one individ-
> ual to move without support and complementarity from the
> others. In effect, I turn the family into my cotherapists.[8]

Minuchin uses and teaches the use of mimesis, the practice of
adopting the vocabulary, tempo, symbols, and gestures of a family. Another form of accommodation, mimesis helps the therapist
join the family and become one of them. This entry eases the way
to confrontation, assignments, or unpopular observations, as well
as supportive understanding.

In one videotape, Minuchin is shown pointedly ignoring a
woman for the entire hour, in order to dissipate her power and
emphasize other subsystems in the family. He will also forge coalitions in the family so he may divide and conquer them, thus
supporting one abused person. About such procedures he says,
with characteristic candor, that he inflicts pain in order to avoid
pain.

Minuchin's method of championing the Identified Patient is
not necessarily to protect him or her from the family. Rather he
places the I.P. in smaller and more manageable conflicts that can
be handled. It remains a superior method for shielding the scapegoat, for it aids growth and experience.

Minuchin's Basic Concepts

The framework for Minuchin's approach is termed "structural
family therapy"; he encounters the individual within the context

of the family. His therapy is openly directed toward changing the structure of the whole family system. Family members typically interact according to arrangements that determine their transactions. According to Minuchin, these arrangements, some of which are implicit and some explicit, form the family's structure and need reordering, if problems are to be solved.

From systemic changes will come alterations in each of the lives within that household, since when a family structure is changed, each individual's experience has to change, also.

Minuchin believes that the normal family has a structure that can be seen only in movement. Family structures are not static, but active. In order to understand a family's relationships, he builds a scenario in the clinic and lets them act out their interaction, rather than just tell about themselves. "Instead of talking about a difficult child, I develop a situation where the child misbehaves," he once told a reporter. In the clinical interview he observes typical transactions among the parents and children and watches how they restructure their patterns to meet a crisis.

Coping families will normally adapt to stress in a manner that maintains their continuity through a kind of "business as usual during alterations." Dysfunctional families (those who cannot cope) will respond to new conditions and crises with rigidity; they can hardly abide restructuring, and will require help.

According to Minuchin, the structure of a family system has the following characteristics. 1. It is an open system, through which change will move from society into the household. 2. It goes through stages of development and necessary restructuring as members are added and subtracted. 3. The system will usually adapt to changed conditions, to maintain continuity and growth. 4. It will maintain homeostasis through its transactional patterns. 5. It contains functional subsystems and such boundaries between them, as we see between parents and children.

The dysfunctional family is so structured that its members blur their boundaries, some parents acting immaturely or some children parentally. Or they may be overprotective of one another or deny the all-too-evident conflict that they experience. Dysfunctional family structures involve a great deal of unwise enmeshment with one another, and therefore a lack of appropriate authority. Dysfunctional families, by Minuchin's definition, require restructuring.

In his family therapy, Minuchin proceeds with impressive confidence. He expects to see prompt change in the first session. To watch him in action is to realize that he trusts his experience and his theory. It is his conviction that any transformation in the family structure will produce at least one possibility for further change. He is convinced that the family has self-perpetuating properties that will aid them in maintaining any new changes, even in the absence of a therapist or in subsequent periods of time.

The Family Model

In the Minuchin construct, the family model is conceived as possessing five related parts. As theory, it is useful for application to therapy, and consists of the following:

• *The family structure* itself is the core of the model. It is the invisible set of functional demands that will organize ways in which family members interact. The children, for instance, may have learned to convey messages to their irascible father through their mother, who acts as an intermediary.

• Their *transactional patterns* are maintained by two constraints. The first is "generic," being the rules that govern the family, e.g., the hierarchy of parents over children. The second is "idiosyncratic" with mutual expectations and trade-offs of family members in a *quid pro quo*. For instance, the wife may offer to press her husband's wrinkled suit if he will drive Effie to her dancing lesson that afternoon.

• *Family maintenance* is a self-starting mechanism, for a family maintains itself and finds alternative patterns for restructure, but will not move beyond their bounds of tolerance. That limit may be reached when a grown son plans to move out to his own apartment and the mother begins to get migraine headaches. In such a circumstance, guilt-inducing maneuvers may begin to appear.

• *Subsystems* within the family shoulder the responsibility for carrying out the functions. For example, the dyad of the parents is one subsystem; they assume the mothering/fathering tasks. Or the children may form a rebellious coalition as a subsystem to frustrate their elders; that, too, is a type of function. Others are conceivable: a subsystem of mother and daughter who prepare the food, and so forth.

• *Boundaries* in the family define who will participate and how. Families have boundaries around their enmeshment (the way they cling together as a mass). They have others around disengagement (like that grown son who is moving out). Coping families have clear boundaries around their relationships. Dysfunctional families may have inappropriately rigid boundaries around their disengaged situation, or diffuse boundaries around their enmeshments.

Stress in the Family

Every family learns how to meet and handle stress, but some learn it better than others. When one member of the family meets stress outside the home, the family can often close ranks to support him. Stress in one person will require adaptation in the others; it is a major function of families to support their members. Thus a man who is criticized by his supervisor on the job may, in turn, criticize his wife when he reaches home. She may be able to provide him the support he needs in their subsystem of the marital dyad. Or the stress may be moved into other subsystems to be handled differently, perhaps even chaotically, as others are affected.

A family adapts to stress in ways that make restructuring possible while maintaining continuity. Otherwise there will be dysfunction—perhaps a runaway child, an infidelity, or a separation. Occasionally, when it has come into such stress that it can no longer cope, a family needs to have its boundaries restructured. One name for such restructuring is therapy.

Stress inevitably shows up at the transitional points of family life: marriage, births, moving, graduation, illness, death. All developmental changes bring new rules, and they offer occasions for adjustment and learning. Likewise, stress will accumulate around any special problem (a retarded child or an illness). Over time, a family will be transformed as it continues functioning under stresses and will need to have its boundaries restructured so it can cope again.

Minuchin represents his therapeutic style as a program to preserve individuation and support mutuality in a family, a seemingly contradictory challenge; yet these are obviously the marks of a healthy family.

An Addendum in Pastoral Theology

Training the clergy for their specialty of pastoral care is hardly the top task to which Salvador Minuchin devotes his energies. Yet he is not averse to aiding the clergy in their work of family therapy, and in fact has guided many of us, along with social workers, psychiatrists, and psychotherapists, through his seminars and workshops. There is no reason to doubt that insights into pastoral theology will come from persons who are themselves not theologians. Minuchin leads us to insights for our ministry through his conduct in therapy and the emphases of his writings.

There is no necessary incongruity between confrontation and good news. Too many clergy back away from what could be therapeutic confrontation of counselees, either because they fear it is discouraging to the counselee or because they find it threatening to themselves. Although they realize a parishioner needs some honest confrontation (say about the treatment of her children or facing up to a damaged marriage), they may pusillanimously skirt around the issue, rather than risk upsetting the person. Yet confrontation is an intervention that can be handled with care. Minuchin is capable of this as well as the more direct challenge. When he notes a father answering questions on behalf of an adolescent son and he challenges the son with, "Did you want your father to speak for you?" he is presenting an indirect but potent confrontation to the father. Yet from such a riposte no upset is likely, little anger aroused.

This technique is useful far beyond the counseling session. Trainees in seminary therapy programs often remark about the effectiveness of their family-therapy training when it is applied to parish business and congregational life. Thoughtfully administered confrontation can be good news in pastoral care.

Many clergy are convinced that our personal attitudes exceed the importance of our techniques in pastoral therapy. It can be a surprise to learn that Minuchin also believes this same principle applies in family psychotherapy. In *Family Therapy Techniques*, he wrote:

> The phrase "techniques of family therapy" poses problems. It brings images of people manipulating other people. . . . Family therapy requires the use of self. A family therapist cannot observe and probe from without. . . .
>
> In my own case, my style has grown softer, and more effective. I feel free to use compassion and humor in joining with families. I have learned to use my life experience and my fellow feeling for families as part of the therapeutic process. Having made my share of mistakes in my life, I don't expect my patients to be perfect. I know that family members do the best they can, and that sometimes the results are very destructive. I am supportive, because I know that I cannot find a wrinkle in any patient's psyche that has not already been pinpointed, examined, and magnified by that person and by every family member. My challenges are sharper and clearer, and at the same time I have learned how to encourage the exploration of alternatives.[9]

In our training of pastoral therapists, we are frequently at pains to convince trainees that the way they use themselves constitutes a most important factor in their work. The teaching of techniques and the imitation of supervisors have notable limitations. It is possible, for instance, to adopt the plan of "joining a family," as Minuchin does in therapy; it is less conceivable to imitate the inimitable master himself. Each of us would do better in our family psychotherapy work through developing the use of himself, rather than trying to use all the techniques of the masters we study. For this reason, as well as others, we are advised not to rush to adopt the measure of "escalating the stress" that Minuchin uses. It is an inspiration that grows out of his idiosyncratic personality, not from mere technique.

This matter of using ourselves leads to another level of personality theory: *being* ourselves. Too many of us expend vast amounts of energy constructing masks and learning character parts in order to represent ourselves as someone we really are not. We clergy are peculiarly susceptible to this temptation. Such ill-advised efforts to "put on an act" come into prominence in clinical training programs for pastors, wherein they begin to adopt the manners and mannerisms of psychiatrists. But that again adopts the medical model in place of the pastoral model for our work. Paul Pruyser draws critical attention to this awkwardness in his *The Minister as Diagnostician*, wherein he regrets the tendency of clergy to enter into diagnosis in the manner of a psychiatrist, rather than in their integrity as theologians. It is well to recall David Roberts's insistence in his near-classic *Psychotherapy and a Christian View of Man* that our first task in ministry is to be theologians. It's a point with which Salvador Minuchin would hardly disagree.

7

Gerald Zuk's
Go-Between Therapy

Go-Between Process does not aim at personality change, which is an unrealistic goal of psychotherapy, but rather at a change in ideas, attitudes, and conduct in family members. It does not deal much with family history but rather concentrates on current events affecting the family and how . . . to alter responses to these events that are proving disruptive, disorganizing, and disorienting to family members.

Gerald H. Zuk

It is typical of Gerald H. Zuk to assign practitioners in family therapy, himself included, their comeuppance. With refreshing candor he characterizes his own Go-Between process as modeled neither after "the computer nor the Wagnerian opera." Without mentioning which groups do fit such categories, he is able to admit that dramatic, operatic reduction of symptoms are not typical among family therapists. Apparently they have a great deal to be modest about.

In the standard *Handbook of Family Therapy*, Zuk is described by M. Duncan Stanton as "a skilled, innovative, systems-oriented clinician who has been active in the field for many years."[1] From

1961 to 1980 he was the associate director of the department of family psychiatry at the Eastern Pennsylvania Psychiatric Institute at Philadelphia, then became professor of psychiatry at the Medical College of Georgia. He is now engaged in private practice, as well as serving as clinical professor in the department of psychiatry and neurology at the medical school of Tulane University and, somehow, as director of the family-therapy program of a large psychiatric group practice in the Los Angeles area.

His work in the 1950s with mentally retarded patients and their families led him to the treatment of schizophrenics and their families. He collaborated with Boszormenyi-Nagy (see chapt. 12) in the writing of *Family Therapy and Disturbed Families,* which was based on a conference he organized in 1964, one of the early national conferences for experienced family therapists.

Zuk has made noteworthy contributions to the literature of therapy, and as founder and editor-in-chief since 1979 of *The International Journal of Family Therapy,* he has influenced the direction of therapists. He has written widely about the disorders of childhood emotional problems, marital stress, delinquent behavior, adolescent acting out, school truancy, depression, and suicide prevention.

In looking back over one of his own cases, in which "reasonably skillful handling" had made "some difference," Zuk rather ingenuously notes:

> At the end, it is possible to report success but also areas of functioning in which it appears success is not apparent. This sort of outcome is far more representative in family therapy than what typically appears in the literature. The dramatic reduction of dramatic symptoms does certainly occur in family therapy as in other therapies, but it is not the typical case.[2]

Among family therapists, a group not famed for modesty, such candor is refreshing and unusual.

The Go-Between Process as Therapy

This therapist, in contrast to some others, offers no great pronouncements as he enters into the transactions of a family hoping to effect desirable change in their relationships. His goal is not conflict resolution but the replacement of "pathogenic relating" among family members. This may require some dislodging of habits or some unbalancing of the family system. He believes the time has come for the family's intimidating behavior and double-binding patterns to be challenged, and for values to be reexamined.

In the Go-Between process, according to Zuk, the therapist may enact three roles at different times and in differing circumstances.

• One is that of *side-taker*, in which he allies himself with (or perhaps against) certain family members in regard to issues that come up in the interviews. To the criticism that this practice is unwarranted or unwise, Zuk responds that families will not allow the therapist *not* to take sides, so the therapist is obliged to do it with awareness and skill for therapeutic purposes.

• Another role is that of the *go-between*, wherein Zuk sets the rules of communication among members of the family. This is done in order to create leverage for a change in transactions and to open the way for new patterns that will change the family's pathological ways of relating. Such mediation is designed to change the cycle of "vicious repetitive" behaviors in families.

• The *celebrant* role is one in which the therapist certifies important family events or crises. In this role he confirms or restores stability and continuity to a family under stress. Zuk compares the celebrant role to that of the priest, the judge, the physician, or the policeman, those traditional societal agents who assure community stability and survival of a system when dislocation has taken place. The celebrant "officiates" at some focal event: a new job (or job loss), an achievement, a hospitalization, a death, or perhaps the emergency caused by a runaway child. Thus a change in life is made significant and labeled, verifying that the experience is important, while enlarging the family's definition of their problem and associating the experience with others who have survived it. When that is accomplished, the role has been fulfilled, and the family no longer feels the need for a celebrant.

Short-term Therapy

In contrast with other advocates of short-term family therapy, Zuk insists that the majority of families limit the time the therapist has for working. He prefers to get on with the work and to complete it, because if the therapist does not move quickly, the family will. He contends that short-term therapy is successful because it does not violate the time frame that the majority of families will tolerate. For crisis situations, he considers six sessions suitable: for short-term family psychotherapy, some ten to fifteen sessions; for middle-range cases, twenty-five to thirty, and for what he allows as long-term treatment, forty or more sessions.

Zuk describes an engagement series of some three sessions to test the family's readiness to undertake the stress of therapy and to assess the strength and limitations of its members. In this period he examines their commitment to the process and determines if there is any possibility of engaging them over a period of time. He has found that working-class families have a somewhat limited openness to family therapy, as compared to middle-class families, and that minority families are especially suspicious of the therapy process, so that the therapist must move rapidly if such families are to benefit from it at all. Zuk doubts the value of family therapy that drags on interminably; with that, a great many of us would probably agree.

The Process of Therapy

Zuk's theory holds that therapy proceeds through four steps: 1. The identification of an issue that has family adversaries arrayed against each other 2. Intensification of the conflict by the therapist and/or the family 3. Efforts to define and delimit one another's positions 4. The reduction of conflict, a redefinition of it, or both.

Zuk knows his task can change many times during the treatment. A family in crisis is going to seek outside control to restore a sense of order in life, while a family in a state of some harmony can react positively to a jovial therapist. The same family may be in both situations during a series of therapeutic interviews, and the therapist will alter his approach to suit the mood of the members, to "resonate" with the family's mood.

Zuk has drawn attention to two dynamics in family interaction, which are instructive to all therapists: the use of silence and the use of laughter. Either one, he notes, may exemplify pathogenic relating. The silent treatment may be used in families to obtain compliance from a victimized member. Silencing is sometimes aimed at making someone a scapegoat. Typically it is adopted by two persons against a third, in what Zuk would label a "triadic" relationship. That such families need assistance in establishing better communication goes without saying.

In laughter he finds a "meta-message" that may disguise and disqualify the primary spoken message it accompanies. All of us have witnessed laughter as a cover for a hostile statement, a way of handling embarrassment, or perhaps as an indication of nervousness. But Zuk, in his essay, "A Further Study of Laughter in Family Therapy," analyzed and explained this phenomenon differently—as a form of pathogenic relating that injures relationships through creating scapegoats.[3] It is his contention that "all family therapies have to do with the masking and unmasking of victims and scapegoats."[4]

Zuk's Conceptual Framework

Over the years Zuk, who appears fond of hyphenated terms, has dubbed his as a "triadic-based" family therapy, or "Go-Between process." With some other family therapists (Bowen, Satir, and Haley, for example), he views family relations as based on triads (he prefers the term *triad* to "triangles"). When tension becomes high between two persons in a family, they will frequently focus on a third member as a means of reducing the tension. Thus parents in a strained relationship might begin to blame their child and scapegoat him. Or they may do something healthier and seek out a therapist to become the third member of their triad, in order to find some solution. More awkward triadic-based involvements may include the instigation of an extramarital affair, the adoption of some activity or hobby that excludes one's mate, or perhaps more frequent resort to the bottle. Indeed, alcoholism is often the third party in marital stress.

In any event, the triad is seen as the basic unit in emotional and interpersonal systems. Triads can shift within the family system. Alliances can change and then return to a previous state. In triadic-based family therapy, the therapist looks for and identifies these shifting triads in order to make a family assessment. All the time, however, he knows that when he is side-taker or go-between or celebrant, he may himself be one corner of a triad. Aware of this, his therapy always takes into account the influence of his own presence.

Certain triads tend to generate what Zuk calls pathogenic relating. Pathogenic relating consists of "tension-producing, malevolent, intimidating patterns of family members toward each other and the therapist."[5] The family may treat the therapist in the same malicious manner they treat one another. Such behavior can take the form of verbal intimidation, doublebinding, scapegoating, unjust labeling, threats, blaming, shaming, or silent resistance. Pathogenic relating is destructive to members of the family. It tends to erupt when value conflicts have reached a state of impasse or have clashed in disharmony. Pathogenic relating has a repetitive pattern that shows up in cyclical behaviors the alert therapist can detect.

Zuk has explicated his own theory about conflicting value systems in family living.[6] He designates values as being one of two types: those of "continuity" and those of "discontinuity." Continuity values express the goodness of emotional expressiveness, of humanitarianism, egalitarianism, wholeness, human interconnectedness, nurturance, and caretaking. As a religious example of continuity values, he uses Jesus and Mary, who epitomize the continuity values of forgiveness and mercy. In daily life, continuity values are more likely to be expressed by wives than their husbands, by children as against their parents, and by the family instead of the neighborhood or community.

Discontinuity values emphasize the goodness of rationality, orderliness, efficiency, law and regulation, analytic procedures, and realism. These are more likely to be expressed by husbands than wives, by parents toward their children, and by the community vis-à-vis families. In another analogy, Zuk likens discontinuity values to the stern discipline of Yahweh, who proclaimed the absolute clarity of right and wrong among his people, and their duty to obey.

Value conflict erupts when one side tries to subjugate the other to their concept of values, which can lead to pathogenic relating. The therapist must avoid automatically adopting one set of values when making interventions. In point of fact, the therapist must not assume that continuity values are good and discontinuity values bad, because both are essential to human existence.

That discontinuity values tend to generate political strength does not mean they are used solely for domination or injustice. Likewise it would be wrong to assume that the nurturance–caretaking stance of continuity values could never lead to contempt for rational understanding and orderliness. Either set of values, carried to extremes, is capable of abuse.

Zuk defines the "truncated nuclear family" as one in which there is an imbalance in the value systems, resulting in the children identifying strongly with their mother against their father. The children experience problems with authority in adolescence and adulthood as a result of growing up in such a family, and also experience hostility to any discontinuity values that have been promoted by their father.

Go-Between Family Therapy and the Pastor

It is not at all difficult to find direct application for Gerald Zuk's family-therapy theory and clinical approach in our pastoral ministry. Anyone who can conceptualize the need for a celebrant role, and even link that role to the priesthood, is our kind of therapist. Zuk's celebrant role reminds us to serve in ways we should have served all along. Whenever the pastor's presence enables families to celebrate nodal events such as developmental stages (births, graduations, marriages, retirements) or family crises (joblessness, illness, humiliations, deaths), these events become certified as significant and influential. There must be a hundred ways of recognizing such events; the church has practiced many of them through the years. They signify that the family is not alone at such times and has the support of the people of God.

No minister of the Gospel needs a reminder of how important it is to be available when death occurs in a parish home. In such a crisis, clergy presence confirms stability and helps restore hope to the grieving relatives. Any loss (indeed, any addition) to a family can produce a crisis. Many of our clergy need reminding that their presence is also appreciated at other critical transitional events: the first job, the new promotion (or a retirement or unemployment), the divorce, the moving day, or the return of a long-absent member of the family. Not only in Sunday worship, but in daily life and normal woes, we need to do theology and relate the life of humanity to the providence of God.

Zuk's example stands us in good stead when we observe his restraint. Note that he neither promises too much for family therapy nor offers dramatic solutions for difficult problems. It is sometimes an error of pastors to oversell the expected benefits of pastoral psychotherapy when they wish to convince church members to enter into counseling. Eager to get help to troubled parishioners, they err on the side of unrealistic promises, especially if they are inexperienced with the process or have become extravagantly enthusiastic about it. The better wisdom may be to assess the readiness of people for counseling and not rush them into an experience for which they are not yet ready. Our seeing their need more clearly than they do will not necessarily convince them. Whenever we, in our pastoral care, work harder on their problems than they are willing to work themselves, the prognosis can hardly be favorable.

Zuk's go-between role is a natural one for the clergy. The position of reconciler is one to which we have become accustomed; in family therapy or community or church action, it is part of our vocation. It is noteworthy that the go-between role is designed to reopen lapsed or blocked communications within a family. Sometimes the most meaningful contribution a therapist can make is to assist stymied persons in overcoming their poor communication habits and frustrations. Exercises in active listening, practice in speaking I-messages, directives on how to set aside regular times for quiet talks, assistance in expressing feelings—these go far in opening up communication.

There are times when the therapist's task is simply to model clear communication. This may call for the pastor to be an interpreter of one person to another: to ask a wife if she heard what her husband said and suggest she repeat it back to him or to ask the husband to repeat his message until both the sender and the receiver agree they understand its meaning. Then it is time to reverse roles and repeat the exercise, with the wife as the communicator and the husband as the receiver. The go-between role, simple though it appears, has profound implications in an interview (literally, it is the view between).

The exemplary value of Zuk's therapist roles requires the clergy to exercise caution with the side-taking role. It has its hazards for the likes of us. Not committed to any particular religious doctrine, Zuk is free to balance the score, so he takes no one person's side more often than necessary. For the clergy, this can be far more difficult. Programmed to seek particular categories of justice among relationships and to right wrongs where we find them, we are too tempted to favor, for instance, the abused adolescent over a blaming father, or the neglected wife in conflict with a heedless husband. In parish life, the hazards of side-taking could have ramifications that reach well beyond the counseling session. Zuk believes no therapist can be altogether neutral in family treatment, contending that even those who try to maintain neutrality are judged by the family as taking one side against the other. His warning points up what a precarious business this can be.

However, another practice of Zuk's can be recommended wholeheartedly, and that is his clarion directive to avoid what he has named pathogenic relating. This malicious intimidation of some family members by others happens not only in counseling interviews but also in household relationships. To put it bluntly, clergy themselves are not above tension-producing and intimidating practices within their own nuclear families and their families of origin.

It will be recalled that Paul, in writing to Timothy, despaired of church leaders whose family life was chaotic. Rhetorically he asked how they could look after a congregation of God's people if they were incapable of handling their own family relationships.

The clergy are not blameless in treatment of their parents, siblings, spouses, and children, frequently making demands of their families that are neither fair nor wise. Pathogenic relating is seen in clergy families in all the familiar ways it is to be found in other families—plus a few more. Some clergy families indeed fit the definition of truncated nuclear families. The concern that clergy have about public appearance and reputation can drive them to a depth of severity, moralism, or guilt peculiar to our profession. The occasional temptation to reform everyone in the family constitutes a tendency to sin that easily besets the clergy. It suggests an imbalance of discontinuity over continuity values. Gerald Zuk has done us a personal service (probably quite unintended, in this case) by reminding us to curb our tendency toward pathogenic relating within our own families. We can be grateful to him, not least, for that.

8

John Weakland and Paul Watzlawick in Brief Family Therapy

Family therapists are an unruly crowd; the quantum jump from original training to family therapy has proved a heady wine for some of them, who in the seclusion of their private offices are experimenting with ideas of yet another jump, this time from the orthodoxy of family therapy to . . . pushing the idea of interaction to extremes, such as taking it quite seriously.

Paul Watzlawick and
John H. Weakland

"Irreverence, irony, and rodomontade": For such varied attributes as these, observers have applauded the innovative membership of Palo Alto's Brief Therapy Team.[1] Two of that team, John H. Weakland and Paul Watzlawick, are presented together here, not because they are ideological twins, but because their contributions and their writings both in books and numerous articles are nearly inextricable. Both of them are veteran staff members of the Mental Research Institute at Palo Alto, California, an agency made famous not only by these two, but also by its founder,

Gregory Bateson, and Don D. Jackson, its psychiatric consultant. Over the years the Mental Research Institute has also had Virginia Satir, John E. Bell, and Jay Haley on its staff.

John Weakland, an anthropologist and researcher, reports that he came to his present role as a licensed marriage, family, and child counselor through the process of reviewing and reworking his own family relations. "In short," he writes, "I became a family therapist by one part good intentions, two parts scientific curiosity, three parts response to challenge, and four parts self-defense."[2] In his anthropological training, he worked with Margaret Mead and Ruth Benedict at Columbia University and the New School for Social Research. He is the author or coauthor of several books and more than fifty professional papers, and he serves as advisory editor to *Family Process.*

Paul Watzlawick is a communication theorist, linguist, and psychologist who was born in Austria and has taught on the faculty of San Salvador National University. An entertaining writer whose style includes numerous allusions from history, literature, and psychology, he is the author or coauthor of some eight books and scores of learned articles. Known as a maverick, his training of students through the one-way mirror is often unconventional. His research work has encompassed a number of unusual projects: for example, a recorded anthology of the mechanics of communication in conjoint family therapy sessions. He serves as a research associate for the Mental Research Institute and a mentor in their Brief Family Therapy unit.

Brief Family Therapy

Brief family therapists have distinctive methods of working. The therapist usually sits at a desk placed against the wall, with the open side toward patients. The patients are seated close together in swivel chairs, so they can turn toward one another. Before them is a low coffee table, placed so it cannot shield their body language, as a higher table might.

The therapy does not exceed ten weeks of sessions; more often it comes to six or seven. Arthur M. Bodin describes six typical interventions used in Brief Family Therapy:[3]

- *Advertising, instead of concealing,* the characteristics or actions of patients. These therapists will not ignore a stutter, a limp, or a spectacular frock, but instead may draw attention to their observation and ask its meaning and possible use to the patient.

- *Prescribing the symptom.* A technique widely used in family therapy, also called the paradoxical directive. In effect, asking the patients to continue to behave in their undesirable ways—to fight more often, drink again, steal more—the objective being to bring about the very antithesis of the injunction and open the way for behavioral change. This, of course, is a version of the "reverse psychology" parents have used with their children for generations.

- *Harnessing of self-fulfilling prophecies.* A design in the form of a forecast that is tailored toward a prearranged outcome, as when a matchmaker speaks independently to both a man and a woman and asks each, "Have you noticed how Sarah (or David) has been eyeing you recently?" The forecast will contain suggestions that can lead to self-fulfilling results.

- *Reframing of incomprehensible behavior.* As in the words of a therapist to a schizophrenic teenager: "I notice that you have nearly perfected a difficult skill, namely, the art of attracting attention to yourself by your ingenious and imaginative range of unusual behaviors. Actually you are to be complimented for your rare ability . . . in drawing attention away from your parents precisely when it looks as if they are in danger of becoming too heated as the discussion becomes an argument."[4]

- *Undermining an existing suspicion by the planting of another and more desirable suspicion.* Thus a quarreling couple may be counseled to keep logs on habits that annoy them and post these lists for both to examine. A matching list of acts that please them is to be kept in secret, with the long-term effect that such an influence will become positive for each.

- *Benevolent sabotage.* For example, parents, worried and angry over their daughter's tardy returns at night, are advised to cease their waiting up and aggravated speeches and try a different tack. They are to come to the door slowly, fumbling with the chain and lock, and admit the girl with a mumbled apology of, "I'm sorry, I guess I was sleeping too heavily. I'll try to remain more alert another night," thus leaving the latecomer confused by a veiled threat that such an encounter may happen again.

Equally unusual is the Weakland-Watzlawick method of supervising therapists. A family case will typically involve not only the therapist or cotherapists, but also three observers who act as peer consultants. The consultants, watching through a one-way mirror, may telephone into the session or even walk into the room with questions and advice. This can work as a ploy to remove stigma from the therapist by having the consultants make an unpopular suggestion and take the blame on themselves. Or it can promote a discussion between consultants and therapist(s) as to whether the counselees are capable of making any change in their style of living. This is a technique that has been honed to a sharp edge by the therapist Peggy Papp, through her skillful use of a so-called "Greek Chorus" (see Peggy Papp, The Process of Change, Guilford Press, 1983).

"Solutions" That Complicate Problems

Weakland, Watzlawick, and their associates are convinced that the real problem is not in the difficulties that families experience but rather in the way they meet their difficulties. Like the behaviorists, they note that many of the problems we face are actually the result of awkward attempts to solve our problems. These therapists have fashioned interventions to cancel that tendency, to alter old habits with new and variant methods that upset the dysfunctional systems in families.

These therapists, in order to elicit the family's participation, establish goals for treatment. Then they seek to reach those goals with the person who is most desirous of change. Using reframing, prescription of the symptom, and other measures, they work with this most approachable person in the family system, thus establishing an ally and an influential colleague within the family.

This approach is direct and pragmatic. It gets down to issues rapidly and unashamedly moves into the presenting problem of a couple or family, regardless of what underlying problems may be discovered en route. Parsimonious in its selection of material, Brief Family Therapy advances resolutely toward problem solving and early termination of treatment. Counselees can return later if their covert problems begin to emerge to consciousness.

Brief Family Therapy has evolved into a new way of viewing human problems. En route, Watzlawick, Weakland, and their cotherapists began to define an entire class of problems that derive from incorrect solutions. Common sense approaches had been inadequate to deal with the problems. As Lynn Hoffman characterizes it, "In almost any problem, when the common sense effort to eradicate it fails, it is probably because the solution itself is part of what keeps the problem in business."[5]

The Therapeutic Doublebind

From the first, when Gregory Bateson and Don Jackson were engaged in theories about schizophrenic communication, the Mental Research Institute has been engrossed with the phenomenon of the doublebind, a two-level communication in which the overt demand at the first level is covertly nullified at the second. "I order you to disobey me" is a doublebind, because to follow through and do the disobeying is already to have obeyed the order. Such a conflicting order prevents people from finding a solution or escaping the conflict aroused by this dilemma.

Although, as we shall see subsequently, this can be an insidious device when used as a weapon in family relationships, the doublebind has its beneficent use in therapy. "The therapeutic doublebind" is described in *Pragmatics of Human Communication*, by Watzlawick, Beavin, and Jackson. A case history is cited, concerning an alcoholic husband and his martyr-type caretaking wife. The therapist gave the wife the astonishing directive to join her husband in his drinking, but *to keep one drink ahead of him.* The expected result was that she would become inebriated before he, thus forcing him into the caretaker role. If he was to avoid the complication, which he could easily foresee, he had to drink far less than usual or nothing at all.

Such therapeutic interventions are puzzling and tend to confuse therapists who work in conventional ways. But then the Brief Family Therapy group has never been very conventional.

The Theory Behind Brief Family Therapy

Weakland and Watzlawick, though often playful and irreverent, can turn quite scholarly, too. This they do in their carefully worked theory that takes seriously the recalcitrance most of us have toward making any change in our living patterns. Based on two abstract concepts from philosophy and mathematics, they emphasize the difference between first-order change and second-order change. First-order change is the sort that can take place within a family and yet leave the family system basically unaltered, while second-order change revamps the entire system.

A case that neatly illustrates these two levels of change is offered by Ronald Levant:

> For example a mother may demand that her son *want* to go to bed on time. It is not enough that he simply go to bed on time; he might be doing so because "he was forced" (a change in behavior induced by the appropriate application of the opposite member, thus first-order change) rather than because "he really wants to be good" (a second-order change in attitude).[6]

Second-order change, preferred by all psychotherapists and mothers because it is the more profound, is based upon the theory of logical types developed by Alfred North Whitehead and Bertrand Russell. In their view, the group (the family) exists at a higher level of abstraction than the individual, and may behave differently from the individual. The group, in fact, may be greater than the sum of its parts.

Seizing upon this theory, Brief Family Therapists compare second-order change to the gearshift in an automobile. Each shift clutches the gears into a new speed—an intervention of a "higher logical type" than merely pressing down on the accelerator. Moving into the "higher logical type" shifts us from the previous accelerator frame of reference.[7]

Inspiration for these therapists' theory of first-order change came from the work of the French mathematician Evariste Galois (1811–1832), whose theory sets forth the differentiation of individuals and groups in yet another way. Four properties, derived from mathematics, measure these differences:

• Any member or combination of members in a group will still comprise a member of that group, and cannot place themselves outside it. They are still included within the whole [family].

• It is possible to change the sequence of operations within a [family] group without altering the result. The randomness of their interactions matters little if they are going to return to their homeostasis.

• If an identity number in a group is combined with another member in the group, the group is going to yield that same member: Four plus zero equals four, but four times one also equals four. The inference is that no permanent change has taken place.

• Each group member has a reciprocal member, and their combination (e.g., four times one-fourth equals one) helps explain why a change that appears to be a large one (for example, family bickering altered to pseudomutuality) may have been a very slight shift, indeed.

Thus group theory offers a way of explaining the puzzling French proverb, "The more things change, the more they remain the same."

Second-order change is the only way to alter the entire system, restructuring the homeostasis of a family. This is a larger order and calls for reframing the reference within which a family has mistakenly defined their difficulties and hopelessly set out to eliminate them.

Lynn Hoffman, who has served as an interpreter for Weakland and Watzlawick, illustrates second-order change handily by reference to a familiar family problem:

To take the example of the mother and food, she may find that lately nothing she serves pleases her thirteen-year-old son who prefers a snack when he comes from school and is then never hungry for supper. It is a good guess that the problem is not really food; the problem is that the rules which govern their relationship are being challenged. The boy is getting to be more independent, more defiant.... The setting for the mother-son relationship has by the nature of things been complementary and unequal; now it is, also by the nature of things, moving toward a more symmetrical or equal one. Some families, after a period of confusion, arguments, and attempts at compromise, will take the leap by themselves. Mother will decide to let the child eat what he wants, or he will go on doing so and she will stop fighting him. Or they may reach some other compromise that gives him more autonomy.

In other cases, the relationship setting may be hard to shift, perhaps because the father never speaks to the mother, and in a way depends upon the boy to put her in her place. Or the mother may feel she is losing her baby, the child she turns to when the father is absent or works late or otherwise distances himself. The escalation of first-order solutions produces a problem that makes the family suffer more and more, and they finally take the son to a therapist on the grounds that they can't control him. The therapist's business is to find out whether, indeed, this is a problem that calls for a [first-order change or] total reorganization.... He will do well to check out the family's previous solutions, to be sure there is not some obvious piece of advice that would set everything right. Perhaps the mother has suddenly gone on a gourmet cooking binge and the son hates spicy foods. If this is worked out, and peace descends, one can assume that no major structural change was indicated.

But if the issue really has to do with the range of allowable behaviors between mother and son, the food is only a symbol of a larger battle. A second-order change has to be negotiated. The therapist might attempt to make this change by asking the mother if she would allow the boy to choose his own diet, at least for two days out of the week. Again, if this solution is accepted no more therapy is indicated; the family is amenable to an outside push to solve the problem. But this is not always true. The mother may resist any suggestion of this kind because it will mean that the boy will "win" and she is angry at his attitude of disrespect. This kind of reaction usually indicates that the therapist is confronted by a self-reinforcing cycle: a behavior (the mother's reaction) that feeds the problem (the son's defiance).[8]

Meanwhile, as Hoffman suggests, there is the problem of the father. He has not been willing to take any stand on the issue, either for the boy or for his wife. It gets complicated:

> The more the father feels one-down to the mother, the more the boy acts defiant; the more the boy acts defiant, the more the mother tries to control him; the more she tries to control him, the more one-down she feels; the more one-down she feels, the more the father will come in to help her; the more the father comes in to help her, the less defiant the boy is; the less defiant the boy is, the more the mother resumes her domination of the father—and the whole sequence starts again.[9]

Hoffman lists some therapeutic suggestions. 1. That the father take his wife to a restaurant one night a week, to reward her for all her misery, and leave their son to forage for himself. This could take the boy out of his place in the vicious sequence and force the parents to face themselves and their marriage. 2. Suggest to the family that they cease trying to eradicate the problem and point out aspects that might make them happier with things as they are. This prescription of the symptom flies in the face of common sense and forces the family to face questions such as: What would the consequences be if the problem were solved? Would the now-spirited home life become lifeless, and could Father deal with Mother's energies, once they were released from combat with her son? 3. Prescribe a new ritual to symbolize the previous closeness of mother and son. Twice a week, she is to prepare the kind of meal he likes best, then sit close to him while he eats, maybe even cutting up his food for him, while Father eats the same meal and quietly accepts any comments about his table manners. This humorous task attacks both sides of the dilemma, viz. the difficulty all three are having in saying good-bye to their former relationship and their intellectualized desire to do just that.

Such therapeutic directions are aimed at the goal of disrupting the cycle. It is hoped that this would break some link in their "game without end" and bring them to the second-order change they so obviously need.

The Mystery of the Doublebind

The doublebind is a concept in common usage today, but it got its start in a now famous 1956 technical paper written by Gregory Bateson, Don D. Jackson, Jay Haley, and John Weakland. "Toward a Theory of Schizophrenia"[10] has had notable impact on family psychotherapy, psychiatry, and indeed the entire mental-health movement. A doublebind demands an impossibility of us, as with a sign that proclaims:

IGNORE THIS SIGN.

There are five ingredients in a doublebind. 1. A negative order that means "Don't do that." 2. A simultaneous order at another level, which cancels the prohibition in a manner conveying, "I didn't mean it." 3. An implication that any comment is forbidden: "We don't even talk about it." 4. A situation of overriding importance, so the receiver must discriminate correctly between the contradictory messages. 5. The guarantee that a mere reminder of the original order is all that is necessary to elicit new frustration or panic.

The receiver of such a communication is in a no-win situation, foredoomed to failure by an insidious system. It would be a mistake, however, to assume that the doublebind is always a transaction between two persons. Weakland has transformed that model into a feedback model that illustrates how a triadic situation (often two parents with one bewildered child) can engage in the doublebind. Moreover, he has pointed out that all of us sometimes respond in multilevel manners, as well as receive multilevel messages.

To make matters worse, the doublebind often keeps recurring

within the same relationship. There are occasions, as the 1956 paper pointed out, when the only recourse for the victim in this game is to lapse into psychosis! Normally the victim retreats and tries one or more of three possibilities. One, the victim supposes that something has been overlooked in the message and begins to search for hidden meaning, but only becomes more confused. Two, the victim tries to literally follow both of the contradictory orders because, since the message didn't make sense anyway, what's the use? Vincent Foley notes that anyone familiar with the army will recognize this response. Three, the victim may withdraw from all human relationships in order to screen out incoming messages, which is schizophrenia.

Okun and Rappaport illustrate the doublebind in a simple family story about a young girl who is constantly given the message that she does not show enough consideration for her parents. When, however, she approaches them to show consideration, she is told, "You are crowding us. Don't interrupt our privacy!" When she retreats to show consideration for their privacy, she is told, "You don't care about us. Stop ignoring us!" She is only ten years old, and does not have permission or the power to escape the family system.[11]

She can make an attempt to escape the family system through a retreat from reality, wherein she may not be held responsible for her behavior. This has happened, and is pathetic.

A Theory of Communication

No school within the family-therapy field has made a greater contribution to communication theory than the Mental Research Institute therapists. Their assumption has been that we can learn about a family's system by studying their communication, verbal and nonverbal:

• You cannot *not* communicate. Invariably, whether conscious or unconscious of it, whether intending to do so or not, everyone communicates something. All behavior is communicative and indicates something about the relationship between people. What passes as a mere shrug may shroud a profound resistance to some suggestion.

• Every communication has content and a relationship aspect, such that the latter classifies the former and is therefore meta-communication. It is not only the substance of the message, but also the intent and meaning of the sender, that make a difference. There is no such thing as a simple message. We even communicate about our communication. A woman may mention that a certain film has arrived at the neighborhood theater, but the relational meaning of that information is that she needs an evening of intimacy with her husband. Relationships are defined by command messages that are sometimes hidden within the content.

• We communicate both digitally (verbally) and analogically (nonverbally). The verbal aspect deals with the content, the non-verbal with the expectation and relationship aspect. We must remain concerned not only with the message, but also with what it indicates about a relationship. Father may say, "That's interesting" to some comment of his daughter, walking away as he says it. The act speaks more clearly than his words about his actual interest.

• All communicational interchanges are either symmetrical (equal or reciprocal) or complementary (in which one leads and another follows). In the first instance, there is equality and equal distribution of power between persons. In the latter, there must be a leader and a follower; one dominates the other. The implications of communication theory for family relationships are obvious. For instance, a marriage that is symmetrical and reciprocal can be a good relationship with a basis for working through differences. However, a marriage in which the complementary relationship finds one dominating the other will need assistance to change. For that task, Brief Family Therapy has been designed.

The Pastor and Brief Family Therapy

Weakland and Watzlawick offer in their Brief Family Therapy the prototype of what the clergy can learn from most family therapists; many of their techniques are adaptable to parish ministry, but some are not. Take, for instance, suggesting to a person that he might not be able to accept a change for the better in family relations. By challenging the spouse of an alcoholic, the parents of a truant, or a squabbling couple, telling them that a solution might be too upsetting, we compel them to take a decisive stand. They may decide to prove how wrong we are and make a quick improvement to show us up. They may, on the other hand, agree they are no longer able to return to stability in their relationships, thereby agreeing with the implied diagnosis that theirs is a systemic problem requiring earnest work with and by the entire family. In either case, the pastoral therapist is well-advised not to be too wise or triumphant in the outcome. It is preferable for the family to conclude that they were the instigators of their own realization. And in many cases, that is probably true.

Weakland and Watzlawick have enunciated a maxim that is instructive for our work with families: Numerous problems in family life derive from incorrect solutions. Alas, many families worsen their interpersonal situations by the very act of attempting to improve them! In those cases where a common-sense effort to solve a problem has not succeeded, it is probably the solution that keeps the problem alive.

These therapists cite a domestic drama in which a wife complains that her husband is not open enough and won't communicate with her. The husband reacts by clamming up more than ever. This propels her to yet more dissatisfaction and questioning of him, which leads to even greater silence on his part, until the wife bursts out with a fit of pathological jealousy. Their awkward attempts at handling their own situation have only exacerbated an already vexing problem. A skillful therapist asks counselees what solutions they have already tried and how far these have gone in meeting their problems. Through evaluating these, discarding the counterproductive ones, and delimiting their repetition (dysfunctioning families have a penchant for repeating their failures *ad nauseam*), the pastoral therapist and family can sort out their more promising attempts and add to them new features not previously conceived.

The straightforward confrontation that Weakland and Watzlawick adroitly use to label meaningful communication will not be lost on many clergy. We, too, can note the stutter, the limp, the new frock, and inquire about their meaning to their owners. We can gently ask about their impact on other family members. Drawing attention to the nonverbal communication going on within the family group and testing its significance constitute a lesson in family education. Watchful for body language during the interview, therapists will help families by teaching them how to observe the meanings of gestures and the impressions they make with their nonverbal movements.

While Weakland and Watzlawick prefer second-order change which improves the family system, over first-order change, which makes limited alterations in some subunit, they do not despise first-order change. Indeed, in their sometimes parsimonious approach to brief therapy, they encourage us to think small. There is no derogation of modest alterations, which can bring prompt relief. Small changes can have a ripple effect, influencing wider circles of change in other aspects of family life. They can make a difference for the time being and later bring the family back for subsequent work on still other problems.

With all the exemplary therapy accomplished by Weakland and Watzlawick, one of their techniques is less than commendable to parish clergy. This is the use of paradoxical assignments.[12] The relationship between pastor and parishioner is so remarkably different from that between these therapists and their patients that it is possible for them to utilize methods that could hardly succeed for us.

If parishioners see through the paradox, it could bring them to question our sincerity. If they follow the paradoxical instruction and it fails in its objective, this could diminish their trust in us. Our prescribing the symptom, by suggesting they go on performing in the same self-defeating way, could bring charges that we are cynical or unskilled. It takes an experienced, well-trained therapist to devise and execute paradoxical therapy. Some clergy do qualify, but the majority do not. With that single *caveat clericus*, it is possible to commend Weakland and Watzlawick as exemplars of high-quality counseling, to take seriously their several warnings about doublebinds, and to cite their writings as useful texts in family therapy.

9

Bunny S. and Frederick J. Duhl's Integrative Family Therapy

Sometimes therapy has been terminated without the goals having been attained. Sometimes, we have felt that we "failed," only to find out later that our clients have used their learnings to reorder their lives away from us.

Frederick J. and
Bunny S. Duhl

Numerous husband-wife teams now operate in family therapy as cotherapists, cotrainers, and coauthors, but few have been at it as long or are known as well as Bunny and Fred Duhl. As co-directors of the Boston Family Institute, they are engaged in delivering service to troubled families, training therapists, and community education. These tasks they perform with a style unlike that of most family therapists. They and their cohorts have a flair for the dramatic: They talk of the family-as-theater. They see nothing improper in paying families to act as the interviewees for their trainees in their rent-a-family program. They shamelessly finger a so-called "magic wand" in their family therapy and let its "magic" reward patients for their willingness to work in interviews.

Frederick Duhl, M.D., is virtually a self-taught family therapist. With no formal courses or direct training in family therapy,
he simply attended workshops on the subject and made this specialty his own. Bunny Duhl, on the other hand, was husband-
taught. She joined the Boston Family Institute training program
incognito in 1969 and studied in the classes her husband taught,
without ever admitting their relationship to her classmates. Now
this pair conducts workshops, writes learned papers, and practices
their innovative educational programs together. Undismayed by
standard practices in the training of therapists, they have pio-
neered such daring innovations as having trainees interview their
own families. They have declined to be identified by any one
method or tool, but candidly say they will use any approach that
can responsibly accomplish the task before them.

Since they will not be typed as proponents of any one specific
modality in family therapy, the Duhls, who draw upon several of
the best-known approaches (systems-based therapy and Gestalt
therapy among them) simply dub themselves as integrationists
and their approach as integrative family therapy.

Integrative Family Therapy

The family-as-theater concept of therapy permeates much that
the Duhls perform. They introduce family sculpting into therapy
and ask patients to pose or act out their impressions. Their role
plays and role reversals enable patients to portray their feelings
and also get inside the feelings of others they fail to understand.
They operate hand puppets and move them to "chat" with children or reticent adults. Their "magic wand" can be tipped im-
perceptibly to cause a small ball to appear to disappear at its top
as an encouragement for openness in responses. Through such
properties and procedures, they highlight behaviors and call upon
both verbal and nonverbal forms of communication.

Reference to the theatrical, of course, is a use of the experiential approach. The Duhls lean toward experience and often away
from verbalization. That gets through to people. They can, for

example, stage an interview that helps patients understand the part that space plays in their relationships, for spatial factors affect all interactions, indicating how much room we need and how much closeness we tolerate.

They have been particularly mindful of the living space in their patients' homes, knowing that the way intimate space is provided in dwellings can define what will happen to people. It is important, they assert, to find out who sleeps where. What doors are missing? Who shares what rooms? A home visit can be invaluable in family therapy, whether it is to slum tenements or well-to-do households.

Goal oriented in their therapy, these therapists assign homework tasks to be completed between interviews. They are educators; being such, they help families procure new information and reorganize it for their purposes. They deliberately (and again with drama) expand the range of roles that husbands, wives, daughters, and sons play in family relations, drawing on these to increase the family's ability to solve new problems. To make certain these educational-therapeutic lessons have gotten across, they will schedule a review at the end of the session, to ascertain what was learned and what has been the effect of therapy.

It is no surprise that Boston Family Institute therapists use quite interchangeably such terms as *patient, client, counselee,* and *helpee.* Theirs is not a doctrinaire approach to family therapy. But they do stand firmly on one repeated principle: respect for the people in therapy. Within that understanding, they reason that:

• Therapists must listen carefully to the patient's viewpoint in stories, language, styles, vulnerabilities, and defenses.

• It is essential to relate the person to the system and the system to the person, if any change is to take place at all.

• It is important to realize that a marriage or a family system is made from real persons who are individuals in their own right, and that they play their own roles and move through their own developmental processes.

• Neither the therapist nor anyone else can touch the family system (in a memorable slogan, the Duhls declare that no one can kiss a system), for it is a hologram and intangible. The best one can do is touch the individual who plays a role within that system.

• There is no valid way of knowing an individual except through her or his impact upon other people.

• Most persons in our society come to know more about power games than they do about intimacy. Unfortunately, the Duhls add, this may also be true about family therapists.

Assessment in Therapy

Assessment in the Duhls' approach involves evaluating the stress, the discrepancy between image and experience, the deviancy, and the resourcefulness of families in therapy. It also involves the fit between therapists and patients. The Duhls' assessment process can be appreciated by means of three categories they have discussed:

• *Families in pain* are defined as those whose resources are stretched nearly to the limit, only to have another crisis strike them. Such families need firmly structured guidelines for coping and techniques to help them connect their family together. To prevent other crises from accumulating, some immediate aid may be necessary—a homemaker to assist in a time of illness, rehabilitation for an injured person, or emergency funds.

• *Families in distress* have managed their lives with some degree of success and problem-solving skills, yet may find themselves in a life or developmental crisis for which they have been ill-prepared. For example, the Duhls record:

> We recently saw one family with three children who were all having various types of problems in a school to which they had just moved. While there were issues within the family system, they were secondary. The main interface of disturbance was the school/child interface and not the family process. The family needed coaching in how to intervene in a larger system which could easily blame and scapegoat it for the child's difficulties in the same way it blamed and scapegoated the child

that did not fit its image. The stance used was more of a coaching one in which we worked *with* them rather than *on* them. The main interventions were to teach them "how to." We provide the permission and teach the skills.[1]

• *Families in need of safety*, on the other hand, require "a net of safety" be thrown over them. Duhl and Duhl describe that procedure in this case:

> Thus a suburban family of four, with an adolescent in school trouble, a father who binge drinks and beats his wife, a depressed and placating mother, and a young daughter who is detached, is in severe jeopardy and requires an approach with interventions which first throw a net of safety over the entire family by stopping ongoing dangerous processes immediately. Only then can such a family slowly learn new behaviors which both respect boundaries and connect across them.[2]

The way the Duhls envision assessment, it can be conceptualized along seven interrelating continua. 1. The situation and precipitating event. 2. The degree of distress as observed or reported. 3. System characteristics in terms of flexibility. 4. Access to information. 5. The family phase of development. 6. Their pattern of relating. 7. The family ambience. These are not uncommon ingredients in family assessment, yet the integration of the seven in combination is a distinctive contribution of this couple.

Some Theory Behind Integrative Family Therapy

With Integrative Family Therapy as the title for their work, the Duhls incorporate features from several types of therapy. The integrative factor is, they say, "our knot in the handkerchief," a phrase they cite from Gregory Bateson. However, they integrate far more than differing therapeutic modalities. They have been influenced by the ecological emphasis of Edgar Auerswald, so they tend to help families see their situation in a wider worldview. In common with the family-therapy movement in general, they view the family as a system, as they put it, "through a zoom lens." It is a complex of systems and subsystems, of physical and intrapsychic aspects in individuals, or relationships worked out simultaneously within culture and with society.

Their theory draws upon several traditions. They use a cognitive construct with their information processing as they trace developmental stages in members of a family. They draw upon Gestalt theory for core images of the past, present, and future that impinge upon individual behavior within families and within other systems, too. They appeal to "third force" psychology, with its concern for pain and vulnerability in the lives of patients. Withal they share of themselves and their experience in that new system that is always erected between therapists and families.

Some Basic Assumptions

Foundational to this integrative theory are certain assumptions to which the Duhls subscribe:

• Human life is sacred, and no violence, physical or emotional, can be condoned among persons.

• Every person, every couple, every family has a story that grounds them in reality and influences their language. So, too, every person has peculiar vulnerabilities and defenses. In therapy, patients share their stories, their assumptive worlds, their angers, and their hurts. Likewise, every person has an idiosyncratic learning style; it is advantageous for a therapist to understand just how this works, if that person is to be reached. But therapists are persons, too, with their own stories, worldviews, growth patterns, distresses, jeopardies, and vulnerabilities. To pretend to be other than human in one's limitations is ridiculous.

• People have a basic right and need to gain information about themselves, as well as about the processes and instruments that can help them guide their behavior and solve their problems.

• People require help in solving their problems by themselves, so they will not need the assistance of therapists—of whom there are not enough, in any case.

• Reality is relative, and it behooves the therapist to be respectful and humble in all interventions, which tend to rise out of their personal version of reality. The lens through which a family views reality must also be respected. Somehow a congruence between the reality views of the therapist and the patient must be discovered and used, if communication is to become effective.

• There is no use in wanting more for clients than they want for themselves. To violate this standard is to end up working harder than they do on their own problem and to veer directly toward failure.

Locating Families on Their Maps

In order to work out interventions that are hand tailored for a family's view of reality, the Duhls draw a figurative map of that family's experiential territory. Aware that families can be located at various points on the map and that they will move from time to time, the therapists use the mapping process to plan approaches and facilitate changes in relationships.

• *Family forms* must be taken into consideration: Extended families differ markedly from nuclear families, one-parent families from two-parent families, and so on. These provide varying types of childcare, adult relationships, and expectations.

• *Geography* makes a marked difference for families. Where a family lives defines the varieties of experience available—for urban families, museums and cultural opportunities, for rural families, experiences in nature. These in turn color the opportunities for understanding and intervention.

• *Economics* also place a family on the map. Their ability to purchase education, a desired life-style, or even therapy depends on their financial situation. Economic conditions may provide stability in living conditions or confine a family to squalor.

• *Social arrangements* likewise influence the family's fit and place. Their social habits may facilitate their ability to talk with one another daily, find opportunities for recreation, and attract friends and social support systems.

• *Educational factors* make a mighty difference for families. The expectations that parents have for their children's education, the parents' own level of education, and the opportunities for learning—all these are determinative for family attainment and welfare. Some families can easily reach out for new information, while others are hesitant about trying anything more than the old patterns they already know.

• *Energy,* both physical and emotional, is required for any change. If a father spends only time with his son, investing no energy, a message of rejection may be communicated.

• *Time* becomes a major factor in how it is allocated and spent. If time is not planned to spend on relationships at home, no amount of therapy will accomplish the job.

• *Religion,* a powerful factor in this mapping, can offer a resource for caring, support, and organization of one's life, or negatively for guilt and a sense of failure.

The map of a family's experience will also take into account their developmental stages and how they pass through them. It will note the "rhythm of the family," enabling a therapist to judge whether they have an even pace or an interrupted, uneven relationship. It will also note their ambience along the dimensions of unselfishness, caring for others, and safety, for the Duhls know that families who are inattentive to others are more difficult to help.

With the educational bent they exhibit, the Duhls are especially interested in the ways families relate to information. Life tasks (and therapeutic tasks, too) are easier with those who have open boundaries that allow a search for new information. Some families lack information and do not know how to find it. They have not learned to learn. Others may know how, but lack the energy or motivation. Their hope is low, and they need to become successful again. Therapy demands an open stance to new information. It may be necessary for a therapist to press new information aggressively at times, particularly in such cases of jeopardy as child abuse.

The therapist must never lose sight of the context of the family. Where they live on that experiential map will make an immense difference in how to work with them. "Context implies the physical as well as the situational and dynamic aspects of one's surroundings, and includes the ability to differentiate and give 'appropriate' meaning to each step in a process."[3]

The Duhls insist that when they do therapy, they work with people, not just with problems. In their eyes, there can be no problem until someone defines an event or behavior as such by contrasting it with an expected image of what should be. Thus a child is a problem (or has a problem) whenever his or her behavior fails to fit the image of parents, teachers, or other adults.

In their treatment of families, as I have observed them, the Duhls often use humor. The capacity for humor in a patient or therapist represents a saving grace. Humor helps a therapist comment on a situation in a way that illuminates it. Humor helps us not take ourselves too seriously. Humor can connect people through mutual recognition of the absurdity of chaos in relationships and context.

Safety is yet another important aspect in mapping. Where communication provides respect and connection, a sense of safety and trust will be present. Safety is the result of knowing our individual boundaries will be respected. If we feel safe with another person, we can risk revelations of who we are and how we feel, even if we are uncomfortable about these matters.

An inquiry that shows a caring attitude demonstrates an ability that makes someone feel special. It may open the way for new information to enter one's mind. "Lost often after courtship becomes marriage, it is essential to connection, novelty, new options, and long caring relationship."[4] When it is lacking, one method of replacing it is to ask one spouse to play the role of a reporter interviewing a person for a news story and question his or her spouse about personal history and important events in life.

Typically, the Duhls express their caring:

> In a world of mechanistic alienation and disconnection, created for us by the technologies of our parents and grandparents, we feel strongly that technique is not enough, and humanistic concern is not enough. . . . Technique is what you do til the therapist comes. And a therapist for us is a person whose intelligence is guided by his/her heart. There is a motto over a

French hospital that states: "Cure sometimes; Help often; Comfort always."[5]

The Pastor's Integrative View

Bunny and Fred Duhl contribute much to the thinking of clergy who are forced to engage in family therapy. Because this is a ministerial task in which we have no choice, the major variable is simply how well we can do it. That, in turn, depends largely on how we use ourselves and our own personal resources. In this, the Duhls point the way through a variety of examples.

To begin with, these therapists are nothing if not active. They get out and visit the homes of families they treat, learning who shares what bedrooms, what condition the property is in, where individuals can enjoy some space of their own, and how house environment may contribute to the family's problems or solutions. They call upon help from other professionals when aid is needed for a damaged family, engaging a homemaker for the sick mother, finding financial resources for the indigent, bringing together school personnel and parents. They promote activity within the therapeutic interview itself, using puppets to interpret, role playing to enlarge the cognitive empathy of patients, and enacting incidents of family relationships.

Pastors, often among the most active of the helping professionals, know how to draw upon community resources for assistance, how to make visits into the homes of parishioners, and how to activate sedentary persons in group experiences.

The Duhl pattern appeals to clerical interest in their sharp inclination toward education. Like rabbis, priests, and ministers, they offer information, they teach persons, they share their own understanding. In many counseling situations, the occasion calls for a brief didactic session. In sexual therapy, as we shall see in chapter 20, a good part of the work consists of helping troubled persons learn what are to them new facts, new ways, and new possibilities. Moreover, both education and psychotherapy share this common goal: They are avenues toward abetting change in attitude, knowledge, and behaviors. This observation is made not as approval for that regrettable habit some clergy have developed of delivering prescriptive lectures, but rather to proffer some permission to do what comes naturally—share relevant information that just might alleviate worry, lessen guilt, or fill in gaps of knowledge. That would not be bad counseling, would it?

In yet another useful model for us, the Duhls frankly profess they have no uniform therapeutic modality, but draw upon many types of therapy and use whatever handy tools will accomplish the job. Slaves to no party line in the current debates amongst the various schools in family therapy, they selectively choose the approach fitted for the need. Thus they can use a task from the behavioral group, a technique from Gestalt therapy, and a communication exercise out of strategic family therapy. In this practice they are in harmony with numerous practitioners of the field. The Duhls just happen to call theirs Integrative Family Therapy. With many of us, they see that several avenues of technique can address the same problem. Their knowledge and experience enable them to combine these in their particular way and apply them with effectiveness. That others scoff at eclecticism and contend psychotherapy is respectable only when based on a unified theory of treatment points up the purist position. The eclectics, or integrationists, would see that stand as too limiting. Most clergy will also find it advantageous to have access to variable methods, as their people's problems come in variant forms needing differing helps.

Most of all, however, the Duhls' philosophy stresses for our clergy a deeply pastoral concern: their caring attitude about persons under stress. It comes out, for example, in their affirmation that they treat people, not problems. Mindful of the fact that they deal with persons rather than cases, they are able to understand the pain and appreciate the need of suffering families. Physicians are warned to speak of a particular patient, rather than "that ulcer in Room 243." Pastors, who ought never to require such a reminder (and yet do), will likewise be alerted that they labor with real persons who are loved by God and who stand in need. The sixty-hour workweeks, the preoccupation with a mass of duties, the obligations to parish and community—all crowd in upon clergy so relentlessly that we, too, become tempted to categorize persons according to their problems and define them by their situation. The Duhls remain a living reminder that we work with people, not just with problems.

III

Multigenerational Family Therapists

10

Murray Bowen and the Bowen Family Systems Theory

To some degree, you never leave the family. But I try to get people to disengage from what has happened to them in the past, and to grow away from it instead of running away.

Murray Bowen

Dr. Murray Bowen is convinced there's bad advice in Thomas Wolfe's title *You Can't Go Home Again*. Not only can we go home again, we should, according to this foremost family therapist. His marital therapy focuses more on the relationships husbands and wives have with their respective families of origin than with each other and their nuclear families. In the recent past, this seemed a wild idea to many; today it is taken seriously by countless family therapists and in many training centers, as well.

Who is Murray Bowen? As a theoretician, he dominates the field of family therapy with his theory and systems; he is widely influential as a teacher and writer. Currently clinical professor of psychiatry and director of the Family Center at the Georgetown University School of Medicine, Bowen comes from a background of psychoanalytic training and innovative experience in clinical practice.

While studying at the Menninger Foundation in 1951, he established a cottage for schizophrenic patients whose mothers were then invited to live-in arrangements. For a month or two at a stretch, the mothers participated in responsibility for the care of their sons and daughters. Within a short time, Bowen realized that others were involved besides the person Frieda Fromm-Reichmann had dubbed the "schizophrenogenic" (meaning "schizophrenia has its start in") mother, so he admitted fathers and siblings to the hospital group, as well. Psychoanalysts had too long overlooked the fact that schizophrenics also have fathers. The program brought Bowen to a new understanding of the psychodynamics of the family, which has informed his work and enriched the entire discipline.

Bowen subsequently moved to the National Institute of Mental Health, where he advanced his experimental work to treating entire families at one time, a bold demonstration then, which excited admiration across the spectrum of mental health. It also attracted opposition. He was soon caught up in administrative hassles, budget delays, and curbs on publishing his research data. He emigrated in 1959 to the more hospitable setting of Georgetown.

In 1972 he anonymously published a case history of his own family. Like Freud before him, Bowen had analyzed himself. But beyond Freud's method, he had discussed his own family crisis, connecting his theories about multigenerational relationships and fused personalities to his personal origins. Against the word of Thomas Wolfe, he went home again. He uses this same method with the families who are his patients and with the students who become his trainees in family therapy.

Murray Bowen's Therapy

Murray Bowen's working area in therapy is the three- or even four-generational family, in whose span of years he watches for traces of triangulation, marital fusion, and problems of differentiation (his terms will be defined shortly). His most successful therapy has been in aiding husbands and wives to differentiate from each other and from their families of origin. As they grow in their ability to deal intelligently with their problems and play down emotional impulsiveness, their family relations improve.

For Bowen, there are four main functions in family psychotherapy. 1. Defining and clarifying the relations between spouses. 2. Keeping oneself detriangulated from the family emotional system. 3. Teaching the counselees the functioning of emotional systems. 4. Demonstrating differentiation by taking I-positions during the course of therapy.

One of Bowen's primary tactics is a selective method of arranging his own interaction with the family. This he does by retaining control of the therapeutic process while at the same time refusing all other responsibilities for them. He emphasizes the futility of attempting to change other people and the obligation for each to take an I-stand on differentiation. The goal, of course, is for the individual to move in an autonomous direction without losing contact with the family.

Techniques of Family Therapy

Bowen's stance with families in therapy is that of a teacher. He spurns the title of *doctor* because it tends to make some patients too dependent. As a researcher, he teaches families to research their own problems. He knows this skill to be essential, and that the therapist plays a vital role in the therapeutic relationship because the introduction of a significant other person into an anxious or disturbed system has the capacity to modify relationships.

He also realizes that, as therapist, he must keep his "cool" and hold himself detriangulated, differentiating himself from the emotional system of the family he is interviewing—as well as from his own family at home. To do otherwise is to overload family interviews with an excessive emotional burden. The basic principle here is clear: Any emotional problem between two people can begin to resolve if they can remain in contact with a third person who is free of their emotional field while actively relating to each. But if that third party becomes entangled, either as a result of emotional problems with his own family or with the pair, a damaging triangulation sets in.

Convinced that any personal change requires time, Bowen and his group believe the recent emphasis on brief therapies is unwise. He meets monthly or oftener with his patients over a lengthy period, and allows a sufficient interval to elapse between sessions to firm up any gains made through therapy.

Unlike many strict family therapists, Bowen does not refuse to meet with individuals in therapeutic sessions. Yet, even when counseling one person alone, he integrates that person's place in the family system. He coaches patients how to understand their family of origin, how to discern triangulations, and how to promote differentiation in their lives. He has discovered that by such means it is possible for one person to change and influence changes in others in the family system.

He characteristically opens a therapeutic session by asking the husband to give an objective report of what has happened since the previous session. Then he turns to the wife and asks her what her thoughts (not her *feelings*, note) were while she listened to her husband. If she should cry, he asks the husband if he noticed, and what his thoughts were as she teared up. The objective is to procure low-key, thoughtful responses; it succeeds. Bowenians believe that highly keyed emotionality in the relationship between therapist and family will bring a quick, but temporary, change. Realism and low-key interactions take longer, but encourage more lasting results.

Bowen and his staff track who talks to whom, and what about; this helps locate the stress level. Learning the paths and patterns of family communication enables them to trace the propensities toward dysfunction and the alternatives that can lead to improved relations.

It was Bowen who developed the now widely used genogram (pronounced jean-o-gram) as a method of taking a family history. This technique, subsequently updated by his interpreters, Philip Guerin and Thomas Fogarty, covers not only the current family, but also reaches back through the previous generations, at least to the grandparents of the adults in therapy. With the family, Bowen plots the generations and significant events, all the time aware of the family's patterns of interaction as they discuss persons and places. He uses this device to discover details about health, religious and ethnic background, deaths, divorces, relationships, moves, and so forth. Through it the therapist can discover transgenerational patterns, broken relationships, scandals, strengths, traditions, ghosts, secrets, and the ever-recurring triangles. Through it spouses learn details about each other they had never known.

The Family Voyage

Bowen regularly assigns his patients the task of returning home to their families of origin on what he calls a "family voyage," so they can trace their roots and reopen contacts. He coaches them on the time and the content of these visits to parents, grandparents (if still living), cousins, siblings, and others. They are to inquire about the family past, retrace relationships, notice tribal patterns, and discover their selfhood on such voyages. What is more, as they notice their family members, they will begin to see new aspects of their own choices, roles, relationships, and patterns of conduct. When successful, a family voyage makes possible the repair of old fractures in relationships and opens the way to more effective family therapy.

Returning home again is the hard part of therapy. Yet basic training in solving a crisis can be found through tracing family origins. What has happened in the past, Bowen claims, has triggered emotional and toxic behavior in the present. The multigenerational transmission system will have set the anxiety level for our emotional fields of tension. Therefore patients who can work out their problems with the family of origin can carry over their solutions to other members of the family and their own descendants. The risk is that unless they clear this early history, they will remain stagnated at the level of insight, without advancing it to necessary change.

The technique is to send the patients back home for gradually increasing lengths of time. Meanwhile the therapist helps them remain calm and objective enough to analyze the experiences that most affect them. These returning voyagers are admonished to deal with only one parent at a time, because parents are skilled at fending off encounter questions and can practice their standard defense: "What do you think about that question, Laura?" One will experience how to interact with the family, which can be done by getting them to talk about their background and learning to be patient listeners to them.

Bowen's remarkable claim is that this process does more for a troubled marriage than working directly with the couples' relationship. When the focus is on the differentiation of self within the families of origin, counselees make as much progress (and often more) in working out their relationship system with spouses and children as do families seen in formal family therapy, where the principal focus is on the interdependence of the marriage.[1] Even if parents are deceased, much is to be gained by sending the patient back to visit uncles, aunts, cousins, siblings, and others.

Moreover, the therapist also will discover this family voyage to be an important aspect of professional life. The training programs at institutions using the Bowen Theory require such visits of their trainees. Other programs adapt the plan and require trainees in family therapy to work out their family biography and analyze its systems, then discuss it in confidence with one colleague. Returning to the place of our origin can free adults from outdated childish bondage.

The Bowen Theory

Bowen's Family Systems Theory, having been expanded and revised over the years, is now parsed into eight basic concepts.
• *The differentiation of self* is "the cornerstone of the theory."[2] Differentiation defines persons according to the degree they are able to distinguish between their thinking process and their feeling process. Those whose emotions and intellect are so fused that their feeling functions dominate their thinking are de-

pendent, problem-prone individuals. By contrast, those who are sufficiently differentiated between thinking and emoting are adaptable, independent, and able to cope.

But those poor fused persons who remain undifferentiated tend to be stuck together in family relations with continuing dependence, repeated conflicts, and anxiety as they strive to increase closeness but only become more confused. Not surprisingly, their family problems erupt and bring them into contact with the helping professions.

Marriage and family therapy would emphasize a mature differentiation between the cognitive and the affective (the thinking and the emotional) phases of comprehending. Bowen appeals to the intelligence of his patients; the better they can think, the better the therapist can use his teaching methods with them.

• *Triangles* are created by dysfunctional families in an attempt to meet their problems. Characteristically, a triangle will have two comparatively comfortable people and one other, who is in conflict. Most common is tension between husband and wife, with their child drawn into the fray. The father may be at the outside position, labeled as weak, passive, and distant. The mother, often labeled as the dominating and castrating woman, will attempt to win the child over to her side, while the child "moves another step toward chronic, functional impairment" by trying to act as the go-between for parents. This is typical family projection; families will replay this same triangular game over and over, as though the outcome were ever in doubt. "But the final result is always the same," Bowen notes. "The child accepts the always-lose outcome more easily, even to volunteering for the position."[3]

Triangles can be composed of one parent and two children. In this trio, if the older child is "parentified," picking on and bossing the younger, the parent's defense of the young victim will only exacerbate the situation. But if the parent works out her own relational problems with the parentified child, the conflict between the siblings will abate.

A fused couple can be predicted to bring in a third force to stabilize their relationship: a child, a counselor, a lover, a bottle, or even a job. Bowen believes triangles provide a flexible, predictable way for the therapist to conceptualize and modify the emotional system.

A triangle enables the therapist to spot the instability and reactions in the couple process. It can consist of scapegoating an Identified Patient. It can mean seeking an extramarital affair. It can also press the couple toward the minister for help. In each case, the triangle is an attempt to work out some therapeutic solution. Like many other therapists, Bowen concentrates on breaking down triangular conflicts into more manageable two-person dialogues.

The therapist can also be drawn into a triangle. Some couples will box in the therapist with their triangulating efforts, insisting that he or she be the judge of who is right and who is wrong. Others want the therapist to be a superparent and adopt them. "Detriangulating," or controlling one's own automatic response in the emotional process, is difficult. It can be done, however, with calmness through assignments (placing the couple in group therapy is a good one) or by working to defuse the most available and amenable person in the situation.

• *The nuclear family emotional system* is confined to just one generation of parents and their children, but it carries replicas of past patterns handed down from grandparents and even more-distant ancestors. We tend to choose spouses, Bowen teaches, who have approximately the same degree of differentiation that we ourselves have. The lower the degree of differentiation, the more intense will be the fusion in marriage, hence, greater emotional outbursts can be expected. Such couples typically learn to handle this problem through establishing emotional distance—a high price to pay for their tense peace.

The emotional problems of a fused married couple may be focused in: 1. Conflictual intensive relations, through which neither is capable of altruism, and their adaptation is minimal. 2. Dysfunction in one spouse, who may be ill, alcoholic, or incorrigible and whose mate is maneuvered into the reciprocal role of chronic caretaking. 3. Impairment of children through the family projection process, in which the younger generation is victimized by the parents' inability to work out their differences.

• *The family projection process*, often used by dysfunctional and fused families, consists of dumping personal resentment, anger, and frustration on some one person chosen as the scapegoat. Of course, even in healthy families, projections of hope, ambition, blame, and worry go on daily. But when the child is scapegoated by the parents in a grim triangle, emotional impairment in that youngster can result. Sometimes the projection is superimposed on a child already handicapped with an illness, thus worsening that condition. It is Bowen's belief that people who have been crippled by the projection process are less able to cope with life and will have low levels of differentiation.

• *Emotional cutoff* is the name Bowen gives to the manner in which individuals separate themselves from past family influences, in order to become solid selves in their own independent living. Any Bowenian therapist would attempt to convert such an isolated person into an orderly differentiated self, free from the family of origin, to "grow away instead of running away." Unresolved emotional attachment to parents has to be handled in some way. By distancing ourselves and cutting off the past, however, we fail to cope with the problem at all. Indeed, we may live to see our own children repeat the same pattern against us.

Yet the person who cuts off the family of origin can be as dependent as the person who never leaves home. Both need help. Such a runaway separates from family influence in the vain hope of becoming a solid self. Oddly, the person who is cut off will tend to duplicate family rituals of interaction from experience and then transfer them to a spouse. Indeed, that marriage relationship is in jeopardy of being cut off, too.

• *The multigenerational transmission process* bequeaths family traditions, values, and problems from one generation to another. Some families, with members who have a high degree of self-differentiation, turn out superior individuals with notable achievements from century to century. Other families pass on dysfunction and difficulties from parents to children and thence to children's children. The therapist who assists patients to re-study their family history will aid them toward self-understand-ing, improved differentiation of self, and a greater ability to deal with the inherited problems of the clan.

In this theory, Bowen can appear to be a determinist, but he insists he is not. His contention is that the less differentiated the person is in functioning, the more automatic and determined that person is. Meanwhile, the differentiated person has far wider choices in life. Bowen's emphasis is on the side of free will, and he is optimistic about human nature. But his study of the emo-tional history of hundreds of families has made him realistic about human potential.

The multigenerational transmission process is largely an un-conscious one. Parents have a tendency to repeat with their own children the treatment they received from their parents. Even if they were abused and hate the very memory, they may experience a perverse tendency to exert the same mistreatment on their own daughters and sons. In Freudian language, this is repetition com-pulsion. In child abuse, it is criminal.

• *Sibling position* in any family can reveal important details about personality characteristics of a child. Bowen is hardly alone in this conviction; Alfred Adler and Walter Toman have ex-panded this idea to demonstrate how markedly different the first child is from the youngest in relationships and life adjustment. Bowen teaches that knowing the position a sibling occupies in family life provides predictive material on how he or she will op-erate in marriage or respond in family interactions.

• *Societal regression* is the name Bowen applies to the theory that emotional problems in society as a whole are similar to those of a family. A family subjected to sustained anxiety will lose con-tact with their intellectually focused abilities and come to rely more on emotionally determined decisions. Something of the same sort is observable in society when it becomes dysfunctional and casts about for almost any legislative or emotional solution. Grimly, Bowen notes that our ecological problems, population explosion, decreasing raw materials and food supply, and pollution may drive us to emotionally charged decisions that are not thought through. Just as a family fused together in a dysfunctional mass requires therapy, so society requires careful therapeutic measures when it nears violence and breakdown.

Throughout all these eight basic concepts, two variables apply: the degree of anxiety involved and the integration of the self. Anxiety has the capability of altering our adjustments and relationships. Likewise, if we are integrated within the self, our relationships are noticeably influenced by that factor. These observations hold for clergy as well as anyone else.

Bowenian Applications for the Clergy

Murray Bowen's considerable contribution to the theory of family therapy carries clear implications for the clergy. These include his emphasis that we understand ourselves and our own family life, that we seek healing for our own disrupted relationships, and that we work out the mutual forgiveness for which these disrupted relationships cry.

The ancient Socratic admonishment to know yourself is fit advice for any pastor planning to assist troubled families. Unless we have some insight into our own personal situation and the ways we relate to our own family members (past and present), we shall be handicapped in our ministry to parish families. For one thing, we could be tempted to project our own convictions, experiences, or hopes upon other families, whom they do not fit. For another, we might be tempted to introduce our own family problems into a counseling interview, in the futile hope we could work on our difficulties along with theirs. Only if we have come to terms with our personal situation can we help others with theirs.

The pastor who has contrived an emotional cutoff from parents or siblings is hardly in an advantageous position to aid others in healing broken relations. The challenge is clear: First return home and mend those fractured connections, *then* bring your gift of counseling to the troubled. This can be done in several ways.

One can seek out a Bowenian therapist for guidance in a voyage home; they are to be found in all major cities. Or one can work through this exercise alone, carefully planning the visits, their objectives, and the means of reaching them. A useful pattern for such a venture is to be found in Bowen's record of his pioneering experience, when he returned to close some gaps among members in his family of origin.[4] Such a work, painful and frightening as it seems at first, can be rewarding in clarifying one's thinking and experience, in drawing family members together again, and in significantly improving the quality of one's pastoral counseling.

In the ministry that Carroll A. Wise has called pastoral psychotherapy, clergy can utilize some of Bowen's aegis as they labor with families who suffer from guilt and broken relationships. We need forgiveness for our own guilt, and we are obligated to forgive others—particularly our imperfect parents and offending kin—for their offenses against us. By then we may be able to forgive ourselves and appreciate God as a divine forgiver, even of clergy!

In any case, clergy hardly require a reminder of the healing power in relationship and in the very attitude of a pastoral counselor. After submitting his therapeutic method to research procedures, Carl Rogers concluded that a therapist's attitudes are more decisive than his techniques. Too many ministers and priests undervalue the weight of the influence brought by their own presence with others. To be fully present to counselees, to relate emphatically, as if their inner world were our own, is to be of immediate healing help. (Those words *as if* are significant, because the assumptive world of others can never be the same as ours.) If for nothing else, we owe Murray Bowen a debt of gratitude for reminding us of our own strengths and possibilities.

With seeming immodesty, Bowen has named his system after himself, and it is known as such throughout the family movement. But his attitude about the concepts and methods he has devised is one of generosity. When others adopt his material, he considers it to be theirs to work with in their way. Not unexpectedly, a variety of therapists have adapted portions of the Bowen

Theory into their practice; Bowen's influence has spread widely throughout the mental-health field.

Underlying the theory is an implicit assumption of freedom and individual ability. People can change. They can take charge of their lives and improve their relationships. And they are encouraged to do so.

11

James L. Framo's Dynamic-Transactional Therapy

There is something about facing and dealing with old issues with one's original family that seems to take the charge out of the negative reactions to the spouse.

James L. Framo

To the astonishment of more conventional therapists, James L. Framo not only counsels with husbands and wives in marital strife, but he talks with their parents, as well. For him, it works. As one of the most familiar figures on the lecture and workshop circuit, Framo is known all over the nation for such unusual methods. He has presented well over 200 workshops for persons in the helping professions. He also carries on a part-time private practice in San Diego and contributes highly regarded books and articles to the literature of family therapy. His latest book project, *The Dynamic Approach to Marital and Family Therapy,* is one of the first on this topic to be written for the common reader, instead of for other professionals in the field.

Framo sees himself as an integrationist, bridging both the older psychodynamic approach and the current transactional approach in family therapy. The transactional aspect is popular in this day of emphasis on systems, but psychodynamically oriented family therapists are in the minority, and Framo's work calls attention to the importance of their place in family theory, thus serving as a bridge between these two modalities. Framo is a past president of the dynamically oriented American Family Therapy Association and also a clinical member and fellow of the systems-oriented American Association for Marriage and Family Therapy. Educated at Penn State University, he received his Ph.D. in clinical psychology from the University of Texas. A longtime leader in the field, Framo organized the first national conference on family interaction and research in 1967. Throughout his career, he has developed innovative techniques in therapy.

Framo the Therapist

Framo works his therapy in a different way from the mass of family therapists. Using three unusual approaches, he presses marital couples into group therapy at an early stage, he moves husbands and wives toward intensive work with their own families of origin, and he does most of his work with a female cotherapist.

He begins first with the married couple. His initial goal, hardly different from that of other therapists, is to establish a level of trust in a series of interviews that may continue for fifteen sessions. If the presenting problem is that of a child's difficulty, the unit of treatment is the entire family. However, the time comes when the child is dismissed and Framo works alone with the marital dyad.

Eschewing such common techniques as questionnaires, personality tests, interview schedules, and experiments, he plunges directly into the task of assessment. For this, several interviews may be needed, during which he and his cotherapist (frequently Mary, his wife) attempt no interventions, even though they are well aware that assessment and treatment become inseparable. They watch for the patients' expectations, reasons for coming into therapy, previous therapeutic experience (if any), the kinds of questions asked, the sense of hope or despair in the couple, and the degree of "connectedness" between themselves and the counselees. Inquiry proceeds about the couple and their relationship through the particulars of age, occupation, length of marriage, children, prior marriages, family reactions to their marriage, fight styles, sexual relations, current relations with parents and siblings, and their motivation for therapy.

In this early stage of therapy, it becomes important to initiate goal setting. The Framos will ask each person to define his or her purpose in coming to this experience. The mere removal of symptoms is viewed as a low goal in this modality. Not infrequently their goals will be incongruous, the wife wishing to leave the marriage without guilt and the husband wanting to stabilize and preserve the marriage. Some may state overt goals that obscure their hidden ones; the stated goals are likely to change during therapy. Yet it is useful to establish even tentative goals and to note the variations between wife and husband.

Then they proceed to a middle phase of therapy. "The essence of the true work of family therapy is in the tracing of the vicissitudes of early object-relationships, and ... intrapsychic and transactional blending of the old and new family systems of the parents."[1] After a period of work with the marital couple alone, they are introduced into a group of married couples somewhat like themselves. That is, a couple in their early forties with adolescent children will perhaps join other couples in the same stage of family life. There each person is asked to reveal family experiences and their views about their spouses. Out of this sometimes painful process emerge concealed areas of stress and covert problems of conflict. The purpose of such dynamic-based therapy is to bring to awareness those former events of personal and family history that are undergirding current distortions and projections. Framo believes each individual carries a nonrational and unconscious truth that can set him free when a real therapeutic encounter occurs.

These couples' groups have rules: No violence is permitted; feedback is to be given constructively; no discussion of the group or its members is permitted anywhere that others could ever overhear; if one member must be absent, the spouse is still to attend; any decision to terminate must be given at least one week in advance, and not by telephone.

In this particular type of group therapy, the therapist engages each couple in turn, while the others look on as spectators. Perhaps because of the similarity of their developmental problems or the commonality of human experience, the couples on the fringe learn vicariously from the procedure, even when they do not participate actively in the process.

Framo maintains that the advantages of placing marital couples in group therapy outweigh those of working with one couple. They get feedback from their peers in the group, and that feedback can have more impact than the therapist. Moreover, the couples discover the universality of their experience and the similarity of their problems, a therapeutic incident in itself. As they develop mutual trust, they come to see one another as models, for the group supplies a wealth of modeling roles that no one therapist could ever provide. Most of all, a caring grows in the groups, and caring, Framo maintains, is always therapeutic.

Enter the Family of Origin

Still more difficult than submitting oneself to group work in marital therapy is the specter of inviting parents and siblings to an intensive four-hour session with the cotherapists. But this is also a feature of the Framos's work with families. The objections are rife to this requirement: "You've got to be kidding!" "My mother would have a heart attack," and worse. Nonetheless, the cotherapists prevail, and early objections drop away as people come to see the value of these sessions. In most cases, extended family interviews help improve the marriage. What is more, the whole family of origin gains from the experience. Framo once declared that one session with the original family is worth fifty regular interviews. It can lead to finding ways that break up old repetitive relational patterns. The reward seems to come when the couple themselves realize that their problems have been alleviated after the family's dramatic visit.

Only one of the couple attends this session with his or her family of origin. The presence of the other spouse could slow the process and serve as an alibi for withholding information or toning down feelings. The absent spouse is kept apprised of the entire session through an audiotape. There must be no risk that the spouse feels excluded or victimized.

Framo and his cotherapist do not preside at these family-system sessions. Trained and readied for the role, the counselee is in charge of the arrangements (timing, travel, sharing of expenses, conducting the conversation, and so forth). In Framo's own words:

> In the family-of-origin conferences the interest is centered on what went on during the life cycle of that family; what were the key events, traumas, happy memories, tragedies, atmosphere; how were the roles distributed, what were the alliances? In these sessions important diagnostic information is obtained on how past family problems are being lived through the present. More to the point, however, opportunities are available for genuine corrective experiences, the discovery of information about the family not heretofore known, the clarifying of old misunderstandings and misinterpretations based on childhood perceptions, and the clearing away of the magical meanings that family members have for each other. This kind of experience also gives people the chance to get to know their parents as real people rather than as fantasy figures who have to be idealized or denigrated. Further, the way is opened up for the possibility of establishing an adult-to-adult relationship with one's parents.[2]

Typically, such a conference begins with a two-hour session on a Friday night, to be followed by a deeper emotional session the next morning. The parents and siblings who enter the scene at this stage of therapy are usually ill at ease and will require assurance. Once again, a trust level must be established. Efforts to achieve rapport are begun with icebreaking conversation about the trip, their work, their hometowns, and the like. Soon, however, the session is turned over to the counselee, who takes charge with the introduction of issues and questions. Inevitably there come "Aha" revelations of "I never knew you felt that way," or

"Why didn't you tell me this before?" Adult children will learn secrets about their parents' families for the first time. Hostility will be awakened, reconciliations effected, new rituals negotiated. In the end, a deeper understanding will have been forged through the hard work of this unusual reunion.

There is a universality of family experience that is—well—*familiar*. We all transfer irrational attitudes and projections onto our spouses without realizing these are steeped in the past experiences of our original homes. We all maintain a loyalty to our family of origin, long after we have begun a nuclear family of our own. We all tend to wait overlong before starting any reconciliation efforts with our original family. Framo admits to having made an appointment for a heart-to-heart talk with his father too late; his father died just before the appointed meeting. Once, in a pensive remark to an interviewer, he ventured that this experience may have influenced him to become a family therapist. Clearly it has had an effect on his methodology.

Without claiming to know quite why, Framo is nonetheless convinced that these family sessions produce profound changes. After the family visit, the couple returns for a while to the couples' group, where they are met with keen interest. They have now survived "the major surgery of family therapy."

From such experience, Framo has learned much about being a therapist, and his students have become beneficiaries of this experience. He teaches them to be active therapists. He suggests that they, like he, use judicious disclosure about their own marriages and relationships with children. He tapes sessions without apology or the machinery of signing permission slips. He gains understanding from the ingenuousness of children in family interviews. He does not refuse social contacts with former clients. He has, he says, broken a number of taboos "without the sky falling in."

And he is not averse to refusing therapy to some persons: "I have dismissed some couples from ongoing therapy who have been using therapy as a substitute for living. I tell them, 'Go out and live your lives and stop examining yourselves.' "[3]

Framo the Theorist

Framo's often reprinted paper "Symptoms From a Family Transactional Viewpoint" offers a representative view of his theory and its features that back up the unusual therapy described above.[4] He begins by stating that family therapy is now centered in a transactional theory of human behavior reaching beyond techniques and forms of intervention. Convinced that families form a reciprocal feedback system that regulates and patterns the individual's behavior, he analyzes those transactions. Disordered behaviors that appear obscure from the viewpoint of individual psychology can often be decoded and understood when viewed as components of their intimate social systems. Even the craziness of psychopathology, traditionally viewed as intrapsychic conflict, is relational in its etiology. Framo would suggest a disturbed person's treatment be within the person's relationships, rather than alone.

Any family-systems theory regards our relationships as a system of reciprocally influenced parts, operating as a whole. Although systems are to be found in numerous other institutions (the church, for example), there is no setting in which human needs and reciprocal influences are so pronounced as in family life. There they make up a continuous process from generation to generation, with struggles over love, hate, rejection, hurt, and gratification.

Framo's theory holds that introjects (memories or imprints of parents and other significant figures) may still be influencing the adult. That is why he prescribes that parents and other family members come in person to the family's therapy sessions. He perceives insoluble intrapsychic conflicts emerging from the original family, being acted out, solved, or defended in relation to current intimates. Therefore, he asserts, the core of his theoretical approach is the relationship between the intrapsychic (what goes on within the individual's being) and the transactional (what goes on between the individual and other people).

Thus, for example, a mother might repeatedly provoke her

daughter to misbehave and then pressure her husband to punish the girl. The mother can then identify with the punished daughter and attack her husband for being too strict. Later in therapy, she may begin to see the connection between this pattern and her own punishing father, whose death she has never mourned and whom she thus revives, to live again in the interplay between her husband and her own daughter. With such angry or aggressive mothers, Framo has learned to avoid paying attention to their behavior, paying attention instead to what they have missed in life.

Children can represent the unfortunate expectations of their parents' introjects: for instance, the case of a child who was conceived in order "to save the marriage." Or they may unwittingly be living out some grandparent's never-realized ambition that got handed down in unspoken family mythology. Even their sibling fights may be expressing parental conflicts that were never opened up. Tragically, we tend to act out the old conflicts of the family and continue the old internal roles in our marriages, and sometimes among our friends and co-workers, as well. Framo notes that a child may incorporate some aspects of parental personality—even those that are unadmired—just to court the parents' acceptance or stabilize their marriage. Families actually find some advantage in delegating one member to be sick, in order to maintain their homeostasis; they may even sabotage a therapeutic improvement in order to maintain their miserable system.

In less extreme ways we all fulfill some family role assignment. Many families have a "quiet one," "the clown," or "the difficult child." These assignments can be reinforced by myths and rules and ritualized in the family structure, with the result that the son or daughter is still pressed into that role, at age fifty-five.

Framo believes that those who are assigned such roles as "the stupid one" or "mother's protector" may incorporate and actually become that assigned role. They may spend a lifetime disputing the role, or may playact it out. Years of training were invested in that part, and maturity has not yet brought any freedom from that introject. That the adult is not necessarily stuck forever with this role is evident in the fact that she or he sheds it automatically with people outside the family or can find release from it in a therapy that includes the family of origin. Such a person may learn to become autonomous and independent of the childish role.

That there are inappropriate ways of escaping these assigned roles is evident in the extravagant way some persons go about making their emotional cutoff from family ties. They may think they have shed all family holds through becoming a runaway, an alcoholic, or a psychotic, or through unrealistic denial. We risk much when we cop out. Renouncing our family of origin is not the solution; these are biological-emotional ties that cannot be completely severed. So "a universal dilemma consists of the question, how can one keep relating to his family and yet stay free of the irrational aspects of the emotional system and be a person in his own right."[5]

Many peculiar symptomatic behaviors could be the result of a person trying to escape his or her family role. It is hardly apparent to what reality or myth a person is reacting when behaving oddly or objectionably. Symptoms, though noxious, may be essential to maintaining some relationships. Intense rage, impossible to vent at home, can be acted out through vandalism, violence, or riot. Belatedly, parents who had been unable to work through their relations with sons and daughters at home are astonished at such behavior.

Childhood problems simply become metaphors for parental stress, Framo holds. Sick though it is, families will permit their members to have symptoms as part of their regulatory system. In doing so, they will make allowances: "Oh, everybody gets peculiar ideas now and then," or "He's so miserable to live with that I figure I have a right to play around."

Crises occur in families not only at natural stages of development (daughter's marriage or Grandpa's death) but also in those subtle breaks in the family system wherein reciprocal relationship has failed. If, for example, a father insists on treating his fifteen-year-old daughter as if she were still nine, he is not only a retarded parent; he has also failed to make the necessary change in himself reciprocal to hers. This problem is a well-known one that leads to hurt, to tears, and to recriminations.

Another symptom is the reciprocal gain that comes from such a system. The alcoholic in the family may be matched by a martyr. The obese may need someone who forbids high-caloric eating. Framo notes that George and Martha in Albee's *Who's Afraid of Virginia Wolff?* find in each other their needed lover-persecutor; Hansel and Gretel locate the witch for their lives; and King Lear appoints his Cordelia for rejection.

But "whenever two or more persons are in close relationship they collusively carry psychic functions for each other."[6] Thus the other one can be a part of the self, so closely are they related. If he's so responsible, then she can be irresponsible. If the wife takes a hard line with the children, then the husband can feel justified in taking the easy.

What the Clergy Can Learn From James Framo

Two rather astonishing procedures in the therapeutic practice of James Framo commend themselves for pastoral consideration. One is the establishment of a marital group for education and counseling. The other is the possibility of inviting a family of origin to aid in a difficult marital conflict. Before rejecting either or both of these out of hand, let us consider how they might be adapted, rather than adopted, in pastoral ministry.

However salutary the standard of marital group therapy, it does present special problems for an average parish. Objections inevitably arise about how such a group can be organized if marital cases are few and so different from one another. Would persons who already know one another be willing to enter so intimate an experience of sharing and confession? Conversely, would parishioners be willing to enter such an intimate experience with strangers they do not know? Despite these objections, it has been verified many times over that such church-sponsored groups are feasible.

David R. Mace, reflecting on a long career as a trainer of family therapists and group leaders for marriage enrichment, has concluded that people in married couples' groups, once they have established openness and trust, are able to support and heal one another. He has convinced many of the clergy that just because counseling with one couple is difficult, it does not necessarily follow that working with five or six couples is complicated beyond reason.

Actually, working with several couples can bring together a collective energy and even a group of amateur cotherapists who ease the burden of leadership.

The course of establishing a working relationship with a group of married couples in the church context is laid out in Richard B. Wilke's book, *The Pastor and Marriage Group Counseling.*[7] He suggests a small group of three to six couples meeting with the pastor for two-hour sessions once a week for a period of approximately three months. These groups can (maybe ought to) be of ecumenical composition, with couples from several churches and cotherapists who are pastors from neighboring parishes. It is wise to form the groups of couples who are from the same stage of marriage (don't try to mix nineteen-year-olds with couples nearing fifty).

Wilke also warns against admitting to the group people who are in catastrophic stress or in need of psychiatric care; they require more intensive therapy than an enrichment-type group for married couples can afford. Pastors will be accomplishing quite enough if they organize marital groups on an educational basis. He also reminds us that the formation of such groups should be preceded by careful preparation of announcements to the congregation.

This enrichment-type program differs from Framo's psychoanalytical approach. The pastor need not (and doubtless should not) probe the depths of pain, conflict, and stress that Framo does. The pastor's objective, let it be repeated, is educational. The pastoral leaders of such groups are facilitators who realize that group leadership is a shared task with members of the group. They will help members make their own contributions to the process, clarify communication, look to one another for ideas, and aid in the expression of positive feelings. The organizing and leading of such a group is a skill that most clergy already have and use.

Consultation With the Family of Origin

Pastoral counseling with a parish couple and their extended family is not everyone's work. It requires both experience and courage. Yet it can be rewarding. Pastors who have used the technique report that the process can be a potent procedure. It necessitates careful planning in advance, and much depends upon the resolve of the person whose family this is. When a marital dyad is stuck in seemingly irreconcilable differences; when the counseling appears frozen, with no change of any kind taking place; when the parties are bored and at the point of giving up, this reunion procedure can be the answer.

A couple in conflict can reach a place where neither will compromise on basic issues without feeling both are giving up something of their very selves. Then the impasse cries out for adjudication and change. Each spouse has basic needs in relation to the other. These needs may not be met, and each is then frustrated in the marriage. It is then that a family of origin conference could help resolve the impasse by clearing up some of the attachment problems each person has with that family.

Arranging these consultations is simpler than most counselors suppose; the procedure can be more pleasant than they expect. In some respects, the consultation with the family of origin resembles a family reunion. That the program does take time is not to be denied. This factor may constitute a major reason why so many pastors are disinclined to get into it.

First of all, the counselee must be coached in the steps essential to the event. Let's assume the wife begins with her family. She will need to sort out with the pastoral counselor who is to be invited, besides her surviving parent or parents. Will it be siblings? aunts, uncles, cousins? The criterion cannot be based on the size of the group or the theory of network therapy, but instead on the degree of enmeshment this counselee feels with individual persons. Her past history with them, their influence on her, left-over ill feelings from former slights and complaints—these come nearer to the basis for a decision about who is to be invited. Invariably the outcome involves one's most intimate relatives in the immediate family. With any special background of relationships (e.g., a child who was reared by an uncle and aunt, or one who had lived for a time with an older sister and her husband), the list may be enlarged or skewed in a different direction.

When the invitations are issued, however, it is the principal party herself who is to issue them. She makes the telephone calls to tell the story and invite her relatives. This is her responsibility, not the pastor's. But the pastor ought to be closely involved, helping her evaluate the invitation list, plan and role-play the telephone conversations, and help her rehearse the lines to be used in those conversations. A pastoral counselor can guide a rehearsal of the event: what issues to start with, how to phrase certain problems. The pastor can talk through with her the scheduling, timing of the event, how costs are to be shared by the family, and attendant details. At this time, arrangements are made to communicate all the experience to her husband, who will not be attending the family session.

In the gathering itself, the pastoral counselor presides at the beginning, but soon transfers leadership to the counselee. Proceedings begin with getting reacquainted and with friendly conversation designed to provide a basis of trust among the family members, the counselee, and her pastor. Remember, some of these people will not have seen one another for some time. That is especially true if relations have been cut off because of previous difficulties. Reacquaintance may need a little time. Soon, however, the pastor can introduce the task of the session, offer a short, selective description of the marital couple's situation, and describe the purpose of the event. Then it is time to hand over the leadership to the counselee herself and proceed with the routine she has rehearsed.

From this point until near the conclusion, the pastor's task can

be limited to facilitating the discussion if it bogs down or refer-
eeing disputes if they happen to erupt. The key issue will be a review of the family's earlier days together, their happy memories,
their sad ones, how they interacted, what roles they played, where
the subgroups operated, and what they did in family life. Old
misunderstandings are clarified. Revelations are opened up. New
relationships are forged. Impressions are corrected and adjusted.
Even if the process confirms that some issues cannot be resolved
at this time, there is gain to be had in the honest facing of that
fact.

Toward the end, the pastor, who has remained a quiet member
of this group, reenters the discussion and assists with the summary. It is appropriate to close with a period of silence and
prayer. The family is then dismissed, but they return to their
homes with different perspectives and new attitudes. Not long afterward, before the spouse calls in his family of origin, the pastor
should make an appointment to see the couple and debrief the
experience. There will still be work to be done on this marriage—and doubtless on others in the parish.

12

Ivan Boszormenyi-Nagy's Contextual Family Therapy

An hour spent working on basic relational trustworthiness can do more than hours spent unraveling symptomatic differences between spouses or even pursuing associations and dreams.

Ivan Boszormenyi-Nagy

It's an unusual vocabulary that psychiatrist Ivan Boszormenyi-Nagy uses in his theory of Contextual Family Therapy. He writes of "revolving slates," "legacies," "entitlements," and "loyalties." All these terms (soon to be defined) point toward one important goal: to build sufficient trust in family relations that members will be encouraged to open up a balance of fairness with one another.

Dr. Nagy (pronounced *Nodge*) was born and educated in Budapest. He served residencies in psychiatry in both Budapest and Chicago. He is professor and chief of the family-therapy section at Hahnemann Medical College of Philadelphia, visiting lecturer in psychiatry at the University of Pennsylvania, and also director of the Institute for Contextual Growth in suburban Ambler, Pennsylvania. For many years he served as director of the Eastern Pennsylvania Psychiatric Institute, where he developed much of his unusual theory in family therapy. He has published seven books and dozens of learned articles. In them he consistently takes a basically moral position, just as in his practice he becomes the representative of morality in an exploration of mutual commitment among family members.

Contextual Family Therapy

An interviewer once asked Boszormenyi-Nagy what he does to help a patient be what he dubs an "active searcher" in psychotherapy. His response was instructive: "I want to make people active rather than myself. I turn to one of the family members in the first few minutes in the first hour and say, 'I want to listen to you. Please tell me why you are here.' "[1]

This psychiatrist listens intently *and takes the side of the person speaking.* This on-the-spot partiality is essential to the process; it is then turned in another direction, as he listens just as intently to another member of the family tell how it appears from a different point of view. Thus a family in therapy is introduced to "multidirectional partiality," a method of flexible side taking that affirms everyone is entitled to attention and guarantees that obligations are going to be reviewed. In time, patients come to trust that their opportunity will come when Boszormenyi-Nagy turns to them.

Gradually he moves on to their relational roots. Inviting them to describe their family story, he urges them toward the goal of mutual trust. Encouraging open negotiation, he makes an assessment of their legacies, the configuration of expectations that originated in their family roots and now affects their generation. Legacy imperatives are the "I oughts" for which we make payments to one another—attempts at balancing the ledger to bring about some fairness in our intimate relationships. Thus one person will feel obligated to take over the family farm because his parents desire it. Another may enter a theological seminary because Father is a clergyman. This is any family's inveterate struggle and the problem on which the contextual family therapist works. Boszormenyi-Nagy, in fact, would maintain that a therapy emphasizing the here and now of current behavior actually colludes with the family's own denial and escapism.

The assessment phase searches out four dimensions of a family's problem: 1. Facts of their background. 2. The psychology they have invested in attitudes and symbolic meanings. 3. Interpersonal transactions, such as power alignments and scapegoating. 4. Relational ethics, the nonmoralistic accounting of equitable fairness, wherever it exists among them.

Of particular interest to more conventional family therapists is the list of common techniques Boszormenyi-Nagy does *not* practice (some of which are the planned interventions of other practitioners described in this book.) He features six prominent negatives:

• He does not relabel actions or attitudes to put them into a better light, because that would be prescribing what people ought to do, rather than eliciting their own intentions from them. He believes those in therapy have already had enough "oughts."

• He does not use criticism with patients. They already have enough experience with criticism. Instead of critical confrontation, he believes patients need a less objective, more empathic therapist.

• He does not prescribe tasks to be performed—either on a transactional basis, which would revise rules about relationships, or on a power basis, which confirms one-upmanship for the therapist (or anyone else, for that matter).

• Nor does he usually ask "why?" questions of his patients. His objective is to broaden the relational context of the events they discuss. Since asking persons why they think or act as they do moves them to defensiveness, it tends to narrow the context, instead of broadening it.

• The contextual family therapist does not search out pathology in persons and their relationships. In beginning therapy, the assessment phase is used to learn about the trust level of these persons, rather than diagnose their psychopathology.

• He does not conceive of therapy as being confined to the time and place of their interviews. "Therapy is not who you see," Boszormenyi-Nagy once said. "Therapy is in the consequences of the work. In classical individual therapy, the difficulty was the belief that therapy was confined to the one who was in the room, just as in medicine there is a body with whom you have a contract and no one else. In psychotherapy that cannot be true. In psychotherapy more is happening than what you do in your office because the effect is affecting other people."[2]

Individuals Within the Context

Considerable debate exists among family therapists concerning how many persons and just which persons of what ages should be included in therapy sessions. Boszormenyi-Nagy, flexible though he is about alternating individual and family group sessions, brooks no compromise on the question of including children. Parents are clearly enjoined to bring their children into the interviews. This is an ethical consideration for him and an important point in advancing his contextual therapy. If persons are to loosen the chains of the invisible loyalties that have been hampering their lives and poisoning their relationships, they must not be helped in any way to pass such handicaps on to the next generation. To give up symptomatic behavior and explore new options may well require the assistance of all members of the family, regardless of their ages.

Thus contextual family therapy allows for treating one person alone or several together, but the understandings are clear and strict. Any individual work will be done in the same context as if more than one person were being seen. There can be no separation of person and context, nor any pretense thereunto. The methods of the contextual approach are based on the theory that leverages can enhance resources in relationship for both personal freedom and for capacity for intimacy. Therapy is aimed at both current problems and a long-range balance of close relationships. The approach utilizes an integrative understanding of the methods of a variety of individual and family-therapy schools.

A Psychodynamic View of the Generations

Boszormenyi-Nagy, coming as he does from a psychoanalytic orientation, leaves room for the transference phenomenon in his theory. For example, he is alert for a wife's attempt to set him up as a *pro tempore* benevolent father figure in treatment. He offsets this common maneuver without interpreting it or calling undue attention to it; he simply quashes it. He deals with resistance in much the same manner, declining to interpret resistance by simply bypassing it.

The key to family problems is sought in the unconscious, internalized models of absent (even dead) persons from the past. Therapy develops an awareness of those past experiences that are supporting current distortions and misbehaviors. Without this search of previous interpersonal experience, repressed material can negatively affect succeeding generations. It will be recognized that this is the theory of object relations applied to family therapy, i.e., to an exploration of the emotional bonds between persons and their need for each other.

All modalities of family therapy somehow take notice of the Identified Patient or scapegoat in a disturbed family, but the Boszormenyi-Nagy approach puts a little variation into the process, a sort of spin on the ball. He does not isolate the Identified Patient or become a father figure to the I.P. Instead, he asks how he can be helpful to the entire family *through* the Identified Patient. Thus the therapist and the I.P. form an alliance to heal family relationships, a process that introduces the concept of loyalty and decisively alters the context.

To accomplish the objective of infusing family relationships with trust, contextual family therapists will not only foster talk about grandparents and the legacies they have handed on, but will also bring them directly into the sessions. With the more complex context of several generations meeting in one place, therapists (and this sometimes calls for more than one) must demonstrate their "multidirectional partiality," which listens to all viewpoints and actively encourages participants to open their

ledgers of concern and complaint. The therapy session is designed
to aid them in balancing their accounts on those psychological
ledgers. Meanwhile the therapists will so frame the experience
that loyalties will be respected and disloyalties opened to inquiry.
Considerable care is given to conserving positive relationships in
this procedure.

The goal of contextual family therapy remains for the therapist
to arrive at the most effective preventive design, to enable the
family to square their obligations with one another and live more
freely in their interpersonal relationships.

Some Theoretical Principles of Boszormenyi-Nagy

Boszormenyi-Nagy's contextual family therapy seeks both individual and systemic growth at the same time. It integrates a multiple level of dynamics with the systemic perspective of
conventional family therapy. But its purpose is to benefit persons
rather than systems, indeed to help those persons within the context of their systemic relationships. The theory has evolved from
individual therapy, intensive family therapy, and intergenerational contextual guidelines—a complex ancestry.

To understand the sometimes involved theory of this therapy,
it is important (as in reading Freud, Jung, or Skinner) to appropriate the vocabulary of the theorist and understand terms as he uses
them. Four repetitive terms stand out of this literature:

• *Loyalty*, whether visible or invisible (overt or covert), consists of the major connective link between generations. This link
can be functional or dysfunctional, but the struggle is to balance
the old obligations with the new. A woman's dilemma may be
that of protecting her loyalty to her mother while also obligating
herself to new loyalties to husband and children—a task that
some accomplish with aplomb, while others fail tragically.

• *Ledgers* consist of the accumulation of accounts of what has
been given and what is still owed in the way of loyalty and obligation. This figurative account book is a statement of two ethical
components: 1. The debts and entitlements from our legacies

(what we are owed and what we owe to our progenitors). 2. The merits we stock up through our contributions to the welfare of others. Any action has the possibility of becoming a value for the group's survival, so the group puts positive or negative evaluations (that is, fulfilled or unfulfilled obligations) on their ledger of merits and obligations. The ledger is a record of a family's concept of justice. Seeking out justice in their interactions is a basic motivation for them. It is justice that regulates the functions of a group and censures the trespasses that sometimes threaten their survival. Over time they will incur and pay off debts carried on the ledger.

• *Legacies* are those obligatory expectations that originate in our family roots and impact on succeeding generations. For example, a woman may feel a special compulsion concerning her vocation or accomplishments, which grows out of the projected hopes of her mother.

• The *revolving slate*, a rather awkward image, is the fated expectation that numerous family patterns will be repeated, against unavailing struggle, generation after generation, as if a father's eating sour grapes set his children's teeth on edge. Boszormenyi-Nagy holds that this aspect of invisible filial loyalty is the outstanding factor in family and marital dysfunction. It can be covert, even unconscious, or it can be insidiously intentional, as when a parent uses a child to compensate for rejection by his spouse or another.

This theory contends that the nuclear family will invariably show the struggle of countless previous generations. For example, Boszormenyi-Nagy asserts that a husband's abusive act toward his wife may have far more dynamic connection to a behavioral sequence of thirty to sixty years ago than to any act of hers that triggered the abuse.

Children and Pathology

The supposed victims of family machinations generally have more power than their relatives recognize. Invisible loyalty commitments to the family may follow rather paradoxical laws, so the scapegoat who refuses to allow others to work off their guilt can be more controlling than the loud, demanding tyrant. So also the delinquent or rebelling child might just be the most loyal member of the family, vociferously defending the others when outside the home. Indeed, that very child can so loyally act out the part of an I.P. that he encourages the family to move against him in order to prove the family's good image! Thus the therapist watches both for overt power-centered behavior and for covert obligation-oriented signs that someone is keeping a hidden ledger of merits, obligations, and resentments. The therapist may help spouses who are bitterly attacking each other to redirect their anger toward their families of origin, once they see that their mutual hostility has been a misplaced loyalty serving as a brake on criticizing their own parents. Therapy can then proceed to balance the ledger more appropriately with those families of origin.

Contextual family therapy contends that invisible filial loyalty is the largest factor in family dysfunction. The literature cites a case that illustrates this point:

> A twenty-year-old girl broke off repeatedly from her fiancé. At age ten she had given the following TAT [Thematic Apperception Test] story:
>
> David and Jane just got married. When Dave came home Jane wouldn't talk to him. Dave said, "Aren't you going to talk to me?"
> "No."
> "Why not?"
> "My sister just ran away." So everybody went out to look for her.
>
> This projective fragment provides a clue to what was becoming apparent in the clinical situation ten years later. Indeed, the girl presented herself as immature, fixated at the preoedipal level, etc. But from the contextual point of view, she was bound to a legacy which compelled her to preserve her commitment to her family at the cost of new relationships. Helping her to face the intrinsically unfair expectations of this "revolving slate" would offer the best chance for therapeutic leverage.[3]

Such pathology is viewed as a flight from facing one's ledger. Nagy told one conference of family therapists, "I think that depression is related to the inability of persons to earn constructive input to care about others. When I cannot accomplish that, then I begin to blame myself." Health, on the other hand, can be defined as the compatibility of loyalty, obligations, and individuation. It shows up as the ability to make compromises and find new forms of paying back loyalties.

Children, of course, may be exploited to rebalance the parents' own previous experience of being exploited. Abusive behavior toward them may well come from unresolved conflicts growing out of negative loyalty obligations.

It would be fatuous, however, to assume that the intergenerational abuses are directed only downward, from old to young. The context regularly includes youth who wrench loyalty payouts from their elders. Such a person can be the parentified child, who assumes mature privileges and obligations to direct her siblings, and sometimes also succeeds in dominating her parents. Therapy tends to replace this kind of petty tyranny with a more appropriate interpersonal relationship within the context of the family, clarifying what loyalties are realistic and what obligations are actually incurred.

Parentification can also mean that the young person has to play a parentlike role (caretaker, provider, incest partner). The key dimension here is possession versus the loss of loved ones in order to avoid any separation from one's parent. The relational foundations are unbalanced ledgers taken over from the family of origin and brought into the nuclear family. Parentification becomes pathological when it is rigid and captivates the children in assigned roles. In order to liberate the children, the therapist has to reopen the older relationship between parent and grandparent. This theory, it will be noticed, partakes of the same principle as that concerning the origins of hostility within a marriage: The background for the problem is to be located in preceding generations. Therapy for pathology is to be found in balancing those old ledgers. By this means, the weary repetition of family dissension can be interrupted. Boszormenyi-Nagy seems to be writing between the lines: "You certainly don't want your children and grandchildren to suffer these same experiences, do you?"

A Pastoral Contextual Perspective

Boszormenyi-Nagy's reminder for the clergy is to always keep the family's context in mind. When counseling with an individual, a couple, or any family constellation, it can be folly to neglect this factor. The background of the counselee, the family's history, the places they have lived, the conditions under which they have conducted a household and reared children—these play an inextricable part in everyone's existence. There are three L's of importance in such an assessment: loyalties, legacies, and ledgers.

In a small-town parish I once served, I became deeply impressed by the heavy hand laid upon individuals by their family past. The loyalty they felt they owed to their parents (never entirely separable from feelings of guilt), the legacies they felt were pressed upon them (enroll at mother's alma mater; join father in his business; take over the farming of wheat), and the invisible ledgers they knew were kept as an accounting of their family loyalty, all weighed down upon them. It became impossible to consider a marital conflict, a parent-child problem, or an emotional difficulty without reference to the family's "L's." If not mentioned by the pastor in counseling, they would nonetheless loom up large and loud in the background.

The implications are plentiful. Have injustices been committed? If so, what are the prospects for a just reconciliation? Are certain entitlements (privileges and recognition owed to someone) being withheld? Have there been crippling offenses, and can forgiveness be procured? Is there an unrealistic expectation of loyalty that prevents someone from getting on with life? Among such queries, and many more as well, the context for pastoral counseling is placed. More than once in my experience, it was possible to confirm what David Cooper charges in *The Death of the Family*: Families, whatever their potential for love and security, can also stifle and tyrannize their own members and turn them toward pathology.[4]

But Boszormenyi-Nagy guides us to other understandings for our pastoral ministry. He makes us aware of all the members in any family. Like other representatives in this multigenerational school of family therapists (Bowen, Framo, and Paul), he admonishes us to admit children into our sessions of family therapy, to include them in the exchanges. Likewise, we should invite grandparents to participate in interviews, both for what they can add to the process and for what they can gain from it.

Almost as a corollary to this point, he cautions us to be on the lookout for the parentified child and to work with that strange dynamic to restore appropriate boundaries within the family, boundaries that can free the child to act her age, as well as aid parents in assuming their own mature responsibilities in relation to each other. Until this happens, such a child can usurp a position from which to tyrannize both siblings and parents—and meanwhile to become miserable herself. The identification of and provision for this need could hardly be noticed unless the therapist is seeing the entire family together, at least occasionally.

But tyranny is a vice that moves both up and down through the generations. What this therapy terms "destructive entitlements" reach their nadir in parental abuse of children. In one case history of a battering father and mother, the therapist attempted to move them toward a more wholesome acceptance of the child. He asked them to tell him something redeeming about their child, only to learn they were unable to think of *even one item.*

The body of all this contextual literature serves as a reminder that families in distress need not only correction but also forgiveness and reconciliation. The pastor who can lead them in that direction—to help them realize that the works of faith are caring, compassion, and mercy—is more than a therapist. That pastor is also a spiritual director.

13

Norman Paul's Therapy: Ghosts From the Past

The quality of one's relationship to members of one's original family forms the unrecognized backdrop for the success or failure of one's marriage.

Norman L. Paul

That Norman Paul, M.D., is sometimes known as an "exorcist" is a friendly jibe at his specialty of helping families clear out ghosts from their pasts. Recognized widely for his theory that unresolved grief in an individual will affect an entire family system, he has built a transactional therapy around that conviction. A member of the faculty in the department of neurology at Boston University's School of Medicine, he not only teaches family therapy to medical students but also conducts a private practice. Because his approach is multigenerational, he teaches his students to first investigate their own families of origin. They then compare their personal memories and impressions with the reports they gather from their relatives. They bring this data into supervised sessions as a concomitant to the cases they are treating in family therapy. It makes for a powerful educational lesson.

Among family therapists, Paul is known as the "conductor type," a vigorous personality who leads and moves his patients. Yet he was once trained as a "reactor type" psychoanalyst, to work individually with adults or children. While he was a first-year resident, however, he began to question this focus on individual therapy. His move toward family-oriented therapy was a natural, gradual one. In the development of his own peculiar emphasis on what loss and grief can do to family relations, he has contributed a specific technical and conceptual formulation of value to all family therapists.

Norman Paul's Transactional Therapy

This therapist's approach to marital couples in stress is through conjoint therapy. Each spouse in the joint session, hearing the other reflect on the past, begins to view the present against that past, with all of its unreconciled losses and problems. Through these joint sessions, it is hoped that husbands and wives will grow out of their old pains and live more adequately in the present. Besides that, each spouse can gain new empathy for the other in such a process.

Paul orchestrates these sessions, spending considerable time on current and past history while benignly neglecting typical transactions within the marital case. Intensive interviewing brings out the memories and fears of each person while the spouse listens and Paul, the onetime analyst, interprets to the spouse the unconscious expectations and projections that he hears in this recital.

In his bias toward multigenerational work, he may bring three generations into the counseling office at one time for this process. In a procedure that must require considerable ingenuity and courage from a therapist, he portrays himself as the transference substitute for the lost person—for example, a deceased mother. He begins to encourage the patient toward a more accepting and open attitude concerning the reality of the loss.

Paul himself serves as the model of empathy for the couples he treats. He thus invites others in the family to emulate this cognitive empathy in depth. The goal is to help them see how they can reach an understanding about one another. His aim is to aid them toward such understanding, rather than simply to observe his practice; for he is convinced that it is far more important for patients to have a good relationship with members of their family than with the therapist.

Paul is not above asking seemingly stupid questions in order to understand the details better and involve the patients more deeply. He says that he has learned,

> . . . to be very dumb and to search for facts without thrusting my expectations into a family scene. My general posture is that until there is evidence that family members feel more comfortable about their lives and their interrelationships, some important information is still missing that could make the family scene more understandable. My general goal is for each family member to be able to cope more realistically with the uncertainties of life and have a sense of joy about being alive. This can occur if one is capable of sorting out the unpleasant, the tragic, and the pain, which, when accepted and then shared with some others, . . . can imbue family members with a spirit of genuine love.[1]

It is instructive to understand Paul's concept of who a patient is. No one-downmanship is involved in this doctor's view of those he treats. A patient is one whose life experience is such that he has been rendered ignorant of the emotional facts of his own life. "To label such ignorance as a psychiatric illness not only demeans the human being, but casts him in a role from which it is very difficult to extricate himself."[2]

Pauline Theories

The concept of object relations is central to Norman Paul's concept of "operational mourning." In this theory, an adult's intrapsychic conflicts emanate from early experiences with the family of origin. That individual may attempt to deal with these conflicts by forcing current relationships to fit internal role models, perhaps the models of parents. No small amount of trouble can arise when a husband pressures his wife to relate to him the way his mother did. Paul's objective is to locate the loss experienced by such a person (for example, that husband's yearning for Mother) through separation from original object relations, then discover the impact operational mourning has had upon that person and his loss. By conducting an inquiry into the past as well as the present, Dr. Paul tries to locate the figure out of the past who has impacted on this person and his family relations.

The Pauline concern about "the unresolved mourning process" moves his patients toward acknowledging a loss that may never have been purged through normal grief work. Now the entire family can return to an arrested mourning for their lost object relations in a symbolic way. Such a procedure, of course, puts unusual emphasis on the past, a marked contrast from those therapists who work exclusively on the here and now. This approach calls up from repressed memories the relationships and values of yesteryear.

The assumption is that family problems involve unresolved internal object relations, and that these are the indicators of pain and problems. As Whiffen Byng-Hall has written, "Family myths may originate in an unresolved crisis such as a failed mourning, a desertion or an abortion; the image of the lost person may become resurrected in a remaining member of the family."[3]

So definite is this method of treatment that patients who have no living family members with whom to communicate about the "ghosts of the past" can be sent to the cemetery to communicate instead with the tombstones of deceased parents and family members. They are advised to take a tape recorder with them and record the words they speak to their deceased relatives. The goal, of course, is to free the family of some of their symptoms through the discipline of grief work.

Since ghosts of the past are forgotten attachment figures who have been inadequately mourned, this lack can obstruct personal development as well as reconciliation with family members. Overcoming the problem enables a family to get on with normal living. It does, in truth, represent a modern kind of exorcism; these ghosts of the past are repressed experiences that can interfere with both marital relationships and the children in the family. Facilitating those marital and parent-child relationships is the heart of Norman Paul's transactional family therapy.

The Pastor in Exorcism and Assurance

It remains for us to ask if the clergy can also act as exorcists for those family ghosts of the past that Norman Paul identifies in his therapy. The clergy are accustomed to the task of comforting bereaved persons in the wake of the death of loved ones. Ministering to such a problem has long been an essential part of the specialty that in *pastoralia* is termed the cure of souls.

The loss of a parent, which is grievous and disturbing for most people, assumes massive proportions under some circumstances. If the death is sudden, if death precedes the working out of lingering disputes and alienation, or if that death is correlated with an unusual emotional dependency on the part of a son or daughter, then the trauma can be all the greater. The loss of a mother or father who seemed to always be there, someone on whom children had counted, a familiar, dear presence now withdrawn from the world, leaves a tremendous void. The long shadow of that parent reaches into the evening of our lives.

Ministers, priests, and rabbis have considerable experience working with the immediate situations of dying, death, and bereavement. (They tend to have less involvement working with those lingering ghosts of the past in retarded, unresolved grief.) Though hard-pressed to say words of comfort adequate to such an occasion, they learn after a time to say little and keep that little scrupulously close to sound doctrine. There should be no hyperbole in this compassion, no promise the Scriptures cannot afford, no pious mouthings of comfort in cheap consolations.

"One simply has to be silent," as John Macquarrie says, "for anything that is said is just too glib and superficial."[4] The separation by death from what Isaiah calls "the land of the living" is too much for superficiality. Enough that our theology of hope holds out the comfort that St. Paul describes: None of us lives or dies to ourselves, and we are hardly those who have no hope, since Christ has taken the sting from death and snatched victory from the grave. First of all, then, the clergy will minister through personal counseling and funeral liturgy in a project of comfort—parsimoniously applied.

Second, we can appeal to the *koinonia* in the parish to come to the aid of the bereaved. The congregation participates in this ministry not only with the very real succor of food for the family and rooms for visiting relatives, but also with the empathy of those who have suffered similar loss. This is where the widow-to-widow program is effective, where parents who have lost children can stand beside those similarly bereaved, where the survivors of a suicide can share the tragedy of others in such pain. These experienced and understanding friends will often identify with suffering at a depth clergy may not be able to approximate, unless they, too, have so suffered.

Third, we shall recognize that there is an ongoing counseling ministry to perform well after the event of death and the memorial service. Some pastors return to the family on a Sunday night two weeks later, to lead them in family worship and remembrance. Some visit again on the anniversary of death.

Parenthetically, it never ceases to astonish us that mature persons, even the elderly, still remain tied to their image of parental approval and disapproval. Fathers and mothers, living and dead, can continue to exert a lasting influence over daughters and sons, long after the launching stage in family living. In some cases, that influence reaches out from beyond the grave and leaves a bequest of guilt to persons who never achieved the individuation expected in adults and designated in the developmental stage Erik Erikson has named "Integrity." Clergy will need to be aware of the need to bring healing to these retarded dependencies.

An ongoing pastoral ministry may also involve the previously mentioned working through of grief and guilt associated with a death long past. Here the clergy concentrate on their priestly function, reminding parishioners of the assurance of God's pardon for their confessed sins of omission and commission. Here, as well, the cure of souls indicates a need for bereaved and guilt-ridden folk to talk out their long-lingering burden, the phenomenon Norman Paul has designated a "ghost from the past."

Some clergy revert to a famed technique of Gestalt therapy and ask the counselee to speak to an empty chair, as if the departed parent were sitting in it. Some, taking a page from Norman Paul's book, send their parishioners to the cemetery, to talk to the grave itself. This is not as ghoulish as it first appears. Many people do just that, without a pastor suggesting it. Feeling a need to relate to a loved one who has died, they travel to the graveside and tell the deceased their thoughts, express their regrets, and organize their adjustment to loneliness. For them, it would be a fresh feature to suggest taking a tape recorder along to preserve these thoughts, or to replay sections of the audiotape in a future counseling session. Recognizing that there is therapy in mourning, we can utilize that dynamic to assist bereaved and guilt-ridden persons through their misery to new resolution. Then, please God, they may be enabled to repair their current family relationships and intimacies so their own survivors need not recapitulate such an experience of guilt, remorse, and loss in some future year.

IV

Psychodynamic Family Therapists

14

Grandfather Nathan Ackerman's Psychodynamic Family Therapy

The goal of family therapy is not merely to remove symptoms or to adjust personality to environment, but more than that—to create a new way of living.

Nathan Ackerman

It is remarkable that Nathan Ackerman, who died in 1971, still continues to influence the family movement. A pioneer in the field, early in his career he combined psychoanalytic theory with his interpersonal emphasis and a systemic approach to family problems. Trained as a psychoanalyst and child psychiatrist, Ackerman was professor of psychiatry at Columbia University and supervising psychiatrist at Jewish Family Service in New York City.

Vincent Foley neatly places Ackerman in historical perspective: "Ackerman forms a bridge between the old and the new. He stands midway between the intrapsychically oriented therapist who is only peripherally concerned with families and those people who are aptly called systems analysts because their concern is that . . . the system is the patient."[1]

Foley dubs Ackerman the grandfather of the family-therapy movement, "a brilliant and articulate spokesman to a rather hostile psychoanalytically oriented community." Ackerman had been snubbed and spurned in the early days of his emphasis on the family. Other psychotherapists, long accustomed to individual treatment of patients from their intrapsychic stance, did not take kindly to the innovations he was practicing and writing about.

One of them having come to recant his earlier criticisms was John Bell (see chapt. 15). Referring candidly to his previous opposition, he recounts how Ackerman's *Psychodynamics of Family Life* impacted on him: "I recall how this book, when I first encountered it, had provoked in me sharply hostile reactions." Ackerman's innovative methods provoked hostility and coolness in others, as well. In the academic strife this contentious, unconventional man experienced at Columbia, his family-therapy conferences were scheduled to conflict with mandatory meetings for the psychiatrists. In the autumn of 1971 when, after his death, the Group for the Advancement of Psychiatry published their annual necrology, this founding member's name was omitted.[2]

Nathan Ackerman's Therapy

For Ackerman, the goal of family therapy was not merely to remove symptoms or adjust personality to the environment, but something more—to create a new way of living. In family therapy, a family learns how to relate to one another in new ways through making changes in their values and relationships. Such a goal is hardly modest. Its very statement implies the seriousness and earnestness of the therapist. Ackerman was a caring person.

He set himself to alleviate the family's current conflict and to strengthen positive elements of personality. He believed that a family changes when it comes into contact with an empathic therapist who helps it deal with its contagion of pain, despair, and doubt. Once a relationship with the family is developed, the therapist can then check out the disturbance and teach members to relate to one another in a more positive manner. The therapist's task, he opined, is to shake up former deviant patterns of alignment and make room for new modes of interaction.

Procedure in Interviewing

Ackerman would begin therapy with one of his troubled families in an informal fashion (he believed formal procedures to be useless in his work). He saw families in weekly one-hour sessions. No practitioner of short-term therapy, he expected to measure significant therapeutic change in from six months to two years.

According to Ackerman, family therapy begins immediately upon the first face-to-face contact with the patients. The therapist makes instantaneous observations about their personalities, their ways of interacting, their adaptation to family roles. How they enter, who sits next to whom, who looks at whom, who looks away, who speaks, who listens, who smiles, who frowns—in these, any observant therapist can note the emotional climate of the family toward one another and the therapist. The quality of appeal that the members project to one another and the existing confusion, distrust, and hostile fragmentation of family relationships are all there to be noted and evaluated.

Ackerman's interest in the family's history was chiefly for what it could teach him about current roles of family members. His emphasis was on the interpersonal and the here and now, rather than on the individual and the past. In any case, he expected historical details to emerge from the interviews in bits and pieces, as patients remembered other items of their family's autobiography.

Out of his psychoanalytic orientation, Ackerman was certain that there is an important exchange of emotion between family and therapist. He is credited with using this exchange constructively, not as mere transference but as a therapeutic value. In his thinking, the therapist's primary responsibility was to mobilize a useful dimension of empathy and communication, to arouse and enhance a lively and meaningful emotional exchange. Figuratively speaking, this lends to the contact a spontaneous and deeply genuine kind of communion. Then, even though the family is pervaded by disillusionment, defeat, and depression, that flicker of hope still present in everyone can be awakened.

Ackerman taught that the therapist should learn the special language of the family, a lesson many therapists have copied. How a family talks, what they talk about, and significantly, what they avoid mentioning constitute the special language of a family. Stage by stage, as the therapist learns the lingo, the denials, and the displacements, the family's rationalizations can be uncovered and stripped away. Then the essential conflicts come into view.

Ackerman's tactic was to catch families by surprise through exposing discrepancies between their self-justifying rationalizations and their subverbal stance. He challenged their clichés and euphemisms; he stopped their fruitless bickering over superficialities; he reached for a more meaningful kind of communication. As a therapist, he considered himself as a reality-testing instrument. Contrary to many another psychiatrist, he identified himself as an educator in the problems of living, pressing patients into an expanded awareness of alternative styles of family living.

Ackerman made home visits to the families he treated. Unconcerned that they might be on their best behavior when he called, he treated this phase as but one integer to be integrated with other findings. He learned there what many other family therapists have learned under the same circumstances: To visit in the home environment of a family is to learn new details about them that would not emerge inside the counseling office. He looked not only for the influence of that home setting, but also for the elements of interrelationships that marked the family's patterns of dealing with one another. More than once, the front a family put on when present in his office fell away when they were at home.

He kept careful and elaborately detailed notes on his cases. The outline for evaluating marital and parental interaction presented in his *Psychodynamics of Family Life* is impressively itemized and goes on for pages. His painstaking notes and labored papers stored at the Ackerman Family Institute run into volumes. A description of the family's behaviors and interactions, a brief profile of each person, an impression of the environment: Such data became direct aids to family diagnosis.

Diagnostics

Ackerman's step-by-step sequence of family diagnosis and treatment involved separate sessions with the primary patient, interspersed with joint interviews of the patient together with other family members. He treated the primary patient or symptom bearer as his usher for interventions into the disorder of family relations. Ackerman learned that one person will reveal what another conceals. The therapist must then distinguish valid secrets from false, pathogenic ones. His philosophy of therapy involved a set of three R's as distinct emphases: reeducation of the family through guidance, reorganization through a change of their patterns, and resolution of pathogenic conflict. Ackerman, ever the teacher, worked through the induction of change and growth by a dynamic approach to the deep currents of family living.

Ackerman's Basic Concepts

To appreciate the basic viewpoint of Ackerman's psychodynamic school of family therapy, it is useful to review something of their psychoanalytic (Freudian) theory.

Freudians see troubled persons as sometimes stymied between the id and the superego, between their base drives and their conscience. The therapeutic task is to aid patients in developing their ego strength, for the ego serves as the personal gatekeeper between the base drives and the conscience. The analyst seeks to free patients from their immobilization through the development of a transference (from the patient to the psychoanalyst). The goal of psychoanalysis is nothing less than the reconstitution of personality. The id is to be replaced by the more logical ego ("Where id is let ego be!" was Freud's dictum); the unconscious must become conscious.

To the psychoanalyst, character is consistent, and it manifests itself in predictable ways through a wide variety of situations. Therefore the therapeutic concept of "working-through" is the same as repeatedly examining the same dysfunctional conduct as it occurs in various contexts of family therapy.

The concept of object relations emphasizes that the ego is in the center of personality, reaching out to objects (typically parents) for support. Beginning with the assumption that a troubled person's inability to maintain ongoing personal relationships is the result of his poor relationship with his mother or father, an analyst then works through the transfer relationship as a second chance to find better object relations. To some extent, the family therapist who subscribes to this theory may temporarily be seen in a parenting role by a troubled family.

The outstanding element to note in today's psychoanalytically oriented therapists is their Ackerman-like shift toward family-systems thinking. Charles Kramer (*see* chapt. 17) writes, "I stubbornly believed that it was both theoretically possible and practically useful to continue psychoanalytic training and practice and concomitantly evolve a family therapy approach based on psychoanalytic principles."[3] To that, Nathan Ackerman could have added an emphatic amen.

Ackerman's Convictions

Throughout his career, Ackerman was to remain basically Freudian in his theoretical constructs and therapeutic assumptions. He made use of psychoanalysis for understanding internal mental processes, but emphasized the adaptation of personality to society and its systems. Moreover, he sought to somewhat neutralize Freud's tendency to separate the individual from others. He wrote:

> I have become increasingly skeptical of traditional clichés and stereotyped formulations regarding the psychodynamic relation of child and family. Such concepts as Oedipus conflict, seduction, inconsistent discipline, overprotection, overindulgence, and narcissistic exploitation of the child can in no way be adequately understood unless the interaction processes of the family, as well as the personalities of each member, are subjected to systematic study.[4]

Ackerman rejected the psychoanalytic penchant for confidential therapy with only one person at a time. The usual approach of psychoanalysis to family life had been indirect, rather than direct. Some psychoanalysts still refuse to know relatives of their patients, lest this interfere with the conduct of the analysis. This can limit the analyst to the emotionally biased views of the individual patient, on whom the analyst remains rather dependent for information concerning family interactions. Ackerman based his impressions of any one family on his direct observation of them and his work with them in the clinic and home. More than that, he had a societal view of families, their history, and their destiny. He once wrote:

> The family is a designation for an institution as old as the human species itself. The family is a paradoxical and elusive entity. It assumes many guises. It is the same everywhere; yet it is not the same anywhere. Throughout time it has remained the same; yet it has never remained the same. The steady transformation of the family through time is the product of an unceasing process of evolution; the form of family molds itself to the conditions of life which dominate at a given time and place. On the contemporary scene, the family is changing its pattern at a remarkably rapid rate; it is accommodating in a striking way to the social crisis which is the mark of our period in history. There is nothing fixed or immutable about the family, except that it is always with us. It is small wonder, therefore, that we accept its role in our lives so naturally, so unthinkingly. In one sense, we have had thousands of years to grow accustomed to it, and yet, in another, each generation in turn must learn again how to live with it.[5]

Psychosocial Understandings of the Family

Ackerman viewed the family as a unique organization, a basic unit of society. He characterized the family's quality of living and functional unity as a "familial organism" with a life of its own. The family has a life history; it goes through stages of development; it has a collective personality. He clearly saw the interpenetrating aspects of social organization and the patterning of the family: Society shapes family functions to its own goals, and the family exerts an influence on the trends of the wider community.

Ackerman was necessarily concerned with the contribution of

culture to the family through the powerful process of socialization. The family is the chief transmitter of socialization; the survival of the family is crucial for any society to endure. Societal goals can be achieved only if the parents are able to do their task and maintain their own meaning in life.

He had traditional convictions about family functions. He understood the specific purposes and functions of a family to be both union and individuation, the care of the young, the cultivation of a bond of affection and identity, reciprocal satisfaction, and training for social participation. The balancing and regulation of these functions constitute a major responsibility of each family. It is hardly astonishing that they occasionally fail to cope with all these challenges.

Ackerman knew that the family bears an extra psychic load. The family shrinks from events in the wider community that it cannot understand or tolerate. Then, to make up for its members' failure to win achievement or emotional satisfaction from the world, the family tries to compensate its members through intimacy and affection. Thus it intensifies the mutual dependence and hostility that feed family conflict.

Roles Within the Family

When the therapist is confronted by a family no longer able to cope, the clinical diagnosis must take into account reciprocal roles, the family group, and their interrelationships. Otherwise the diagnosis is faulted. Roles always carry involved interpersonal relationships. To talk about a mother necessarily involves a child; to discuss the role of a husband implies that of a wife. A role relationship concept has to mean some degree of reciprocity.

Roles in a family can also include some rather sick functions. There are the roles of attacker and victim, but also of healer. From time to time, these roles can be exchanged, for families are divided into competing emotional alliances. They want different things, and they wage battles around the felt threats of their differences.

A great deal of marital conflict, according to Ackerman, arises from role competition. The corrective, he realized, was to help the husband and wife better understand that their life was complementary rather than competitive. This they could learn rationally through conscious, cognitive processes. Ackerman's independence from psychoanalytic orthodoxy freed him from assumptions that spouses act competitively only from unconscious motivations. He could accept that the unconscious impinges upon family life, and he probed into this aspect whenever it was necessary to family treatment; but he realized other methods of therapy are useful, too.

From experience, Ackerman learned about the dichotomy of enmeshment and individuation; he called this "togetherness" and "separation." He also held that a true development of autonomy can be superimposed upon a satisfying union of wife and husband. It is possible, he insisted, to be yourself and also be in deep union with another. The failure to see and act upon this understanding is the foundation of considerable family conflict.

Nathan Ackerman's keen observations about family life and his wise directions about family therapy arose neither from research nor secondary resources, but from the arena of therapy itself. He put it succinctly: "All that I know about troubled people I have learned from treating them, both as individuals and as families."[6]

Implications for the Pastoral Counselor

It would have been a surprise to Nathan Ackerman that his writings have enabled church leaders and psychiatrists to communicate better with each other. That was hardly the purpose of the 129 papers he left as a bequest to today's family therapists. He would be astonished to learn that Christian pastors and church leaders look to his principles and practice for guidance in treating the troubled family. Nevertheless, this creative and irascible grandfather of the family psychotherapy movement has left us with a half-dozen lessons from his own experience.

• For Ackerman, therapy had a purpose beyond that of aiding patients in personal adjustment; his goal was to lead them to new ways of living. Pastoral counselors, being theologically grounded, have long realized that their task is to reach beyond the immedi-

ate goal of alleviating pain and assisting persons in life adjustment. Many of us are convinced that our obligation is to point
the way to redemptive possibilities, to help counselees strengthen
their spiritual resourcefulness. Without this essential extra step,
our work remains unfinished.

• Ackerman was convinced that it is a primary responsibility
of the therapist to mobilize a deeper dimension of empathy and
communication, arousing and enhancing a lively and meaningful
emotional exchange. This, he found, led to a genuine level of
communion. There is hardly a pastor who can read of such contact without being reminded of the spiritual bond that can be felt
by persons with mutual faith in Christ. Indeed, this is a quality
upon which the minister can count in pastoral counseling, an experience to be purposefully sought. It is the accompaniment of
genuine and appropriate prayer in the therapeutic setting. It is
the synergistic product of a shared faith, the cause of heartfelt
thanksgiving from counselor and counselee alike when they realize that God is present in their midst.

• It amazed Ackerman's contemporaries that this eminent
psychiatrist would leave his office and take the time and trouble
to make home visits to client families. He did this because he was
convinced there are important lessons to be learned in the setting
of the family's life and being. That many social workers now follow this same practice is tribute in part to the example of this pioneer of family therapy. If routine calling in parish homes has
fallen into neglect in so much of today's church, it is a sad com-
mentary upon our congregational mores, because calling could
contribute to preventive screening of family problems, as well as
to a natural setting for immediate work on visible conflicts.

• The relatively simple scheduling technique used by Ackerman has imitable value for many others working with families. It
will be recalled that he interspersed personal interviews among
whole family sessions, so he could meet with individuals at times
and in conjoint sessions at others. There are times in marital therapy when the therapist may find it advisable to see the husband
without the wife or the wife apart from the husband. This gives

the lone spouse an opportunity to express thoughts that are difficult to voice in front of the other. It may offer the more reticent person a chance to have a "day in court" uninterrupted by the partner. Whatever the reason, it is useful to follow these individual interviews with joint sessions. This way, although it is not indicated in all or even most cases, the best features of conjoint interviews and personal sessions are realized.

- The three *R*'s that are described in Ackerman's *Treating the Troubled Family* are likewise immediately useful for others who treat families in distress. To view the task as one of reeducation, reorganization, and resolution is to see a holistic approach to such counseling. It encompasses in a trice a masterful description of the work, which is educational, systematic, and teleological. As so much of our counseling duty involves teaching, changing relationships, and providing help in maintaining that change, this example can be of value to us all.

- Last, this early master left us a psychological construct of importance in his description of family roles. To conceptualize the reciprocal roles of family members in the terms he used may exercise the obvious, but it still draws sharp attention to a truth often overlooked. Of course when one is counseling a husband, somewhere a wife has to be involved. Nor are there any parental problems without children's participation. But to highlight these reciprocal roles is to remind ourselves of the need to work with the whole relationship and to assist persons, as Nathan Ackerman did, to enter into complementary roles instead of competitive shackles.

15

John E. Bell's Family Group Therapy

Not all problems are solved, nor can they be. . . . But I have learned that carrying my intent as a group therapist into action with a family can lead to change, can reduce isolation, can free communication, can deepen trust, can promote fun, can lead to fulfillment.

John Elderkin Bell

As he tells it, John E. Bell worked in child-guidance clinics for years with a primary orientation toward the individual child. He confesses that he thought of the family as just part of the support structure. In his view, the child was the product of parental relationships and sibling rivalries.[1]

When he converted his therapeutic practice into family therapy, it was done with some apprehension. He worried whether parental presence might affect children, how transference and countertransference problems would obstruct treatment, and whether he would be able to include fathers, a class of patients he had not often seen in his work.

Previous to the 1950s, he viewed parents as a negative influence, the very cause of pathology. His position had been that fostering independence in a child takes precedence over integrating the child into family life. In any case, he doubted that parents could be changed much by family therapy. Being rigid adults, they would need skilled, individual therapy themselves.

Yet in 1951 Bell began to work in a new method, with the entire family present for treatment. To his astonishment, it did not prove an impossible task. Fathers did cooperate. Children were often relieved rather than upset by stormy sessions, if or when they occurred. And changes did take place in families. Imagine his surprise!

Today John E. Bell is semiretired, serving as a psychologist consultant with the Palo Alto Veteran's Administration Hospital as well as adjunct to the faculties of the Stanford University School of Medicine, the University of California (San Francisco), and San Francisco Theological Seminary.

Described by Ferber, Mendelsohn, and Napier as a lone and original figure in family therapy, Bell's quality of leadership is gentle, sympathetic, and courteous.[2] Currently he works not only with effecting change directly within the family processes, but also as a family-context therapist who is a planner and a coordinator for change within the community on behalf of family well-being.

John Bell's Therapy

In his first step in a series of efforts to build relations with the family, Bell develops the quality of therapist-patient interactions. A step-by-step process starts with the adults—commonly the parents, but also others who are closely involved day by day in the life of the family. Because the adults will have sought the therapy, they expect to tell the therapist about problems they are experiencing. Bell listens sympathetically, but regards their information giving as a preliminary effort to establish a relationship with the therapist, a process that will remain one-sided until children are present.

Bell insists on seeing both parents together that first session, if the marriage is at all intact. If one parent wishes to come alone, Bell simply indicates that he does not work that way when both parents are potentially available, but will be happy to work out arrangements to see them together. He quickly learned that it was a canard to say fathers would not come to therapeutic sessions about their children's problems. Indeed, he began to conclude that fathers are not only at times more motivated to work on family problems than mothers, but that they resent being left out.

In the event that an individual protests this demand for both parents to enter therapy, Bell politely suggests they seek some other clinic. Usually their protest is minimal, and the couple and their children are soon coming together.

In this first session, Bell introduces his expectations and lays the groundwork for succeeding interviews. In a wily maneuver admired and imitated by other therapists, he introduces at once a paradoxical contract with the parents. Explaining that he will expect them to make some changes that may be inconvenient for them, he procures their advance agreement to revise the ways they sometimes operate. He urges them to accept some suggestion that a child will make in the next interview, when the entire family is to be present. This "puts the parents in the position of control as co-strategists with the therapist, but paradoxically their first move is to agree to see what happens if the child is put in control of a limited aspect of the family's rules."[3]

The Second Interview

The second interview in Bell's family cases will bring the parents and children together. It opens with a time of orientation for the entire family group. This orientation has four special functions: 1. To review what the therapist's role is to be. 2. To clarify the obligations of the family while in therapy. 3. To anticipate with them what is likely to happen during therapy. 4. To make the practical arrangements for family therapy conferences.

It is in this phase that Bell makes two points clear. In the first, he describes himself more as an umpire than a father figure. In so doing, he encourages family members to express their feelings, even when some guilt may attach itself to the process. In the second, he makes it clear that he is a friend to children. He addresses the children, reporting that the previous week he had met with the parents and saying something like, "We're here to talk about the family and why it isn't working as well as it should, and what can be done to solve problems to help it work better." Into this meeting he introduces that opportunity for a child to suggest some modification in family rules. In this session he especially talks with the children; the parents had his exclusive attention in the previous interview. He can be quite plain with children in understanding their plight. Parents are sometimes strong and bossy, he tells them (as if they didn't know), thus identifying with their feelings of defenselessness. He pledges that although he is a grown-up, he will protect their rights in these sessions. He tells the children he's on their side—as are their parents, in a different way—and that he's there to help parents change things in order to make everyone in the family happier. As a therapist, he wants to help persons learn how to act in new ways and see that everyone gets a chance to talk things out.

This is a skillful, empathic beginning. Then, as if to demonstrate his points, Bell invites a child to state his wishes, grievances, and fears while the parents, cautioned not to dominate or interfere, are listening.

> But the primary problem is to convince the children that it is safe to talk in the therapy. They have to learn two truths: first, that they cannot use acting-out behavior as their primary way to communicate here, and second, that it is safe to talk. The first requires control; the second, security.[4]

His solution for this problem has been to work through the parents, with the aim of placing the parents in control of their children's acting-out behavior at the interview (insofar as possible). The goal, obviously reinforcing the parents, is to help the youngsters communicate and control themselves when they want to express something through their muscles: "Here we talk. Here, we don't play," says this therapist. Although it may take one or two conferences before a child begins to express himself on a verbal rather than a motor level, Bell is there in the meantime to protect the child from an overcritical parent.

He begins now to enlist the adults as cotherapists. He cautions them to expect some emotional crises, and he establishes the rules with them. For example, if one or more members will be absent, the session will be cancelled. In this interview, Bell moves conversation away from the Identified Patient and toward the family as a whole. He points out that the disturbance may show the family is not right for the individual and there may be some problems in the family that somehow affect the person who is acting out.

Parents will often seek a private session with the therapist in order to discuss the problems of their children. This Bell will not allow. In one instance a mother attempted to schedule a private interview with him, which he refused, mentioning that she could, if she wished, work with another therapist. Then she attempted to elicit therapy by telephone, but he had these calls deflected. Next she turned to writing letters. These he brought to the next session and read to the family. "The mother went into a rage," he reports, "but this was the end of her efforts to communicate with me privately. . . . In all families I have to hold the line against the efforts of individuals to break up my communication with the total family, and center it in a therapist-individual relation."[5]

Tapping Family Resources

Bell displays strong confidence in the resourcefulness of families. He remarks that he notices a family commonly makes an effort before the end of a session to seal off explosions, to pull themselves together, and to provide a basis for continuing the next week. Moreover, he is impressed that changes at times take place with impressive speed. "One week you have the problem, and the next week you don't. But now I understand that there is a lot building up to the stage where there is this rapid shift, sometimes happening after what seems a minute shift in the position of one of the family members."[6]

This approach, he stresses, is toward the family rather than any individual. He does not discuss a child's enuresis, delinquency, or school problem. Instead of emphasizing such topics, he speaks of family problems. "If the parents turn toward discussion of an individual's symptoms at the beginning, then I say, 'Yes, these are problems, but we're not here to talk about these difficulties but about the family.' "[7]

Parents are sometimes pleased by the ways in which a child can take a central part in solving problems. The child sees the parents somewhat from the standpoint of an outsider and can bring perspective, information, and insights to the parents, to help them in resolving their difficulties. Bell writes:

> I recall a boy, Skippy, about 11 or 12, whose father was a lumber salesman for a wholesale firm. He felt the only problem in his position was that he had great difficulty getting warmed up on Monday. He called his problem his "Monday neurosis." During six years of work for this particular company, no Monday had, in any way, come up to the level of the other days of the week. He brought in the problem for family discussion. Skippy said that he knew what to do. He proposed that, on the next Monday morning, he and his father would start the day with a game in which Skippy would be the first customer. Though he did not know anything about psychodrama, he suggested just such a drama in the family. The next Monday morning, he and his father played this game. The father was greatly amused; he had a hilarious time with Skippy, got a lot of whimsical enjoyment out of it, and to his delight that day was superior to any Monday he could remember. The back of his Monday problems was broken.[8]

A Final Phase

Bell then observes and facilitates the family toward a new phase, to consider sibling relations, roles outside the family, and eventually termination. Finally the family plans how to handle their affairs using old methods they have concurred are worth continuing and new techniques they have learned within their discussions. The time has come for the family to take over, and they themselves decide the next steps: the functions they might perform for one another, the patterns and values they will adopt, and the goals toward which they will move.

Bell's Basic Concepts

All therapists come to some convictions about how they are able to influence change within families. Bell realizes that family interaction is structured within operational limits that produce stereotyped patterns of reactions and restrictions upon individual behavior. They may use cynicism, mutual depreciation, and unrealistic appraisals. But he also knows that most parents and children have a range of behaviors beyond those they use in the family.

With such background of habit, individual family members begin to react to the therapist without the intense anxiety they might use with their relatives. This is the beginning of change. But then other family members begin to respond to the new patterns they see revealed in one another. They revise their stereotypes about family members, reevaluate them, and respond with new attitudes and accommodations in their own behavior. They begin to test out the possibilities for change that prove successful, and abandon those that do not. From this point onward, they can support one another by mutual commitment and consolidate the new patterns that replace the old, unusable patterns in their behaviors.

The nature of family changes brought by therapy has been described by Bell in cogent steps.[9] The first change he spots is a fluency in conversation and increased participation in communication. This may be followed by an improved understanding of the roles required or permitted in the family. The family begins to see that behavior has meaning and that symptomatic behavior can make psychological sense. Gradually they can reduce the tendency to blame one another and decrease the habit of assigning all the responsibility for change to someone else. Now new communication patterns become capable of demonstrating love and respect in the family. Their bonds of union gradually strengthen and overcome the disintegrating tendencies that had driven the family into divisive segments.

Bell has his convictions about how a therapist works:

> The therapist is using a conscious and disciplined technique to assist family members to accomplish the job of solving their own family problems. The difference between a family's own efforts or casual attempts of friends, neighbors, and so on to help a family, and a therapist's attempts, is that the latter is following a technique; he is in control of himself in some predetermined ways in realizing the job he has to perform. He uses himself as an instrument in helping to accomplish that. He develops particular ways of relating to the family that bring about certain therapeutic consequences; he can facilitate the changes, and speed up the change process, when his technical competence is such that he can handle the treatment. . . . The therapist's overall activity may be described, then, as an effort to promote social interaction through communication within the family unit, permitting it thereby to experience, appraise, define and reorder its relational processes.[10]

The Family as a Group

Among his presuppositions, Bell has two that come to the fore. In the first place, he is purposeful about working with the family as a whole. Although he will make reasonable exceptions for those who are too young, ill, or out of the area, he prefers to have the entire family together at the sessions, and he pressures them into attendance. As he sees it, no individual is more significant than any other in the family, regardless of age. In therapy, each is part of the other's system, so none would remain the same if removed from that group. His approach requires that the participants have developed a concept of themselves and others as differentiated individuals, but also some understanding of the family as a unit. Knowing that everyone who is left out is potentially an enemy of the treatment because he may not have been a part of the emerging agreements, Bell works for inclusiveness.

In the second place, Bell has traditionally placed his emphasis on a group theory of family relationships. Some therapists mix their work in the family group with individual therapy; not he. Because he perceives persons in relationships, for him the individual exists as an aspect of memberships, and the self is defined as an aspect of social relations in action—the sharing of ideas, aims, efforts, and experience.

Disorder and Pathology

Some families habitually fluctuate between turmoil and harmony. Their times of tension may serve the grim function of breaking up antiquated patterns that have lost their usefulness and uncovering patterns more responsive to the family's needs. Although painful, such tension has a process meaning: The old is being discarded, and a way is being prepared for the new.

Family disorder is seen by Bell as an effort (awkward though it may be) to disrupt some rigid system in the family or revise patterns that may have hardened. If forces for change cannot prevail against rigid family patterns, pathology may occur. Change, of course, is inevitable, whether it results from crisis or development. Yet when the change threatens the family, the family is going to strive to conserve its balance, even if it means continuing disorder within the home. The astonishing explanation for this is that family members have learned the adaptive values contributed by behavior disorder, and have found their procedure useful!

For example, they may be scapegoating some family member as a regular ritual. A weird logic holds that this practice will concentrate the family pathology in just one person. The scapegoat's symptoms may then progress to perform a new value, namely to provide a means of relationship and communication within the family. They can talk about their mutual problems and at least agree on victimizing him or her. Sick though it is, it performs a gratifying function for some.

A child with problems is often pushed forward as the family representative to legitimize their entrance into therapy. If the therapist were to accept this finesse at face value and begin to work only with the child, the opportunity would be lost to treat the whole family system; family therapy would have failed.

Family Environment

Bell's therapeutic technique has grown and expanded with the passage of years. After considerable experience, he came to the conclusion that family group theory was not working broadly enough to meet his standards. He has now extended his earlier work to include a family-context model that makes provision for family functioning in a still larger perspective.

His family-context therapy attempts to change environmental conditions that cause or accentuate family difficulties, constructing contexts that promote family well-being. Such a theory will necessarily involve intentional transformations of the world beyond the family, to lessen or remove the problems that context builds in physical, economic, and social ways. This form of advocacy and community organization is seen as an extension of family therapy. Its ultimate aim, explained by Bell in an article he wrote for *The Journal of Marriage and Family Counseling*, is to improve family competence in confronting problems, redirecting resources, and improving family efficiency—an ambitious objective. But John Bell has led the way for family therapists for years without trimming his objectives or waiting for others to join him.

The impact of the housing industry, the location of industrial plants, the service of transportation systems—all have profound influence upon family functioning. The essence of family-context therapy is moving the site of intervention from the clinical office into the greater society. Bell sees this as an advance within his own theory because he has discovered how problems that could not be solved by family therapy alone find some remedy in the larger contextual approach.

Limitations of Family Therapy

For Bell, family therapy is not the only avenue of relief for people's problems. Along with other therapists, he discovered certain factors predisposing against conventional family therapy. The family's own perceptions may get in the way. Their priorities can also sabotage therapy. Or the very nature of the problem (for example, chronic violence) may make family therapy inappropriate. Bell cautions that not all individual symptomatic behavior is removable through family therapy. His major criterion is whether a person's symptoms have been primarily the product of disordered family interaction. If so, family therapy is indicated as the treatment of choice.

Bell has performed a service for all family therapists in his definition of the middle ground where family therapy belongs. Located between individual therapy on the one hand (where intractable problems are lodged in the handicaps and disabilities of persons) and community action on the other (where the immensity of social disorders cannot be solved by a mere family), family therapy is in that wide range where the family system is at the base of the problem and can be used as the solution.

Therapists, he points out, have their limits in competence, acceptability, and power. Wryly this experienced therapist tugs at excessive zeal in family therapy: "Behavior which appears pathological or deviant to a professional person may not be of concern to the family."[11]

A View From the Church

Beels and Ferber once noted how John Bell anticipated the contributions his contemporaries in family therapy later developed. His blending of Don Jackson's paradoxical instruction, Virginia Satir's establishment of communication as the focus of therapy, the positive interpretation of Jay Haley, and the planning of phases that James Framo uses show his careful eclecticism in family-context therapy. What Beels and Ferber did not cite when they identified these strands in Bell's therapy is his basic Christianity. He is theologically educated (Union Theological College of British Columbia) and served in United Church pastorates early in his career.

John Bell has deep concern for the individual. His advocacy of
hospital patients, children in foster care, and families who have
an ill member comes through his writings again and again. For
example, he champions the cause of beleaguered parents with
this ringing exhortation of hope:

> Let us get away from thinking of parents as evil. Let us
> abandon thinking of all child patients as victims of their par-
> ents, or of circumstances. Let us remember that children do
> terrible things to parents, and, whenever we have a disturbed
> individual in a family, the whole family is probably embroiled
> in the problem. Let us remove from our thinking any bias
> against involving fathers in treatment. Let us get away from
> fixed ideas that adults are inflexible and unready to change;
> adults have potentialities for change that are not thought of
> when we are looking only for pathology; they can change and
> in major ways. They have a non-pathological side where readi-
> ness to change comes from, and family therapy works with the
> strengths among all family members.[12]

As a champion of the victim, Bell is ready to resist the family's
tendency to push their Identified Patient forward as the cause
and locus of their problem. Instead, he treats any scapegoated
symptom bearer as a respected person within the system of his
family relationships. Gradually he helps the family see that their
Identified Patient just might be the exhibitor of their collective
insecurity.

Bell's keen sense of the social context in which families live
and move and have their being has propelled him into becoming
an advocate. Like a veritable liberation theologian, Bell calls attention to the needs of families in our industrial-urban complex.
The helplessness of the family unit in this context is inevitable,
unless they are united and their problems can be heard. He knows
the limits of family therapy if it is offered within an inimical society; much of the gain from the therapy can be thwarted or
wiped out by the conditions of the living situation.

Any view from the church must take into account John Bell's
profound sense of disorder in human relationships and world

events. Convinced of the imperfect nature of humanity that theologians call original sin and aware of the tendency of persons to infect their associations, Bell is impressed by the way tension enters into daily life. He is not hopeless about tension; he sees it in positive perspective. The process meaning of tension, as he sees it, is that new ways of meeting experience and new demands to give up old patterns are revealed.

There is a new and growing appreciation of the value of tension and its contribution today, even in church life. Christians are showing somewhat less intimidation from the prospect of stress within the congregation, society, and family. In this they will find an ally in John Bell, who is able to see through disorder to the point where tension can present one method (albeit awkward) of altering rigid systems and preparing the way for new procedures.

Throughout his work with troubled families and even with recalcitrant institutions, John Bell has maintained a continuing hope. His goal as a therapist is to aid families in reordering their resources and to improve their relationships. His fresh evaluations of their situations mark a way for them to discover new possibilities in each member of the household. His balance helps us understand something of the needs, the possibilities, and the challenging context in a ministry of family therapy.

16

Lyman Wynne's Exploratory Family Therapy

Functioning in grossly disturbed families should help provide insight into the functioning of other families where those processes usually proceed so quietly as to remain unnoticed. The difficulties experienced by the families of schizophrenics . . . differ in degree, not in quality, from similar problems encountered by all families.

Lyman C. Wynne

Almost everyone now realizes that dysfunctioning families have more in common with normal, functioning families than they have in contrast to them. It is one of those humbling truisms that comfort the disturbed, inform the public, and aid the therapist.

It was Lyman C. Wynne and his team of researchers, however, who demonstrated in what particulars this realization is true. A major theorist in family therapy, he is also a pioneer who has served, and continues to serve, as mentor, consultant, and especially as researcher for the entire field of family psychotherapy. His influence upon the practitioners of family therapy has been so significant that many professionals use his insights (and even his vocabulary) without knowing where these have originated. The term *pseudomutuality*, for example, has enriched the speech of therapists the world over; it is but one of a number of colorful neologisms coined by this psychiatrist.

Wynne brings to his work both a medical degree and an additional doctorate in sociology. His studies with Talcott Parsons at Harvard, his experience as medical director in the U.S. Public Health Service, and his record in research have informed his psychiatric understanding of the person in the context of family relationships. At historic meetings of the American Psychiatric Association in 1956 and 1957, he joined forces with Murray Bowen, Nathan Ackerman, Don Jackson, and Theodore Lidz, a group from which we can date much of the subsequent flowering of this field. Thus began a lasting collaboration of knowledge and experience about still-new methods of treating troubled families.

Dr. Wynne is chairman of the editorial board of *Family Process*. His psychiatric practice includes a component of cotherapy with his wife, Adele Rogerson Wynne, in the treatment of families. Now professor of psychiatry at the University of Rochester School of Medicine and Dentistry, he continues to challenge those who write and practice in family therapy.

Lyman Wynne's Therapy

In Wynne's approach, exploratory family therapy amounts to a new transactional relationship. The mix of therapist and family must always bring a unique interaction, for no two are ever alike. Any description of a therapist is incomplete without a description of the family in treatment. This psychiatrist asserts that he is not the same therapist with a Jewish upper-middle-class family as he is with a family from the slums, for the therapist will become part of the family system for the duration of the therapy. Studying therapy out of context is unrealistic. That family makes the difference, and the therapist is there to promote change.

In his practice, he considers exploratory family therapy to be the treatment of choice for "relationship problems in which all of the participant family members have a vital and continuing stake on either a conscious or an unconscious level. Ideally, a central part of each family member's life should be absorbed in wrestling with, fending off, or coping with the shared problem."[1]

In common with other therapists, Wynne conceives of his treatment beginning with an entry phase, a time of introductory liturgy. In this, as in all that follows, the therapist is to be active and assertive, rather than reactive and passive. Unless this is the case, the family, which has maintained a long enduring system prior to this encounter, has the power to resist, absorb, or sabotage the process from the very beginning. Wynne is convinced that the family therapist must be comfortable with utilizing the aggressive, active, limit-setting aspects of this task from the outset.

Consistent with that conviction, the therapist provides a workable structure for the interview and delineates emphatically who is to take part in these sessions, when they are to be held, and what regulations are to be followed. Wynne sets up an inclusive membership of the nuclear family at first, and continues for some time with this larger group. During this period he remains alert to the "absent member phenomenon," a subtle form of resistance by one member or another. Under such circumstances, he is wont to cancel the interview unless everyone shows up.

Wynne utilizes a number of treatment standards in his family psychotherapy. He finds it essential to tailor his approach to the family's specific problems. It will not do to use only one approach in therapy for all kinds of families, even though such a measure has the appearance of consistency. With his comprehensive grasp of the work, he has the ability to revise and adjust his technique to the needs of the family and alter methods according to his research data.

He spends little time in discussion of the family's past history. Unless considerable work has been done in noticing and understanding current experience and interaction within the sessions, working over the past could become a mere intellectual exercise.

The Limits of Insight and Interpretation

Despite his original psychodynamic orientation, Wynne has limited regard for the value of insight in treatment. He believes the grasping of immediate subjective experience is a more critical issue than the attainment of insight. Insight has too many divergent meanings to make psychological probing for it profitable; in any case, it is chiefly useful to the therapist, rarely to the family. "Insight has lost its reputation as the primary agency of therapeutic change even in classical analysis; I suggest that this dead concept be left in peace," he writes.[2]

He has long advocated avoidance of premature interpretation or clarification by the family therapist. Although observable dynamic material may be impressive to the therapist, the family could become confused or defensive if he outdistances them in what they are ready to admit into their own awareness. A therapist may need to use every bit of empathy available to understand the ways in which family members are experiencing the interview, lest he leap too far ahead of them.

This active therapist sees his role as steering a family toward new values, ways of communication, and relationships that can survive when the therapist is not with them. When they are together, however, therapist and family comprise a "therapeutic culture" in which it is safe to express their opinions and feelings with candor. The therapist's task is to step back from and comment upon the interactive process of this culture, in what Wynne calls focused observation. As an example, he cites a certain family in treatment:

> Every time the parents began to quarrel, or later, to express positive feelings, they turned away from each other to the elder son. Reciprocally he actively interceded with pithy attacks on one or the other until their quarrel or incipient love-making was temporarily disrupted. Despite the regularity with which this interaction pattern was manifest, none of the family members had been aware of it.[3]

Focused observation can apply to nonverbal exchanges, as well. Wynne cites the example of a mother who became increasingly disorganized whenever her husband and daughter would signal solicitous glances toward each other. It is precisely then that a therapist could add a new factor to the transaction by stepping back from and commenting upon this interactional pattern.

But the intent of exploratory family therapy is to set up conditions for interaction to take place as freely as possible. This method looks for the immediate impact of observable interaction, a phenomenon familiar to all those who practice interpersonal psychiatry. In this setting, the therapist can (if desirable) quietly draw attention to a transaction that has passed unnoticed by the family. At other times, however, the therapist may decline to comment upon what is unnoticed but inferable.

Resistance and the Family

Long inured to the phenomenon of resistance, Wynne characteristically teaches that grumbling during a treatment session could belie a really deep involvement on the part of the grumbler, even an indication of the unspoken feelings of others in the family. One way for a therapist to explore such behavior is to wonder aloud if that person is voicing the wishes of the others as well as his own.

> In effect, the therapist raises the question whether the grumbling, compliance, silence, or whatever, serves a purpose or function for the family as a whole. For example, it may represent a style of warding off or of encompassing the "outsider" therapist. This inquiry may lead into consideration of feelings and difficulties family members have about making relationships which go across family psychological boundaries. Then, too, the therapist may observe that the interaction between himself and a family member is also manifest between family members, as an aspect of intrafamilial relationship difficulties.[4]

Dr. Wynne admits it is inevitable that a therapist will become involved in a family's confusion and distress, but even this can be turned to therapeutic account. The therapist, in fact, can demand that the family help clarify the situation and aid him in overcoming the confusion. This places responsibility on the entire system, and does not leave the therapist in lonely exposure.

Less doctrinaire than many theorists in this field, Lyman
Wynne advocates a judicious mixing of individual and family
therapy where such an admixture is indicated. This therapist believes that family diagnosis and accompanying conjoint interviews can serve as adjuncts to individual therapy. For him, it is
reasonable to engage in the treatment of an individual, either before or after family therapy. As he sees it, family therapists frequently err in not giving sufficient attention to the individual,
while certain other therapists err when they treat only individuals
to the exclusion of relationships within the family system. He
plainly sees that conjoint family therapy is usually the treatment
of choice. This conviction, now widely accepted among family
therapists who view their work systemically, displaces the individual as an isolated patient.

Lyman Wynne as Theorist

It just may be the fate of Lyman Wynne to be remembered
more for his colorful terms than for some of his foundational research. There are at least three terms he originated that are in
wide parlance today because they are so expressive of common
conditions.

• *The rubber fence*, an apparently yielding but often tricky
boundary that families set for their relationships, manages to keep
their members uncertain and their place unclear. In that confusion, the rubber fence serves a useful, if nefarious, purpose.
Wynne sees it as the psychological boundary that is maintained
partly through shifting the fence's location without opening up
any genuine transactions. The family rubber fence can be
stretched to include or exclude others, but it is known in the long
run more for its impermeability than for its openness. It serves to
prevent the recognition that the family has any conflicts that
could threaten its mask of mutuality.

• *Pseudomutuality* is that common experience that preserves a
mythical appearance of open, friendly relationships where such is
hardly the case. So great is the perceived need to fit together into

their expected roles that persons will feign an understanding relationship, even at the risk of losing their individual identities. Thus some families maintain an unspoken rule to return to the grandparents' home for Sunday dinner with a cheerful countenance and superficial zest, no matter how much they may sometimes dread it. Pseudomutuality is but one of a trilogy of terms including *mutuality* (the open and reciprocal understanding in interpersonal relations that we find in the fulfilled marriage) and *nonmutuality* (an official or formal complementary concept that expresses the equally open and reciprocal matter-of-fact minor relationship that might exist between a customer and a salesperson).

• *Pseudohostility* is to be found at quite the opposite end of experience. This is the expression for a superficial split between persons, a split that appears deeper than it is. As Wynne describes it, it is a shared defense against recognizing or experiencing potential tenderness, affection, or sexual attraction. For those who fear intimacy, it operates as a collusive defense against the anxiety of achieving real relationship. Pseudohostility has an unreal quality about it, but it remains an effective arrangement to keep others from getting too close.

Utilizing his Parsonian sociological theory, Wynne early noticed the individual's dilemma in the context of family therapy: the tightrope walk between affirming autonomy and encouraging relationship. In a dysfunctional family, these two goals seem to always be in conflict. The therapist's objective is to aid persons to realize themselves, while at the same time improving their ability to be cooperative and understanding with others. When the therapist has led the family to achieve some balance in this issue between identity and interpersonal competence, therapy can move toward termination; the work is about done.

Wynne has not been drawn into the trap of championing the underdog in family relations, befriending the scapegoat or identifying with the Identified Patient. In his writing he has been clear that the Identified Patient (perhaps schizophrenic) is not simply the victim of parents or others in the family, but is caught up with each of them in reciprocal victimizing. It is for this reason, though not this alone, that he has consistently contended the family in therapy must be approached from a standpoint of strategic-systemic theory. He sees his function as one of normalizing such individuals and their family systems. For him the family system, rather than an individual, is the unit of intervention or engagement.

The dilemma points up the continuously conflicting needs of the individual to develop a healthy "can do" in identity and relate significantly to others. The dysfunctional family confuses these, just as they also mistake their interpersonal boundaries, making them too rigid or altogether ambiguous. Wynne, again reflecting Parsonian theory, views the family as a social subsystem. Seen systemically, the family has everlasting problems of role structure, and that structure needs restructuring at times. The roles require change with new occasions and duties. Reciprocal relations necessitate understanding and flexibility.

It is often the therapist's task to teach just such role performance. For that task, the therapist needs considerable energy and sustained interest in the treatment, because families can be marvelously resistant; they have a staggering capacity to remain the same. This remaining in the same position is what the family therapist (borrowing a term from biology) calls homeostasis.

Indications and Contraindications for Family Therapy

Family therapy is indubitably indicated as the treatment of choice when a family's reciprocal patterns of interaction involve one another. Wynne has discovered it is unnecessary for all members of a family to acknowledge their part in the system in order to gain from family therapy. They might stoutly deny that the Identified Patient's presenting problem (say, alcoholism or anorexia) has anything to do with them, and still realize some value from the collective experience of therapy. Experienced therapist that he is, Wynne is willing to go along with this charade as a way of reaching an entire family.

Of the special problems for which family therapy is indicated, Wynne designates these in particular:

• *Problems of adolescent separation,* such as identity crises, rebelliousness, continuing dependency, and acting-out delinquency.

• *The trading of dissociations,* where each person sees himself or herself as having a specific, limited difficulty that is attributed to another family member and can be alleviated only by action of that other person. "It's all your fault!"

• *Cognitive chaos and erratic distancing,* where the family's transactional sequence may be bizarre, disjointed, and fragmented, and where fractured communication requires repair work and coaching by a therapist.

• *Fixed distancing* with eruptive threats and episodes: a condition of emotional cutoff in families who share a sense of being unable to reach one another on a level of human feeling.

• *Amorphous communication:* the vaguely defined expectation that drifts off with unclarity of expression, messages of pointlessness, and words that fail to inform.

For all these conditions, and others as well, family therapy, with its emphasis on relationship, reconciliation, and communication theory, is clearly indicated as a way toward improvements.

In certain other types of intrapersonal and interpersonal problems, it may not be indicated. Wynne specifically questions whether family therapy can be useful for depressed persons, for masochistic individuals, or for acute schizophrenics. It was with such patients that he and his colleagues gained so much of their early expertise and conducted considerable research. It is to be questioned whether the clergy have any justification for doing family work with these categories, or even with some of those for whom Wynne believes family therapy is more clearly indicated.

A Pastoral Perspective on Exploratory Family Therapy

Once more we are confronted by the theoretical concepts and therapeutic example of an experienced psychiatrist and realize that clergy are less equipped to take on the same work in the same way. We are constrained to inquire what elements clergy can derive from the patterns and practices of the psychiatrist. Still, because of his own contacts with the clergy and his appreciation for our point of view, Wynne's therapeutic theory and practice can offer several hints for the minister, even though they may not have been designed for that purpose. Certainly a number of insights from his experience are adaptable and do have relevance for us.

For example, we can agree with the wisdom that family therapy is but one therapeutic approach among a group of several available for treatment and referral purposes. That very realization will aid us in recognizing indications and contraindications for its use. With Wynne, we can turn to individual counseling when that is the treatment of choice, and to family therapy when that is clearly indicated.

Second, Wynne's influence has led others toward the systemic view, to see how the family system works and what to do in therapy. This could perhaps be the single most important lesson for pastors, prone as we are to regard problems in a personal or even moralistic fashion, instead of an interpersonal, contextual fashion.

Third, we can keep ourselves aware of role relations, to better understand what goes on among the persons in a family when their interpersonal transactions are repeatedly conflictual. The objective observer can often note specific features of these transactions that the family has not noticed. They might, for instance, have entirely missed the repetitive pattern of a daughter who takes to her sickbed with nauseous headache the day after her parents have had a harsh quarrel, and how her headache impels the husband and wife into another truce.

Fourth, we can use Wynne's reminder that a particularly difficult stumbling block of countertransference arises in family work when we find ourselves in competition with any member of the family. The clergyman may be tempted to take over some of the decision making and leadership generally reserved to the *pater familias.* If he succeeds in being warmly regarded by the family, this may defeat his work as a therapist when the father drops out or leads his entire family away from the interviews. Needless to say, the exact same condition obtains between the clergywoman and the mother of the family.

Fifth, and like unto it, we need to make sure that any problems we have with our own authority figures do not intrude into our counseling relations. Although we must remain empathic, we dare not exclude from attention those who resemble someone out of our past and therefore threaten us. We must deal with our own relationships, if we are to be of aid to the relational problems of parishioners.

Sixth, an overidentification with any member of the family, or the ignoring of one of them, may also create difficulties. Partiality toward the Identified Patient, the young, or the abused in the family could not only stop any progress in the case but also blind the pastoral counselor to reciprocal activity within the family constellation.

Seventh, we must not allow an already confused family to take charge of the sessions. Clergy have practiced a nondirectional form of counseling for so long that this idea looms as a revolutionary idea for some, but it is one compatible with family therapy.

Lyman Wynne leaves us with a word of encouragement:

> Many of the difficulties can be reduced to a manageable level by quite workable means, such as establishing as definitely as possible the conditions for treatment of each family, clarifying the therapist's expectations about such matters as who is expected to lead the sessions, and maintaining an orientation to those problems which are shared concerns of the *entire* family. . . . Finally I would like to state that it appears easy to exaggerate the possible hazards in family therapy. The likelihood of bringing about drastic or precipitous changes unintentionally is actually extremely low.[5]

17

Charles Kramer's
Integrated Family Therapy

Therapy is an induced crisis. The therapist's intervention in the crisis the family brings to therapy creates a new crisis with the possibility of a corrective experience.

Charles H. Kramer

Charles Kramer, M.D., has to be numbered among that early group of medical psychiatrists who turned from psychoanalytic practice to marital and family therapy. Since the mid-1950s, he has treated families in groups, supervised other family therapists, and taught the subject of family therapy to mental-health professionals, including the clergy. Founder of the Center for Family Studies at Northwestern University Medical School, he not only teaches medical personnel but also conducts growth workshops with his wife and cotherapist, Jeanette Kramer. He is a founding board member of the American Family Therapy Association. But perhaps he is now best known for training those in the helping services to develop a therapeutic style and understand themselves in relation to families in distress.

Family Therapy in the Kramer Style

With his characteristic candor, Kramer denies there is any personal charisma that makes a family therapist successful, Virginia

Satir and Nathan Ackerman notwithstanding. Instead, he asserts plainly that successful family therapy is composed of a number of interrelated ingredients that are essential, teachable, and largely independent of the therapist's personality.

Physician that he is, Dr. Kramer conducts a preliminary diagnosis of the family's problems. In this he is careful not to reinforce the family's mistakes by repeating their attempted solutions that have already failed. In sequential order, he: 1. Outlines the family system and how it works. 2. Redefines their presenting problem, to show its interplay with what else goes on in their family life. 3. Affirms the family for their strengths, even while acknowledging some weaknesses. 4. Reviews their therapeutic experience of the interview.

This opener enables families to reduce anxiety, learn some new communication skills, begin to hope that solutions are possible, and gain a sense of safety within this process with the therapist in charge. As the inevitable model for his patients, Kramer listens to everyone in the family, observes both himself and the others, communicates clearly without taking sides, respects each person, protects tham all from attack, demonstrates humor as well as solemnity, and explains frankly what his role is in the therapy.

From the very first contact with the family, Kramer believes, any therapist must keep in mind the system with which he or she is dealing. Even if talking with only one person, it is essential to view that individual within context. It is equally essential to establish rapport at the outset with the most powerful figure in the family, if interviews are to continue beyond that first session. He goes to great pains, however, to maintain equal contact with each person in the family, speaking as often to one spouse as to the other, explaining his techniques to them both, glancing at one as frequently as at the other. By the end of the first interview, he arranges with the couple or family a mutual commitment to the process of assessment and treatment. This contract includes such items as who will come and in what combinations, how many meetings will be held and where, and general agreement on their goals.

In this phase he subscribes to Carl Whitaker's expectation that there is a "battle for structure" (*see* chapt. 2) because the therapist is outnumbered the moment two or more people walk in the door. He will press the issue of authority to the limit, if necessary, saying something like, "I have tried it the way you are suggesting, and I have tried it my way, and I have come to the conclusion over many years that the way I am proposing works better. I guess you will just have to trust me enough to go along with me on this. If you can't trust me that much, then perhaps you should see another therapist whom you can trust."[1]

Convinced that a powerful empathy develops in this process, he says, "the rising pitch of a violin shatters a goblet when the frequency of the sound vibrations exactly match the corresponding latent resonance of the glass. Families struggle with so many different conflicts that sooner or later their 'vibrations' will evoke sympathetic vibrations in the therapist."[2]

Becoming a Family Therapist

Following years of work as a trainer of evolving family therapists, Kramer has assembled a number of aphorisms from his experience. In his book, *Becoming a Family Therapist,* he delineates these:

• There is no way of learning a new technique without changing yourself. In adopting the family perspective, one simply must change one's view of self and one's place in the world.

• It is necessary to learn how to admit it, more or less gracefully, when you are wrong. Therapists too often tend to be perfectionists who have difficulty acknowledging or even recognizing their errors.

• You can get yourself out of your family; but you cannot get your family out of you. Unless you have worked on your own family relationship and understand it, you will be handicapped in this work.

• Get help for yourself. It is no disgrace; indeed it could turn out to be the best thing that ever happened to you to enter treatment for yourself and your family. By this you will also learn a great deal about how it feels to be on the other side of therapy.

• Every action can be expected to elicit an equal and opposite reaction. Beware of resistance, for it is a subtle and powerful maintainer of the status quo, yet the binding element in a structure that is erected against chaos.

• Never underestimate the power of helplessness. The newborn baby, the helpless invalid, the manipulating dependent person: All these have the potential to influence others. Yet sometimes the best way for us to help is to decline help in the way that a family demands, standing by while the family learns to help themselves.

• All behavior is understandable—which is not the same as saying that it is permissible. The mental-health professions have contributed to the perpetuation of problems by confusing acceptance of a person with approval of the person's actions.

• No matter how loudly the family members protest to the contrary, any pair that stays together deserves each other. Seen both negatively and positively, this means that both spouses in a conflict gain some gratification from their destructive quarrels, the caretaking parents may need the sickness of a child as he needs them, the victim requires a victimizer.

• Reassurance is not reassuring. Even though it is well-meaning, it will solve no family problems. Speak the truth openly if you know it and the family is readied to hear it. Meanwhile it is useful to be benignly evil-minded; suspect the worst and be empathic when you find it!

• Family therapy is designed to deal with relationships, and not especially with content. Families struggle for hours over money, in-law relations, child discipline, and religion before they learn that there is a repetitious pattern of pathology running through all their complaints. The key is in that pattern of their relations with one another, rather than in the substance of these issues. If the therapist is drawn aside to deal with the substance of each complaint, little will change.

• Hidden conflicts are more harmful than open conflicts. Besides that, they are more likely to trigger symptoms. If a family feels safe with the therapist, they can tolerate the probing for their unmentioned tensions and bring them out for examination and possible alteration.

• Do not overlook medical matters. Family problems can have physical as well as psychological etiology. Obesity, alcohol abuse, and sexual dysfunctions may be at the cause—or in the effect—of family problems.

• None of us is all-giving or all-understanding. The price to be paid for that super responsibility that got you where you are might be exacted from your own family relations. Know your limits and be good to yourself, lest burnout leave you and your relationships in tatters.

• The goal of the family therapist is to put oneself out of business. The therapist serves as a temporary, perhaps necessary, aid to the family, who must learn to stand on their own feet. It is our task to aid people to take command of themselves.

• When you begin to feel that you are becoming a pretty good therapist, remember that family therapy accomplishes precious little. This is meant both ways: It doesn't change much, but what it accomplishes is very precious.

Kramer as Theoretician

Kramer has a thesis, and it is blunt and clear: The family is a more important and influential unit of mental health and mental illness than the individual. In the total psychoeconomic balance of the family, the marital and family relationship processes play the major role in the genesis and maintenance of a child's psychopathology. The family is the basic unit of treatment, and therefore seeing families together in therapy has a special therapeutic advantage. He has gathered these convictions from the experience of his emmigration from orthodox psychoanalysis as a child psychiatrist into systems theory and family therapy. Kramer's writings now reveal such a family-therapy approach based upon psychoanalytical principles.

His family paradigm is this: It is predictable that any intervention that produces changes in the relationship network of an intimate human system such as a family will lead to changes in members of that system, and vice versa. Grasping this system's point of view has enabled him to look at behavior in a new light. In this light, previously isolated and seemingly unrelated psychological phenomena have become more understandable. Kramer holds that meeting with the total family is the treatment of choice when there are difficulties of relationship among family members, regardless of whether individuals therein have a diagnosis such as manic-depressive illness. It is likewise the treatment of choice whenever work with their relationships is necessary to produce change or to maintain change, regardless of the presenting problem.

Advantages of Family Therapy

Kramer holds that the methods of family therapy are superior to those of individual treatment in a variety of ways. For one, they allow for the development of technical and conceptual skills for producing predictable system changes that could not be predicted in individual treatment. For another, a family therapist can facilitate improvement in someone thought unreachable by working with the more cooperative members of the family. "The first time this happens it boggles the mind: major symptoms and personality change take place in someone who seldom, if ever, came for appointments. . . . Often symptom reduction has occurred faster than would be expected if the patient were actively involved in the interviews."[3] This ripple effect is part of the feedback loop in the family system. It illustrates that the promotion of change in one person will likely change others in the same household. Surprisingly, efforts that are directed to asymptomatic members of the family can also produce lasting changes in the symptomatic ones. The therapist who learns to produce change in the more remote parts of a system has learned a valuable clinical skill.

Having lived through a variety of treatment techniques and

having tried them, too, Kramer is firmly opinionated. He holds that treatment of the family within their system is significant and crucially different from other forms of psychotherapy, such as individual and group therapy.

Kramer, a true believer, amasses an array of evidence to indicate the advantage that family therapy can claim over the psychoanalysis he once practiced. Based on studies published by Gurman and Kniskern,[4] he notes the efficiency of this method in five separate aspects:

• Therapy for couples produces positive change about sixty-six percent of the time; that for individuals less than half (forty-eight percent).
• Some two-thirds of the studies that compare family therapy with other therapies show it to be superior; another one-third find no differences. No study, however, has showed individual therapy to be more effective than family therapy.
• Short-term, time-limited, goal-oriented, problem-centered therapies appear to be at least as effective as treatment of longer duration.
• Fathers, traditionally absent from child-oriented psychiatry, play a major useful role in family therapy.
• For clinical problems and goals such as treatment of childhood behavior and psychosomatic problems, anorexia nervosa, and sexual dysfunction, systems therapies are the treatment of choice.

In addition, Kramer theorizes that family-systems therapy is more efficient than other modalities. It has the advantage of revealing sabotage by family members far sooner than individual therapy, wherein the saboteur is often out of sight at home. Because it is of short-term duration, family therapy goes faster than individual psychotherapy. That, in turn, allows for a prompter termination of cases and readier resources for new families awaiting assistance.

In his *Becoming a Family Therapist*, he highlights still other advantages of the systemic approach:

- Dependency on the therapist is less than in individual therapy, and the patients begin to take charge of themselves
- Major and abiding changes often occur outside the sessions
- More technical options, such as family sculpting, are available when additional family members are in the room
- The behaviors between persons can be observed directly in therapy, rather than simply being described by one patient.

For his purposes, Kramer puts the whole matter straight by writing, "The thesis of family psychodynamics holds that by and large the family is a more important and influential unit of mental health and illness than is the individual. In the total psychoeconomic balance of the family, the marital and family relationship processes play *the major role* in the genesis and maintenance of a child's psychopathology."[5]

What Kramer Can Teach the Clergy

Charles Kramer has much to teach the clergy, and he has been doing just that for years. Note, for example, his conviction that all behavior may be understandable and yet not permissible. He could not countenance that occasional error of pastoral counselors who confuse acceptance of a person with approval of the person's actions.

Numerous rabbis, priests, and ministers have attended the workshops and university courses Kramer and his wife teach. In these as well as in his writing, he has recognized that the clergy in their normal pastoral work perform considerable preventive and remedial work with families. His theories include much that is immediately applicable to pastors everywhere. Of these, the following four are noteworthy.

Therapy for the Pastor

The advantage of beginning therapists contracting for therapy for themselves is frequently pressed in training programs. Occasionally the point is debated by those who, like Jay Haley, maintain that no research shows the practice makes trainees into better therapists. However, Charles Kramer maintains, and I tend to agree, that experience on the receiving end of therapy is useful for therapists in training.

Therapy assists in the development of cognitive empathy, for the trainees begin to understand the position and the feelings of the counselee. As they select how much they will share with the therapist, trainees begin to appreciate that their own counselees may also choose what to reveal and what to conceal, how to shade the truth, and when to withhold data until greater trust is established. They learn from such experience what resistance is! This is a powerful lesson in how their own counselees will take in the experience of counseling and feel the welling up of resistance in their being. Moreover, the trainee, through watching the therapist and taking in the effects of the work, will learn techniques to use and eliminate from his future practice. This turns out to be a lesson not only in what to do, but also in what not to do.

But seeking therapy as an experiment in field-based learning is not the entire reason for such a recommendation. If that were all, it would, of course, be a debatable plan, but the therapy in and of itself can be advantageous. All of us have inner conflicts to work out, secret concerns we need to evaluate, and alienated relationships that trouble us because we never seem able to settle them. A brief experience in therapy could go far in attacking such difficulties.

Pastoral Conflicts and Conflict Management

Kramer apparently knows our ecclesiastical pitfalls—obviously shared by a great many others—as is shown by his observation that hidden conflicts can be more harmful than openly admitted ones. Those ordained to be spiritual directors of the faithful frequently hope to quell disagreement by ignoring it. Or they may deny a conflict exists, in the hope that it will not break out and have to be faced publicly. In fear of controversy and in expectation that an ignored issue will go away (an expectation that is occasionally fulfilled, it must be admitted), many clergy avoid difficult issues.

In doing so, they risk a double loss. First, there is the odds-on chance that a congregation can learn and grow through an experience of resistance and change. In point of fact, many parishes have emerged from conflict as reconciled, stronger institutions. The second possibility is that an issue ignored and denied may break out in some unexpected and damaging way at another time or another place. A covert issue breaking through into the open can emerge in a new and different form. Thus a world-peace issue promulgated by the social-action committee might have been quickly settled by a split vote and a small majority; and the issue may appear to have been quelled. Yet it could be followed by a disappointing response to the annual financial campaign.

The clergy may carry a self-image of those who are peacemakers and meek. (Blessed are both those categories, according to the Gospel of St. Matthew.) Bearing this passive image in public, some clergy are known to brook no open disagreement within their own families and admit no contention with spouse or children. It hardly befits them to become pastoral therapists if they cannot honestly face up to their own conflicts. In fact, this may regrettably drive them into modeling and encouraging a similar head-in-the-sand bias on the part of counselees. Thus do we project our unfinished predilections onto others.

Interventions to Note

Interventions, meaning the direction or influence a therapist exerts on a counselee to make changes, begin the moment counselees enter the room. A pastoral counselor will intervene in some manner or other. The outstretched hand, a proffered chair, our very smiles: Any or all of these might encourage or block change.

Planned interventions include educational instructions, confrontation, assigned tasks, and much else. Kramer's example illustrates that this process starts at once with the family in therapy. It will be recalled that he begins with a preliminary survey of their presenting problem, reviews their attempts to meet it, connects their concerns to their family system and shows how these interact, then affirms them as a family for the assets they do have. This gambit generally has the effect of reducing anxiety, increasing hope, and building trust. Intervening has already begun through the influencing of altered attitudes.

Kramer makes a second point about interventions. He advises the therapist working with a family to measure interventions in short steps toward an explicit long-range goal. For instance, if the ultimate goal is to restore badly fractured relations between a father and his son, the answer is hardly to establish a reunion event in one large step, but rather to work out a series of more modest interventions. These might include such straight directives as to take a brief shopping trip together, a paradoxical suggestion or two expressing the doubt that they could ever readjust to an improvement in their compatibility, a larger assigned task (say, attending a ball game together), followed by other mounting assignments, until they can stand each other in a scheduled conversation about meaningful events and plans in their lives. The cautionary element here is that one great intervention does not make a happy family; it requires careful programming.

One other pointer, selected from among many in the Kramer stock, is of importance to pastors: Keep all interventions in balance, because people may discontinue cooperating when they expect to be hurt. This would seem to argue against confrontations, but Kramer could hardly mean that to be his goal, because he uses confrontational interventions himself. Instead, the message is to alternate confrontations with more welcome relationships of support, humor, and encouragement. That constitutes a balance; it makes the occasional necessary confrontation more acceptable.

The System as Context

Old-time parsons, intimately acquainted with the families of their people, needed no reminder about the contextual environment in which their congregants lived. Aware of extended family relations, and even of the previous generation's shadow over the current one, they were alive to the issues of context. Under contemporary pastoral conditions—our briefer pastorates, our more complex network of reconstituted families, congregant job changes and family moves—such an understanding of context is more difficult.

Yet context is so essential to understanding the vector of family therapy that it dare not be neglected. The extended family must be kept in mind, not only when engaging in counseling a whole family, but also when counseling an individual. The extended family's pervasive power over the individual means that a person can be understood only as part of the system from which she or he comes. Inquiry about that contextual factor, about family of origin, about relationships, will advance the therapy. None of us exists in splendid isolation, but always in nexus with others. Without reference to these links, no one can be understood or effectively helped.

The contextual model includes an important corollary in systemic therapy. Dubbed somewhat inelegantly the "ripple effect," it reaches well beyond the person in therapy, to effect a number of other persons and problems. A change in one person will ripple out to the other persons in the system, because it is impossible to change one part without affecting another, and yet another. Even a small alteration will reach well beyond the counselee, to persons who may recognize neither the new factor in their lives nor its origins.

The second manner in which the ripple effect casts influence is within the individual. One of the beautiful results of productive therapy, when it works well, is the rippling continuation of solving one problem after another. Stimulated by a new technique that helps solve the presenting problem, such a person can move on with renewed confidence and newfound competencies to utilize a problem-solving technique, or adapt it, in other similar situations. Thus the ripple effect has aspects that promise progress in therapy well outside and beyond whatever takes place during the interview. But it is in that outside area where most family psychotherapy takes hold, in any case—either there or hardly at all.

V

Behavioral
Family Therapists

18

B. F. Skinner's
Influence on
Behavioral Family Therapy

Our only hope lies not in making people feel emotional but in showing them what can be done and giving them reasons for doing it.

B. F. Skinner

B. F. Skinner has two outstanding distinctions: He is recognized both as the most prestigious and also as the most controversial of American psychologists today. Although he has been preceded by others influential in behavioral psychology, it is to him that current behavioral therapy owes its inspiration.

Born in 1904, this lawyer's son grew up in Susquehanna, Pennsylvania, where he received a solid education both in public schools and a Presbyterian Sunday school. He entered Hamilton College with intentions of becoming a writer, but soon concluded that he "had nothing important to say." Feeling his failure as a writer, he tried psychology in a graduate course at Harvard, and there found his real field. He was later to teach psychology at both the University of Minnesota and Indiana University, but returned to spend most of his career on the faculty of Harvard. There his teaching and experiments in behavioral psychology

have attracted wide interest and influenced an entire generation.

Like many celebrities, Skinner is sometimes better known for
his idiosyncrasies and his unusual experiments than for his solid
theory. When he designed an air crib, or glassed-in roomette, as a
controlled environment for his infant daughters, some critics
were outraged, dubbing it the "Skinner Box." Nonetheless, those
two babies, Julie and Deborah, grew healthily and normally and
did not, as persistent rumor has it, end up in mental institutions
or as suicides.

Skinner stands in the tradition of Ivan Pavlov, John B. Watson,
and E. L. Thorndike, all of them behaviorists. Unlike them, however, Skinner has been less interested in the sequential connection between stimulus and response than in how behavior can be
regulated by the use of rewards. In this theory, these rewards follow an action and are given the name of "operant conditioning."
A toddler, for example, learns to walk by receiving congratula-
tions for those first stumbling steps. It is rewards like these that
Skinner would use for behavior modification, a method he sees as
urgently needed, because the whole world is in crisis. There is
danger that our contemporary culture will not survive, he la-
ments, and we have learned we cannot count on Christian compassion as a restraint. Behavior modification is now required,
because the world is so confused that we spend hundreds of bil-
lions of dollars on armaments each year!

To the criticism that behavior modification can be abused,
Skinner's response is that the method is neutral; those who employ it have the choice of being autocratic or democratic. True,
totalitarian governments use behavioral modification, but so do
schoolteachers. Our central issue, he contends, is to adopt an approach of behavioral technology to solve the problems of society.
To do that, we must move beyond the customary concepts of
freedom or dignity, even if it means curtailing individual independence.

His novel, *Walden Two*, remains a vivid portrayal of how such
a Utopian society might operate. It has inspired more than one

group to imitate it by inaugurating a commune along its lines. In the novel, in accordance with Skinner's philosophy, the people develop environmental conditions that reduce disease, pollution, and social ills, while promoting socially beneficial goals. Utopian it surely is.

The critics converge on Skinner's philosophy with accusations of determinism, manipulation, exploitation, and opportunism. They aver that he is too simplistic in assembling data about experiments with rats and pigeons and then generalizing about humans. But he deftly defends his stance, noting that "a technology of behavior" is an attempt to attack the nearly hopeless problems of modern society by means of a scientific investigation of human conduct. In any case, Skinner keeps insisting, our only hope lies in showing people what can be done to avert catastrophe and motivating them to do it. To accomplish that, we may be compelled to sacrifice some freedoms and our vaunted dignity that we hold so precious.

Taking this debate into consideration, Professor James Woefel, of the University of Kansas, has noted: "Skinner's work is an invaluable, if clearly limited reminder to Christians of some of the radical implications of our earthly creatureliness and interdependence within the web of nature and society."[1]

Behavioral Therapy in the Service of Families

Behavioral therapists have more interest in how persons act than in how they communicate; more interest in what they learn than in what insight they gain; more interest in the outcome of their behavior than in their reaching understanding. This is the Skinner influence.

The behavioral therapist will seek to work through a series of therapeutic stages with a family under stress. Step-by-step progression of treatment in behavioral therapy includes:

• A preliminary stage of assessment and description, in which the undesired behavior is specified and defined.

• A second stage, in which the problems are observed, counted, and recorded.

• A third "on task" stage of collaboration, with family members choosing alternative behaviors that will appeal as more desirable to the family as well as to the Identified Patient.

• A fourth stage of intervention, in which the family is coached how to reinforce behavior through positive and negative means (through encouragement of the desired conduct and extinction of unwanted behavior).

• A final stage of coaching and practice in ways to consolidate the new behaviors and intrafamily relationships that have been learned.

It all began, in a manner of speaking, with Ivan Pavlov's (1849–1936) slobbering dogs. He had so conditioned the dogs in his laboratory, by ringing a bell each time he fed them meat, that they would salivate at the sound of a bell, whether the meat followed or not. This stimulus-response sequence convinced him and a generation of experimental psychologists that our human social learning is a similar product of conditioned response to the stimuli of our environment. It took B. F. Skinner to refine Pavlovian theory with the correction he calls "operant conditioning." In this version, no bells ring and no glands *anticipate*. Rather the learning *follows* the event, as when a child quickly withdraws a hand from a hot iron.

Utilizing not just one, but actually both of these compatible theories, the behavioral therapist modifies the behavior of persons and groups through a series of steps and a variety of techniques. This begins with a clear record.

The keeping of records is essential to the therapeutic plan. Unless records are maintained, progress cannot be measured. Record keeping is given over to the couple or family; theirs is the responsibility for knowing about changes that are or are not taking place. Theirs is also the responsibility for making those changes. A quantitative record of arguments, wet sheets, or pounds gained is a step toward a change in the frequency of these unwanted behaviors. For his or her part, the therapist helps counselees define and reach appropriate goals about their quarrels, enuresis, or weight problems. If such quantification appears too mechanical and simple, note this criticism voiced by Gerald Patterson:

> On the face of it, observing and counting just do not seem to be the kind of things you do when you wish to help someone. Behavior can of course, be changed without anyone carrying on these activities. However, strange as it may seem at first, you are more likely to be successful if you take the additional time and care involved to observe and to count.[2]

The goals of behavior therapy are notably specific. They customarily deal with habits that are to be extinguished (patterns of drinking that have led to marital discord, eating problems, sexual malfunctions, and so forth). By maintaining this count of unwanted behaviors, a family may be enabled to move on to collaboration in methods of reinforcement and change.

The behavioral therapist uses record keeping in other ways. Aware of Festinger's teachings about cognitive dissonance, the behavioral therapist also seeks to reduce conflicts within the counselee's thinking and acting. If there is dissonance between the couple's expectation of romance and their routines in marriage after eleven years, some consonance can be worked through self-investigation of their marriage and writing down a record of their thoughts to each other. This is similar to a practice that Marriage Encounter leaders prescribe for wives and husbands in training sessions.

Implosion, a technique common to behavioral therapy, sometimes offers a firm dose of anxiety as a step toward reducing anxiety. As used for phobias and other problems that involve maladaptive anxiety, it amounts to toxin-antitoxin. The therapist exposes the counselee to the feared object or situation in order to demonstrate that it is less harmful than feared ("You can get used to it"). Presented either in imagination or in real life, these stimuli are continued until they no longer trigger the old anxiety.

If, for example, the fear of flying impedes a woman from visiting her son's family, the behavioral therapist may ask her to imagine taking the very flight she dreads, picturing its specific details—from making the reservation to deplaning at the terminal where her son is to meet her. They would work on such an assignment until the prospect no longer holds the panic for her that once it did. Under some circumstances, the therapist might even introduce her *in vivo* to the flight itself and press her into an actual airplane trip to dispel the phobia. In this more stringent measure, the technique is sometimes known as "flooding." The expectation is that either the imagined experience or the actual experience of a routine flight will move the patient toward the solution of her flying phobia.

A similar technique common to behavioral therapy is *desensitization*. Desensitization begins from the other end. Anxiety-producing situations are ranked according to their severity for the subject, and the behavioral therapist begins by suggesting the weakest concerns first. This procedure, combined with relaxation exercises, then advances to progressively stronger anxieties, until such phobias no longer have the power to frighten. For example, the woman who is afraid of flying might begin imagining she is packing her suitcase for the trip, then proceed gradually to imagining she is on the way to the airport, thence to ticket purchase, to the boarding area, and at long last to the vision of entering the aircraft itself. This way, it is possible to increase therapy by increments, just as the allergist increases the rose content in desensitization injections until a patient with rose fever is able to smell a dozen roses and not sneeze. Knox explains it this way:

> The basic premise of desensitization is that anxiety and relaxation are incompatible. When relaxation is substituted for tension, positive behavior becomes a more feasible possibility. One of the most prevalent uses of desensitization is in the area of sexual behavior in which positive, appropriate sexual behavior tends to be inhibited by an undesirable increase in tension. In effect, desensitization assists the client in engaging in sexual behavior without anxiety.[3]

Extinction, a term in frequent use among behavioral therapists, refers to the elimination of some unwanted behavior—an older brother's teasing of a younger sister, for example. In order to extinguish this behavior, it is important to supply two reinforcements, one to lessen the teasing, another to displace it with a more constructive activity. The children's mother, who may not be aware of such traditional constructive procedures, is coached to ignore the teasing incidents (attention to them in the past has reinforced the little rascal's habit) and be prepared to supply an alternative activity of more positive quality, such as an attractive game (simple enough, but honored more in the breach than in the observance by scolding, spanking parents). Extinction thus cancels the negative reinforcement parents have so often used when they unthinkingly rewarded children for an undesirable behavior. Instead of merely shouting, "Don't do that!" they fill the new void with an alternative, constructive experience.

On task is the name given to complete attention toward an assigned intervention, that is, practicing a new habit. If a couple is to improve communication, a time will be set aside and a place determined where they can concentrate on being present to each other for the practice of their communication skills. The therapist is adapting from academic psychology the concept of an on task performance, in which each spouse gives undivided attention for a definite period to the assigned project.

Behavioral therapists also use the *Premack Principle* in their methods. This trade-off system is a tradition with many people who have never known or applied the term to a practice they've followed for years. It consists of contracting for some contingency, as when I tell myself that a high probability behavior (an evening with my woodworking hobby) is contingent upon a low probability behavior (completing an article one week before deadline, so ample revision time remains). In marital stress, the behavior may be contingent upon the spouse. A wife who resents her husband's business trips out of the city may save up certain enjoyable activities for herself (shopping, concerts, or telephoning her sister in Hawaii) for his absences and, through enjoyment of these, learn to displace some of her resentment about his absences. Any high-frequency behavior can be used to reinforce some low-frequency behavior: "Finish your peas, Junior, then you'll get your Twinkies for dessert." (You see, most parents already use some behavior modification.)

Exchange contracts in marital therapy have recently come into prominence. They represent a different kind of trade-off for the Premack Principle. Indicated for reasonable, realistic people who are capable of negotiation, such contracts provide the reinforcement of a *quid pro quo.* A husband agrees to reduce the number of nights he goes out with his cronies by a total of three each month if his wife, in turn, will agree to greater frequency of lovemaking and initiate intercourse a corresponding three times a month. Too calculating? It must be remembered that much of life's satisfactions come from reciprocal relations, even though such reciprocity may be far more covert than these open contracts. But any couple's contracts may grow more subtle as they move toward mutual satisfaction through implicit arrangements that need fewer explicit terms than these.

Modeling also plays a large part in behavioral therapy. Although hardly unique to behavioral therapy, it is important that modeling be consciously programmed by the therapist and others. The model of a positively regarded person demonstrating how he or she deals with conflict, anger, or pressure is a valuable learning asset. "The principles of imitative learning," behaviorist Robert Liberman writes, "have been exploited with clinical success by researchers working with autistic children, phobic youngsters, and mute, chronic psychotics."[4]

Modeling is enhanced through role playing, sculpting, and simple example. It is useful as observational learning for teaching social skills, control of one's conduct, and negotiation between persons of opposing views. Modeling is impressively effective in assertion training, where it enables persons to say no graciously. It will also help a child learn from an adult how to act when in difficult circumstances.

Basic Behavioral Concepts

Theoretically, couple and family situations offer a fertile area for behavioral modification because of the intimate, everyday relationships and encounters of the household, wherein persons constantly influence one another. Working with a therapist, families can lift their ways of dealing with one other into new patterns of reinforcement. Instead of rewarding maladaptive behavior with attention and concern, family members learn to give one another recognition and approval for desired behavior.

Family behavior, like most behavior, is learned in the daily education of the home environment. It is reinforced by an intricate but largely unnoticed system of encouragement and dissuasion over a period of years. By the time a family gets to the therapist for help, their patterns of interrelationships are so habitual that it requires a new learning process in order to shape fresh patterns in their daily communication and contact.

Both desirable and undesirable behavior are learned. It is a basic assumption of the behavioral therapist that deviant behavior is subject to the same principles that govern all human behavior. Therefore the procedures useful in changing any kind of behavior can be applied to deviance as well. Saints and sinners become what they are, this theory of social learning holds, through precisely the same method—education. The behavioral therapist, more than most, is an educator. Learning theory remains basic to the methods used in any behavioral modification. These therapists will seek to change those contingencies around and through which some misbehaving family member is receiving concern or attention from others.

This application of learning theory is neatly explained in a now famous essay by Gregory Bateson, Don D. Jackson, Jay Haley, and John Weakland:

> The simplest level of this phenomenon is exemplified by a situation in which a subject receives a message and acts appropriately on it: "I heard the clock strike and knew it was time for lunch. So I went to the table." In learning experiments the analogue of this sequence of events is observed by the experimenter and commonly treated as a single message of a higher type. When the dog salivates between buzzer and meat powder, this sequence is accepted by the experimenter as a message that "the dog has *learned* that buzzer means meat powder."

But this is not the end of the hierarchy of types involved. The experimental subject may become more skilled in learning. He may *learn* to *learn.*[5]

Such learning theory can be applied directly to family therapy. The assumption is that stimulus reinforcement operates to prompt undesirable behavior inside the family system. In this work, the therapist educates the family in the modification of pathological behaviors. Behavior modification is used for school phobia, quarreling, and overeating. "It is useful when the mono-symptomatic person is unwilling or unable to operate consciously with the therapist or family members: e.g., a young child, mentally retarded person, brain damaged elderly, or rebellious teenager."[6]

Behavioral modification, in its purer form, is positioned in contrast to the communications school of family therapists, in that the behavioral therapist will be more intent on how persons act than on how they communicate or relate to one another. In like manner, the behavioral therapist contrasts with the psychodynamic therapist in regard to the function of insight. For the behaviorist, insight is not vital to therapy. In this modality, as Robert Liberman notes, the counselees are not diagnosed as "sick," and the medical model of treatment hardly applies at all. The potential for blame is reduced, and there is no point in having family members acknowledge weaknesses or irrationality. In many instances, behavioral therapy has become a preferred alternative to psychodynamic treatment oriented in psychoanalysis. In common practice, however, therapists are seldom so exclusive in their treatment. They can and do combine such modalities as behavioral therapy and psychodynamic methods through an interactionist theory.

Reinforcement has consequences, namely the possibility that such behavior is going to be repeated. Behaviors are strengthened when they are reinforced. David Knox reminds us that the husband who voices appreciation for the peach pie his wife has baked is likely to discover peach pie again as a dessert. Selective reinforcement (gratitude, compliments, warmth, affection, even smiles) remains an important learning device, not only in behavioral psychology, but also life in general.

The irony, of course, is that many a family reinforces exactly the wrong sort of behavior, the type that is counterproductive for their very relationships. The youngster at the supermarket learns he can get away with a tantrum and even influence purchase by his wheedling. Rather than rewarding maladaptive behaviors with shock and reactions of concern, parents and other members of a family can learn to offer positive attention at times of more approvable behavior.

Although the maintenance of a behavioral problem in the midst of a family life is enervating and difficult, it can also be somehow satisfying to members of the family. It enables them to maintain homeostasis. They may feel, in a term familiar to the behavioral therapist, reinforced.

Contributions of Behavioral Therapy

It is typical of dysfunctioning families that little social interaction of a positive nature takes place. The disapproved person inevitably feels isolated. Such interaction as does occur all too often is on the level of irritation, nagging, and blame. The sad result is that even this type of negative attention is perversely sought by the deviant person; it acts as powerful reinforcement. Better to be condemned than to be ignored! With behavioral therapy, a deviant family member, such as an enuretic child, begins to appreciate attention with positive concern from relatives.

But behavioral therapy with families also has some noticeable limitations. The behavioral therapists must choose their cases with some care. Unless the symptom is quite specific, there can be some deterioration while therapy is going on. Complaints about this approach include: 1. Those of Identified Patients who feel they are manipulated. 2. Ethical issues about the values and rights of changing a person who is identified as the problem person in the family—often without an open agreement on the part of that person. 3. Mechanical application of quantitative techniques. Some believe this approach to be too mechanistic and simplistic for the immense complexities of contemporary family pathology. Such critics have dubbed behavioral modification as "a teaching machine approach."

Behavioral Therapy in Pastoral Focus

Nevertheless, from the sizable school of behavioral therapists, clergy can learn to keep aware of the effects of unconscious learning, a process that the educator calls "conditioning." In many homes, parents reinforce undesired behavior through their attention to it. It should be reemphasized, both in education and in counseling, that spouses elicit responses via the kind of "strokes" they give or withhold. Skinner is right: All of us utilize rewards in our relationships with others. Our positive and negative use of such reinforcement makes a difference in how others respond in our intimate relationships.

Knowing that behavior can be influenced by a variety of measures, and that these methods are of use in the pastorate, opens a way for clergy to apply some of the principles of behavior modification in their work. We, too, can ask our counselees to make a quantitative count of the problems about which they are concerned. Keeping a chart of the time and nature of each quarrel during an entire week can instruct a sparring couple on the patterns of their interaction. Applied internally, for any one of us to keep a count on the number of times we allow interruptions to terminate our study or the number of hours we spend in meetings, will reveal new understandings of our work habits. Applied to therapy, this method is an eye-opener to the frequency of a problem and the ways it might be solved.

From behavioral therapists we can also learn to keep our own careful records. A succinct summary of the interview, some brief notes on the telephone call that followed it, some reminders to get in touch with the guidance counselor: These make for more effective pastoral therapy, because less gets lost between sessions. Such records need not be long. They need not even reveal by name who the persons are in the case; a code can cover these identities, in the event that the case would somehow be read by another. The point is (and behavioral therapists are hardly alone in this practice) the conscientious practitioner is purposeful about records and scrupulous about confidentiality.

We can also learn something about making contracts for *quid pro quo* expectations from behavioral therapists. Their familiarity with establishing agreements has led them to develop this method into a high skill. It is difficult for some persons, especially when hurt, to compromise and move toward each other with altruism. Yet if they feel there is some reciprocal movement on the part of the other party, and if they can conceive of that movement as arithmetically just and equitable, they can begin to change their style of operating. Pastors sometimes find themselves in the position of negotiators in what amounts to conflict management between married couples. In such negotiation, they might also use a contract that starts a couple toward new movement when other methods do not appeal.

One other device of the behavioral therapist is handily transferable to the pastor: the assignment of a readily achieved goal. In this selective use of desensitization, the pastor can move persons toward a desired goal via tasks of gradually increasing difficulty. A couple long alienated from each other and cold in their relationship is advanced toward greater intimacy through a progression of assigned tasks. They may begin with the resumption of simple dates, such as eating out occasionally at a restaurant, and finally progress to a resumption of lovemaking.

Behavioral therapists, of course, are not alone in recognizing these modalities and using them. Today there is a wider sharing of techniques among the several schools of therapists. Indeed, there has grown up an "Interactionist" group, who combine behavior therapy and psychoanalytic psychology, two groups once considered to be mutually exclusive. Nevertheless, it is these Skinner-influenced behaviorists who remain best known for the consistent use of such behavioral techniques. Pastors would do well to adopt those that are workable in the parish.

19

Richard Stuart's Social Learning Theory and Therapy

I was taught that every client gains more from the process of forming a therapeutic relationship with a caring professional than from any specific activities of the professional. I have since learned a countertruth, that "Love is not enough." A benevolent caring therapist is needed to help each person learn to accept responsibility for change in the interaction, but his major shift in perspective will come about only when the therapist bets more heavily on the deployment of technical skills than on being an accepting friend.

Richard B. Stuart

With their marriage on a downhill slide, the couple had entered their first appointment with Dr. Richard Stuart, ready to cite their complaints and problems. He disappointed them, however, inquiring instead what was positive in their relationship. Then he directed them back into establishing "caring days," the ritual of one daily, modest pleasure that each partner would desire of the other. Abruptly they found themselves off to a new start, different in hope and in actual behaviors.

Behavioral modification came into its own as a respected modality in family therapy in the 1960s, in no small part due to Richard B. Stuart's theory and practice. Stuart is now known as the father of behavioral marital therapy. Carlfred Broderick, a leader in the field of family studies and professor at the University of Southern California, has written an appreciation of Stuart's contribution:

> He emerges as a committed behaviorist who is nevertheless in touch with the power of cognitive reframing, a theorist whose concepts are tempered by systematic research as well as by clinical experience, but most of all as a man rich in ideas.[1]

Dr. Stuart is professor of family and community medicine at the University of Utah. A widely traveled trainer of family therapists in workshops and a prolific author of more than one hundred learned articles, he has also written eight books in this field. He is a clinical member of the American Association for Marriage and Family Therapy and visiting lecturer in psychology at the University of British Columbia.

Stuart's Therapeutic Approach

Nothing if not candid, Stuart opens his important study of *Helping Couples Change: A Social Learning Approach to Marital Therapy* with a disclaimer of four clichés he had been taught and had once half-believed about the practice of family psychotherapy. First, he found it necessary to cast aside the psychodynamic assumption that gathering facts and taking history in the traditional way are essential to the task. He became convinced that fact gathering occupies too much of the therapist's time when the goal is to get on with efforts to change behavior.

In the second place, he soon came to doubt the veracity of a dictum he had once been taught: "Start where the client is." That method, he holds, simply allows a client to direct the flow of therapy and places responsibility for the restorative process in the hands of the sickest person in the room! Perhaps the client is an expert concerning the goals and content of personal relationships, but he can be a miserable failure at developing any technique for reaching those goals.

Third, Stuart soon came to doubt the assumption that clients gain more from the relationship with a caring, empathic professional than from any specific therapeutic skills or activities. It was his experience that couples enter into therapy not to effect any change in their marriage, but in search of a confederate who will help each to hold himself blameless, while fixing full culpability on the other partner. A therapist concentrating on positive regard instead of on behavioral change can simply compound that problem.

In the fourth place, Stuart had been taught that every individual is unique and that this uniqueness must be understood, if treatment is to succeed. As he sees it, this canard has led to devoting twice as much attention to the categorizing of client distress as to its relief. We are more alike than different, he maintains, so the process of treating marital distress is actually generic. Treatment can thus be offered as an action program that is not noticeably different from case to case, and significant change can be accomplished in the very first session.

Timing and Structuring

Given such iconoclasm, it is unsurprising that Stuart has a straightforward approach to his therapy. His, in common with others in this behavioral-oriented group, is geared to short-term treatment. A typical course of marital interviews will range from five to ten sessions. Time-limited treatment, he has discovered, offers greater benefits to marriages than does that of longer duration. Citing a number of research studies as evidence, Stuart cogently argues that short-term treatment has both a favorable benefit-cost ratio and a point of diminishing returns that indicate it should not be unduly extended. Long-term therapy, he is convinced, offers too much of a good thing. Forthrightly, he avers that therapists who hold to long-term treatment do so more as a factor of their own preferences than of their clients' distress or any support from research data. Setting short-term limits, on the other hand, can help crisis-prone persons mobilize their resources quickly and get on with the job of working with the therapist.

A couple is going to enter into therapy with a good deal more confidence if they can see some structure in what their therapist is doing. They have come into this experience because they are in a muddle and cannot solve their problems, so they need to gain some sense of organization in the contract they are making. Stuart believes a recognizable and usable interviewing structure is as important as a positive attitude on the part of the therapist or a good relationship between therapist and couple.

However, structure is not naturally or instinctively formulated. It requires four conditions to make headway in marital treatment. 1. It must be goal oriented, so both the couple and the therapist are agreed on the objectives of their work together and the appropriate means of reaching such objectives. 2. The therapist's role must be carefully described in a way consistent with these procedures, for the therapist's roles are multiple: mediator, reeducator, director, model, plus Gerald Zuk's categories of side-taker and celebrant. 3. The client's roles must also be explicit in short-term marital therapy. They are expected to keep appointments, follow directives, assist in their own evaluations, and complete written and active assignments. 4. The structure will necessitate a series of independent, interrelated stages that cumulatively increase the couple's skills.

Such a structure shows counselees that the therapist knows what she or he is doing, and also serves as a guide for what tasks to undertake, which ones to defer until later, and how to tackle them.

Making Treatment Programs Effective

Carefully organized as this social learning approach is, it is to be expected that Stuart has worked out procedures for effectiveness in couple therapy. He begins by making sure the very first session will be productive. This reduces the time involved and helps make short-term treatment feasible. At the outset, Stuart explains how he works and what the couple might expect from the treatment, instead of the contrary practice of expecting the couple to open the session with a description of their position as they see it. Next he requests each of them to cite some positive aspects of their marriage and of their partner. This leads to a brief abstract of the behavioral change goals they would have already noted on the application/information form he requires couples to complete. At the close of this first session, Stuart and the couple should have arrived at a concept of their roles, an agreement about the means of intervention in their problem, the instigation of an early behavioral change, plus a commitment to each other and to the possibility of prompt change. No small order, that.

He also establishes a treatment contract, either verbally or in writing, that specifies the privileges and responsibilities of the couple and the therapist. He has found that formal contracts signed or initialed by all parties facilitate the completion of assignments and behavioral innovations in the couple's relationships. They make for clarity of expectations and for confidence in the process.

Stuart is meticulous about making an audiotape of every session, to study progress and insure quality service. To this practice can be added two variations: the use of a videotape instead of an audiotape, and the presenting of the tape to the couple, to be taken home and reviewed prior to the next interview.

It is also important, Stuart teaches, to make certain that everything clients are asked to do is consistent with the general goals of treatment and that their compliance is consistently monitored. For this purpose he uses a treatment planning worksheet that checks on objectives, their fulfillment, and the timing involved in that process. In addition, he uses an evaluation instrument to check with the couple at the end of a therapeutic session.

He does one thing more, an unusual feature in marital therapy: He shares with the couple some of the reactions other (anonymous) couples have experienced in responding to their own therapeutic programs. It is of no small comfort to a couple to realize that others in this process have passed through a "beginning awareness stage," an "awkwardness stage," a "testing stage," and a "conscious-skillful stage."

In all this, the therapist plays an active executive function, directing, correcting, modeling behaviors. With consistency and firmness, he makes sure this is conjoint therapy and not simply individual work with the one partner who happens to be willing to participate. Marital therapy is designed for mutual change, not for one spouse "fixing" the other. If one member of a couple seeks personal aggrandizement at the expense of the other, an unjust situation results. Likewise, if only one partner is willing to work on the marriage in therapy, the prognosis is grim—that relationship is out of balance. Stuart uses persuasive measures to bring in the unwilling partner, more often than not, the husband. First he offers the rationale for conjoint therapy. If the man still refuses to come in, he suggests the wife invite her spouse for just one session, in order to help set goals and define the agenda. If the husband still holds out, Stuart (with the wife's consent) contacts the chap directly, again explains the rationale of treatment, summarizes the intervention program, and assures him that he need not return after the first session. Stuart contends that it is the rare husband who can resist this onslaught.

Caring Days

Stuart's most ingenious contribution in family therapy, and that for which he seems best known, is a technique called "caring days," designed for building commitment to faltering marriages. These days are integral to his assumption that despairing couples enter into therapy with expectations that the downhill slide of their marriage can hardly be arrested; their hope and their confidence are damaged. Such expectations must be shifted toward positive anticipation and success-oriented tasks. Caring days offer a way.

In his own words, "On caring days couples are asked to act 'as if' they cared for one another in an effort to elicit more frequent, small, specific, and positive investments by both spouses in the process of building a sense of commitment to their marriage."[2] The outstanding advantage of this plan is that it offers couples the unprecedented opportunity for some immediate alteration in their relating to each other. In fact, "the positive changes mediated by this approach provide the energy that fuels subsequent efforts to make more demanding changes."[3]

A key to the impact of caring days is the principle that positive actions are likely to induce positive reactions, just as openness invites openness, disclosure inspires disclosure, and so on. The technique is innovative. Each spouse is expected to answer the question, "What would you like your partner to do to show that he or she cares for you?" A written answer is called for, and it must be positive, specific, and modest enough to be accomplished once a day. It must not have been the subject of a recent sharp conflict. Stuart suggests that "Please ask me how I spent my day" is a positive request, far preferable to its negative form, "Do not ignore me so much."

In an explanation of why the technique works, Stuart reminds us that couples are asked to offer each other something inconsequential and modest in the way of caring behaviors. This is rather like the "foot-in-the-door" technique that begins small and builds from there. Gains from caring days advance through positive feelings toward new trust. The nonconflictual behaviors are (to use a behavioral term) reinforced, and commitment is strengthened.

> In summary, the caring days technique helps the couple to step aside from the weighty, negative interaction that occasioned their request for treatment. Without forced apologies for past wrongs done, without the assignment of blame, without the fruitless search for the first negative causes of chains of stressful events, caring days offer couples an opportunity for relatively risk-free change under the skillful guidance of a therapist whose perspective is valued. . . . The instigation of changes consistent with caring days techniques helps to move the couple from an aberrant course back into the mainstream of constructive and facilitative social experience.[4]

Basic Concepts Behind the Stuart Therapy

To begin with, Stuart's basic concepts are firmly seated in social learning therapy. This, he explains, uses a threeway analysis of human behavior: the person, the environment, and behaviors. These are viewed as reciprocally determined: The environment impinges upon the person, and the person communicates through behaviors. This dynamic interaction involves "a physical being with thoughts and feelings, a series of covert and overt behaviors, and a set of environment factors that set the stage and provide the consequences for these behaviors."[5] In this complex interaction, cognitive forces play a major role, but the behavioral change process is more important.

Therapists founded in social learning theory use two types of therapeutic skills to achieve change: 1. The skill of modifying thought and feeling patterns through relabeling experience and modification of expectations. 2. Skills of transmuting these attitudes into new and more acceptable behaviors.

The plan is to encourage clinicians to relabel experiences of counselees to help reduce emotional impact and to encourage clients to change their expectations to more realistic ones, which makes new behaviors possible. Stuart holds it is possible to utilize techniques to change the details of social interaction in a way that positively influences couples to handle larger issues in their marriages.

Relabeling, a technique shared by many family therapists from nearly all schools, enables us to treat some actions as if they were not problems. A two-year-old's misbehavior may be relabeled as appropriately aggressive. A critical mother can be said to be one who really cares. Stuart cites Watzlawick's (see chapt. 8) suggestion to a husband that his wife's withdrawal is not motivated by dislike of him, but by an effort to respect his privacy. This is then matched with a countersuggestion to the wife that her husband's doubts are the result of his genuine desire for closeness, not an attack upon her actions. Skillful relabeling of this kind has power to turn a case around.

The modification of expectations is another technique Stuart teaches for the behavior change process. All of us change in our expectations over the years of a marriage. It is important that some flexibility be developed, to adjust to this phenomenon. Expectations that are incongruent (she wants a career of her own; he wants her to remain a homemaker) or unrealistic (her yearning for her husband to become a millionaire) require adjustment that will reestablish marital harmony, if that union is to persist.

The Case of Bill and June

Mindful of the systemic aspect of family relationships, Stuart insists that contextual relevance be employed in the assessment of a case. To be useful for marital therapy, all assessment data must lead to an understanding of the role that each plays in the relationship. He presents a case example of a couple in an intense exchange the night before the husband's real estate agent's exam:

> June: Would you please help me get dinner on the table?
> Bill: Why don't you have some understanding once in a
>   while? Can't you see I'm up to my ears in landlord and
>   tenant rights?
> June: You've had six months to study for that exam. If you'd
>   watched ten fewer football games, you would have been
>   ready for it by now. I've worked all day and I need some
>   help from you now, exam or not.
> Bill: (Storms out of the kitchen, grabs his coat, and heads for
>   the door.) I've got to get out of here or I'll go batty.
> June: You can get out of here all right—and you can stay
>   out, too!

When Bill describes this interaction, he describes the way in which June's actions precede and follow his, a scene in which he is the helpless victim of her excesses. He might point out that (1) she blew up at him; (2) so he said he was going out for a while; and (3) she told him to stay out. June does the same. She might tell a friend that (1) he accused her of bothering him while he works, so (2) she did point out that he put off his studying until the last minute and now she needed a few minutes of his time and a little consideration; (3) to which he responded by just storming out of the house. It is only when Bill and June add one element to each of their stories that they begin to have the ring of truth. Bill should have added that he prompted June's blowup by accusing her of lacking understanding, while June could have completed her tale of woe by pointing out that she did ask for help at a time when he clearly was tense and busy. Therefore, the clients' descriptions of their experiences are useful to them only if the therapist helps each to render more of the complete story. Instead of three-element tales—other did, I did, other did—tales of four or more elements are needed. This is the only way in which clients can be helped to learn useful things about their roles in their own interactions, and . . . these data are available only when collected during the conjoint session.[6]

Communication Theory

Bill and June are having a frightful problem with communication. The case cites their verbal exchange. Stuart's theory holds that couples should be taught to use both nonverbal and verbal messages whenever they wish to express positive feelings, but to rely heavily on words when they wish to communicate negative feelings. He holds this procedure to be important because nonverbal messages permit one to avoid taking responsibility for messages, even if they may be the most accurate glimpse of true emotions.

If Bill comes home in the evening, opens a can of beer, and slumps into his chair to read the evening paper, he is clearly communicating to June that he would rather be left to himself for the time being. If she calls attention to what she is now experiencing as his indifference, he can self-righteously respond that he meant nothing of the kind, that he is merely tired from a hard day at the office and is, of course, interested in her.

> The sender of any nonverbal message always has this quick and ready escape from acceptance of the responsibility for the message sent, because it is always very easy to hide under the cloak of misunderstanding. Therefore, in the interest of fair play, any negative messages should always be put into words so that the message sender has proper responsibility for the message sent.[7]

Recognizing the importance of communication training for troubled couples, Stuart has designed a program that involves five communication-change steps: listening, measured self-expression, selective request making, provision for positive corrective feedback, and clarification of intended meanings. Underlying this program is a conviction that when any conflict exists between the nonverbal and verbal levels of a message, the former has greater impact than the latter. Along with that goes a second conviction that couples must develop the ability to express their offers and to hear and understand the mate's counterbids, if they are ever to bring their relationship under reasonable, negotiated control.

Stuart has been able to test his communication theory and his therapeutic methods through a variety of outcome studies. In one such survey, he reviewed the progress of four couples who were on the brink of filing for divorce. Through seven sessions of conjoint therapy, these couples were taught to initiate behavioral change, to request three positive, specific changes of each other, and to improve their communication skills. The outcomes were a self-reported increase in daily hours of conversation and frequency of sexual interaction, plus an improvement in marital satisfaction reported through a marital inventory administered by the therapist. A subsequent follow-up at twenty-four and forty-eight weeks later confirmed that the conversational and sexual improvements had been maintained and that changes in global rating of marital satisfaction had continued.

What the Clergy Might Learn From Richard Stuart

Clergy can be appreciative (and many are) for Richard Stuart's practical pointers for the conduct of family therapy. Of his wealth of suggestions in Helping Couples Change, five stand out as eminently useful in pastoral work.

• Stuart favors short-term treatment, which is to say a series of about five sessions. Such a duration suits a pastoral schedule for several understandable reasons. Priests, rabbis, and ministers keep a demanding schedule of multiple duties and cannot devote an elongated period to each family case, as can some family therapists who specialize in this one work. In addition, not being specialists in such psychotherapy, many clergy will run low on resources and methods after a time and will find it difficult to sustain a lengthy series of interviews. But their most realistic reason may arise outside themselves, in that the married couples and families who seek them out for help in distress are generally unwilling to continue in treatment for more than a few meetings. They are frankly looking for quick results. These reasons lead to a decision (indeed, a necessity) to adopt short-term counseling as the norm in church work.

• It may not fit our pastoral orientation as easily, however, to remember that Stuart advises the therapist to work out a structural plan. His belief is that counselees gain confidence in the process when they see a structure, especially when they feel their own affairs to be lapsing into a state of disarray. To some clergy this will be difficult. Accustomed to "going with the flow," they usually begin where the couple is. This approach has been formalized into a standard method and is taught in courses and workshops. The busy pastor finds such an idea appealing and thus enters counseling sessions with only an approximate idea of what will develop. Systemic theory and family therapy have done much to revise this notion, and many counselors who once were reactors to the lead of counselees have become initiators deliberately instigating the flow. Stuart's structure provides for a goal that both he and his counselees agree on, for a definition of his role and theirs, for an incremental series in skill learning that advances toward a goal, and for careful records in worksheets that track their progress. A similar pattern can be recommended for those clergy who wish to gain proficiency in their therapeutic ministry with families.

• In an example that commends itself to all counselors, clergy or lay, Stuart accentuates the positive. Although standard practice follows a propensity for getting all the complaints out on the table right away, in order to analyze what is wrong with the marriage or the family, Stuart turns that procedure on its head. He asks a husband and wife to tell him what is *right* with their marriage. He continues by asking them to cite positive aspects of their relationship. Led to rethink the better elements of their mutual experience, they can begin to believe it is possible to work on and expand these positive characteristics and rebuild their lives together. Whatever goal they choose for their counseling, this augurs well for its success, because they are already on the way.

• Perhaps the most suggestive of these measures is that Stuart innovation known as caring days, which represents behavioral therapy at its optimum. It involves a carefully selected specific request, a positive approach, and a reinforcement. Besides all that, caring days can lead from little to much, through gradually increasing expectations and satisfactions. Subsequently the couple may begin to care more deeply about each other, simply because on these days they have been acting as if they *do* care. This is B. F. Skinner's operant conditioning in process, a theory many have seen demonstrated in therapy. It is appropriate to the ministerial model of counseling.

• A telling example of professional therapist and mentor, Richard Stuart leaves us with memorable observations. For one, he artlessly questions the qualifications of any family therapists who have been unwilling to work on their own marital problems sufficiently to preserve their marriage—as they expect their counselees to do. This candid point constitutes a shock among some marriage and family therapists who are in their second or third marriages.

In another observation, Stuart's assertion that a therapist's love is not enough to help his counselees pulls us up short. At first it seems to be a harsh opinion, until we read it again and combine with it what we have learned about his careful attention to workmanlike methodology. Certainly it requires more than a benevolent personality to help people make changes in their ways of living. It takes prayer, planning, and practice. It will also likely involve some direct confrontation; even that can be good news, within this learning experience.

20

Helen Singer Kaplan and the New Sex Therapy

When sexual conflict is severe, all phases of sexual response may become impaired and the person becomes totally asexual. . . . To repair these various malfunctions efficiently one does not simply "kick the television set"; one intervenes at discrete points with specific therapeutic tools.

Helen Singer Kaplan

Dr. Helen Kaplan is not one to "kick the television set," nor the patient, either. Hers is a practice in sex therapy at once scientific and compassionate. Marriages troubled by sexual malfunctions can be miserable, as any pastor knows; the correction of these problems has long been elusive and difficult. A remarkable breakthrough occurred in the early 1960s, when William Masters and Virginia Johnson began to study human sexual response under the same kinds of laboratory standards customarily used for any physiological function.

Building on their research, Kaplan, who is one of the second-generation of sex therapists, has developed a treatment program that combines behavior modification, psychotherapy, and physiological methods in what is now known as the new sexual therapy.

As clinical professor of psychiatry and director of the Human Sexuality Program at New York Hospital–Cornell Medical Center, she has organized a team of therapists who treat those who are troubled by sexual problems and coach them in the now-accepted solutions to such problems. Whatever else it may be, this sex therapy is considered a form of family therapy.

Dr. Kaplan is a diplomate of the American Board of Psychiatry and Neurology, a fellow of the American Psychiatric Association, a member of the American Academy of Psychoanalysis, the author of scores of professional publications and several books, and the editor of *The Journal of Sex and Marital Therapy*. She is the mother of two sons and a daughter, and like others in this book, she conducts a private practice in psychoanalysis and sex therapy.

The New Sex Therapy

Within the context of marital conflict, there may often be found some sexual problem. The clergyperson who counsels with the couple is well advised to make discreet inquiry about that possibility. But whether to continue and discuss that sexual problem or to refer the couple to another therapist is a matter for decision to be based on personal experience, training, and ability. Only a minority of the clergy are equipped and willing to engage in sex therapy, although their number has been gradually increasing. Even if they refer couples from their pastoral practice to others for sex therapy, it is advantageous for them to know what it consists of and what these therapists do.

How the Sex Therapist Proceeds

A sex therapist like Helen Kaplan will proceed with treatment along the general lines of almost any family therapist, with assessment, history taking, and the establishment of goals. Those goals and the means of reaching them will loom more prominent here than in some types of therapy, because of the specific nature of sexual problems and the standard exercises for meeting them.

Assessment of sexual disorders will involve a careful inquiry into the nature of the couple's dissatisfaction and necessitates a deep sense of trust in the therapist. These are questions of intimacy, fraught with emotional content; counselees must be made comfortable with the process, if they are to be candid. Even in this era of explicit sexual content in print and films, and of considerable sexual experimentation, it can be expected that couples will still be selectively reticent and reluctant in some of their revelations. For this reason, though not for it alone, the choice of the sex therapist is of prime importance. This must be a person in whom the pastor has confidence and whose skills, sensitivity, and ethical stance are certified through personal acquaintance. In this therapy, certainly no less than in other types, the therapist himself or herself is a major component of the therapeutic experience.

The manner in which assessment is conducted is of no small importance. Empathic inquiry is by far the most frequent method, although a few sex therapists do study the couple's sexual interaction through videotape, live observation, or via surrogate partners. That some of these procedures are questionable, at the very least, can be appreciated by a moment's thought. Couples with sexual problems are less likely to enact them in typical fashion if they know they are to be closely observed or directed. To that least question the pastor would add concerns about ethics, sensitivity to feelings, and modesty.

History taking in sex therapy follows along the usual lines of family therapy. The therapist will inquire not only about the practices of the couple, but also about their background, their rearing, their relationships in family of origin, their health, intake of alcohol or drugs, their relationship with each other, and so on. Kaplan's *New Sex Therapy* offers a detailed guide to the search for historical antecedents to the problem. Ever since Alfred Kinsey's precedent-breaking sex research of the 1940s and 1950s, his inventory of questions has been widely adopted and adapted for this purpose. Many clergy have learned the gentle, matter-of-fact approach that such inquiry entails.

Goals in sex therapy invariably include the reduction of tension and anxiety, some new way to handle the presenting problem (say, disputes over the frequency of sexual intercourse), an improvement in the couple relationship, and a healthier experience in their sexuality. Much of sex therapy involves a cognitive-behavioral approach with couples. Its components will include points that are biological, psychological, attitudinal, behavioral, moral, religious, and relational. It makes for a complex form of family therapy.

Three Sexual Disorders Among Women

Of the most common sexual disorders, three occur in women, three in men. The success rate in correcting these disorders has improved in recent years, perhaps somewhat less for women than for men. Women with complaints of sexual dysfunction are likely to suffer from general sexual dysfunction (sometimes unfortunately and pejoratively dubbed *frigidity*), from orgastic dysfunction, or from vaginismus.

• *General sexual dysfunction*, often accompanied by a reluctance to enter into the sexual relationship at all, calls for a nondemand ambiance on the part of the couple. They will need to relax their high expectations and demands, in order to reduce the ineluctable frustrations this condition creates.

The exercise Kaplan prescribes begins with "sensate focus," a form of unclothed petting that temporarily precludes intercourse. It calls for a patient husband, willing to forego his desire for orgastic release, and an opportunity for the wife to take initiative with the confidence that she cannot be rejected by him for her assertiveness. They both are encouraged in this noncoital genital playing and body caressing, until they work into nondemand coitus. This means the woman is relieved from the pressure of producing a response but is simply able to lie back and enjoy. Her desires are to dictate the movements, the pace, the technique. In charge of coitus, and uncoerced by her own or her husband's expectations, she can begin to enjoy the experience. Her own needs and requests govern their sexual lovemaking, perhaps for the first time. In more than fifty percent of the cases treated, marked improvement is attained.

- *Orgastic dysfunction* is the plight of a considerable number of women who have not known orgasm in their own bodies, despite their deep desire. The Kaplan approach is to coach such a woman in self-stimulation with the use of a vibrator, until she is more aware of her own physical sensations and can bring herself to climax. Meanwhile the preorgastic woman (note that positive term in place of *nonorgasmic*) is assisted to resolve unconscious fears and to understand better the muscular factors in her own organs. Here the method is to distract the distractor by aiding the woman to eliminate negative thoughts and reduce worry about failure. (The inorgastic woman has something in common with the man who suffers erectile dysfunction. He also suffers from worry about failure.)

The final step in treatment is necessarily to transfer orgasm from self-stimulation to orgasm in coitus with her husband. Success is achieved with thirty-five to fifty percent of preorgastic women. The condition is now understood by Kaplan and her colleagues to be "a normal variant of female sexuality."

- *Vaginismus*, on the other hand, is a condition alleviated in more than ninety percent of the cases researched in sex therapy. This is a conditioned response associated with pain or fear connected with any vaginal penetration. Physical pain and psychological distress are therefore the invariable situations accompanying the disorder. The marital problem that results is the inability of the penis to enter the tightly constricted vagina. Sexual intercourse is impossible.

A modern and simple technique introduces catheters of graduated size into the vagina over a period of time, beginning with the smallest and proceeding to others of ever-larger diameter. Meanwhile the therapist works with the patient to reduce phobias, eliminate intrusive distractions of worry and pessimistic thoughts, and move toward feasible coitus. When at last the husband's penis is inserted into his wife's vagina, it is to be held there motionless for a period before the movement of intercourse. This belated penetration by the penis is therefore the introduction of a different catheter into a vagina already accustomed to round, firm shapes. Vaginismus is a fairly rare disorder, with relatively simple treatment and a high success rate in therapy.

Three Sexual Disorders of Men

The three common sexual disorders from which men suffer today are premature ejaculation, erectile dysfunction (known negatively as *impotence*), and retarded ejaculation.

• *Premature ejaculation,* the definition of which obviously relies somewhat upon the couple and their desires, is the tendency of the male to ejaculate his sperm before fulfillment has been experienced by wife and husband in intercourse. Frustrated by the brevity of the experience (and it must be remembered that in all of sexual desire, our hopes have been elevated in the past three decades), men have sought longer staying power and increased satisfaction for themselves and their wives.

The Kaplan approach to this problem is to use the Seman's start-stop technique (so named for J. H. Seman, an early sex researcher), which consists of the wife's stimulation of her husband's penis until he feels a premonitory orgastic sensation. At this time he signals her to cease the stimulation until his excitement has abated and his organ is again flaccid. Then she is to resume the stimulation while he concentrates on his sensation until the fourth time, before coming to orgasm. Following the repetition of this exercise, the couple is then encouraged to attempt coitus. At intervals of every two weeks, however, they are to repeat the start-stop exercise to maintain their gains. It is to be noted that the advice here is the very opposite of locker-room counseling, which says one should keep one's mind off the sensation by concentrating on the batting averages of baseball stars, or (in the case of clergymen) repeating to oneself the Greek alphabet. Instead, the strategem is to awaken consciousness about penile sensation, to learn at what point ejaculation is likely to occur. This leads to better control. The success rate claimed for this therapy is the highest for any of the therapies for sexual disorders, something above ninety percent.

• *Erectile dysfunction,* sometimes pejoratively and unhappily dubbed as *impotence,* is common to men of all ages, but found in greater frequency among those who are older. The inability of the penis to reach or to maintain engorgement results in failure to achieve intercourse, since a flaccid penis cannot be entered into the vagina. The treatment for this condition begins with nondemand pleasuring of the husband by the wife, a form of petting in which the goal is to fondle the penis into erection, desist until relaxed, and then resumed until it is again erect. The patient is monitored for any distracting worries about failure or concern about what is happening in his wife's attitude. This, as Kaplan says, "distracts the distractor" and facilitates concentration on the exercise. After repetition of this simple exercise and the resultant confidence that an erection can be gained, lost, and regained, the couple is encouraged on to coitus. A success rate of some sixty percent has been logged for the problem of the erectile dysfunction.

• *Retarded ejaculation* occurs in a man who is able to achieve erection, erotic feeling, and coital experience, but who cannot come to orgastic release and ejaculate. The therapist conducts a careful investigation phase as to cause and characteristics, offers information and detail about the orgastic reflex, and prescribes an exercise. The exercise consists of intense stimulation by the wife, sometimes using an electric vibrator and glove, in which the coital act itself is preceded and followed by a variety of excitation that brings ejaculation through one means or another—intravaginally or extravaginally. Meanwhile the therapist works on a systematic reduction of the phobia in the male, who may be plagued by self-doubt and low self-esteem. This combination of wifely encouragement and therapeutic assistance to reduce anxiety brings about success in more than fifty percent of the cases of retarded ejaculation.

Theoretical Assumptions in Sex Therapy

Descriptions of corrective treatment for sexual disorders have a way of appearing all too carnal and mechanistic. In point of fact, these tactile techniques are closely interwoven with emotional factors and interpersonal responses. Always present in a marital couple's sexual adjustment are issues of trust and commitment, of openness and intimacy, of erotic attraction and love. Beneath physical feelings of sexuality are concerns of responsibility, flexibility, and devotion. It is healthy to achieve sexual pleasure, to enjoy frequency and variety in the marital relationship, to reach orgasm, and to know the peace that envelops a love relationship that is sexually adjusted. Our sexual well-being is an important part of human experience, but it remains only one part.

Yet if the research of Kinsey, Masters and Johnson, and Kaplan means anything, it is that sex therapy can also be predominantly physical in emphasis. This research has corrected an assumption of yesteryear that any serious sexual pathology would require long-term psychoanalysis. Sexual dysfunction may indeed be linked to deep-seated emotional problems, but not necessarily so. Newer, brief forms of sex therapy are sometimes effective precisely because a straightforward behavioral approach can be used, without recourse to long-term personality counseling. Sex therapy has differed in this regard from other modalities; it can be limited to the sexual dysfunction itself, and primary therapeutic attention can be applied to the sexual complaint and its concomitant communication features.

Sexual response is largely contingent upon positive, loving feelings toward the partner. Although the male is capable of sexual arousal with less genuine relation to his partner than is the female, both sexes are dependent upon a positive interaction to stimulate sexual awakening. As Kaplan has explained it, any unconscious conflicts about sexuality, shame, guilt, and fear can be instrumental in the genesis of sexual dysfunction. So can a rivalrous and hostile marital relationship, concerns about rejection, a fear of losing control, or conflicts about aggression and passivity.

Clearly the war between the sexes contributes to a no-win outcome. The sexual phobias of male and female differ greatly. Women tend to dread rejection by their partners, men to worry about their performance ability. Such phobias and any conflict about them will affect the possibility of sexual arousal and increase anxiety. The result sometimes is the virtual destruction of sexual desire, a common problem with which psychiatrists have been working more and more in recent years.

There is no exaggeration in repeating the cliché that the most important sexual organ is the mind. It is in our desires, our imaginations, and our relationships that sexual behavior is rooted. The personal relationship between partners, their communication factors, their emotions: All these can loom larger than any physiological data. Take, for example, the communication problems of wives. Their physiological responses are more internal and cryptic than the male's. Women sometimes require a long time to learn how to communicate their sexual needs clearly and without hostility. Often, in ill-advised dissimulation, they may pretend satisfaction they do not feel or forfeit control of their sexual relationship out of fear of abandonment or rejection. Culturally conditioned to hold back from candor about their sexual preferences, they can grow to resent the very act of sexual intercourse. What they and their husbands both need to learn in sex therapy is how to communicate about sex without defensiveness, resentment, or guilt.

Therapists like Helen Kaplan have contributed materially to marital happiness with their research, treatment plans, and education. Her description of sexual response, for example, has allowed for an organization of education useful to therapists and couples alike. She describes a triphasic staging of desire, excitement, and orgasm as categories in which to understand both the problems and the treatment. These categories also aid us in bringing essential information into the counseling experience. A large part of sex therapy consists of education. It is astonishing how many otherwise sophisticated people still lack knowledge of the simple facts of sexuality and thus need elementary instruction.

Because sexual pleasure requires relaxation for erotic enjoyment, the intrusion of anger, resentment, or out-and-out quarreling has a psychosomatic effect in the sexual relationship. A host of interruptions can alter this fragile experience: fear of discovery by the children, worries about unwanted conception, moralistic concerns planted by parental or religious prohibitions, guilt over past sexual experiences, misconceptions and ignorance arising from poor information, lack of desire or of stimulation, medical problems (coronary, diabetic, or alcoholic diseases), fear of rejection, hostility, bad memories of previous encounters such as incest. All of the above harm the relationship and contribute to its failure.

In all therapy, success can be fraught with threat. In sex therapy, this is especially true. Can the fragile accord between these partners survive the therapy itself? Will possible cure bring on new crises in relationship? If people improve in sexual response, can spouses adjust without terror, or will they both be threatened by the very success they have sought? Many spouses have felt secure in their marriage simply because of the sexual problems of a partner. What if they begin to worry about the possibility of infidelity in a sexually cured husband or wife? These are some of the misgivings that attach to sex therapy, unless it is also accompanied by effective marital counseling that takes into consideration the whole relationship between wife and husband.

With such a complex relationship, it is little wonder that marital stability could be roughly shaken by even a minor sexual dysfunction. It is, however, of more than passing interest that some marriages can achieve a stable and happy level even in the face of poor sexual performance.

If sex therapy is to succeed, certain prerequisites must be met:
• Both partners must be in agreement that they wish to improve their sexual relationship.
• Each spouse must take responsibility for personal pleasure in orgasm, and for letting the partner know what is pleasing and displeasing about the experience.
• They must learn that sexual engagement is a loving activity *with* each other and cannot be as effective when they think of it as something they do *to* each other.
• They must work on communication skills, to convey clearly

to each other what they need in cooperation through sexual love. Mind reading, guessing, and sheer assumptions cannot avail.

Dr. Kaplan's research and teaching have materially advanced sex studies and treatment. Her integration of behavioral therapy with psychoanalytic practice and systemic counseling puts all the helping professions in her debt, not least, the clergy.

The Clergy and Sex Therapy

Can the clergy extend their pastoral counseling to work with sexual dysfunction? The question is irrelevant: They do it with frequency. Congregants expect clergy understanding and assistance with what Tolstoy called "the tragedy of the bedroom." This is because they associate their sexuality with the marriages the church has blessed and because they will respect pastoral guidance for a referral to specialized treatment. We must now discuss how these concepts of sexual performance, failure, and success apply to pastoral care; which ones we can use and how; and which ones we need to know about, in order to make effective referrals to specialists who treat sexual pathology.

Pastoral First Aid

Pastors themselves are a first recourse for aid to the sexually dysfunctional, for they are not without resources. By tradition, they tend to refer troubled parishioners to useful literature on such subjects, and this bibliotherapy is not without merit. Numerous useful books are published that deal with this theme. Helen Kaplan's own *Illustrated Manual of Sex Therapy* is an explicit yet tasteful example of the literature. The information in such a book could be what the parishioner needs.

From the clergyperson, though, the parishioner often needs something more than bibliotherapy. An exploration of the problem and some aid in its clarification, a measure of warmth and understanding, a bit of education, even a degree of permission to enjoy marital love: These are within our clerical province. When a troubled person inarticulately presents the sexual question, we can respond with patient probes. "Can you describe it more plainly?" "What has been the most difficult part of this situation for you?" "How is it different from previous experience?" As Kaplan notes, other techniques can be designed to assist persons. These include "expressions of warmth and understanding for the problems of both partners, openness regarding sexuality, and the dispelling of myths and misinformation regarding sexual behavior."[1]

Virginia Adams has described the Kaplan approach:

> The eclectic method begins at the surface and goes deeper only if necessary. If a sexual difficulty comes from a learning deficit, for instance, information and instruction may be all that are needed. If the trouble is minor anxiety of recent origin, a series of guided sexual tasks may be enough to desensitize patients. If it turns out that a couple's sexual problem comes from . . . power struggle . . . then marital therapy may be tried. In any case, the first approach is behavioral. "If emotional conflict surfaces," Kaplan says, "you may go to interpretation," giving the patient at least some insight into the deeper layers of his or her personality.[2]

In referring for such sex therapy, the pastor must be knowledgeable. It is essential to know something of the techniques and ethics of the sex therapist to whom referral is made. In this, as in other therapeutic areas, mountebanks and charlatans can be found. But more than knowledge of the therapist's qualifications is necessary. The limits of this (as well as any) therapy must be taken into consideration. Successful therapy can eventuate in new difficulties. It could alter relations in the marital dyad, creating new anxieties about the increased libido or ability of one's partner, bringing new expectations for performance, or opening recognition of underlying problems that had previously gone unnoticed when sex seemed to be the chief malady in the marriage. The pastor will want to work with the marital relationship while the sex therapist is working with the dysfunction. The pastor, in fact, will want to pay attention to the state of the marriage when the therapy is completed.

Solving sexual problems will not bring total happiness to a marriage; sex therapy does not create love. Such therapy works best when a husband and wife already love each other. This the sex therapist knows, and any pastor of even a year's experience will know it, too. Sexual experience, like any element in systemic theory, is but one integer in the total context of marriage.

The pastor, however, has arrows in the quiver that few therapists possess. His or her professional work is not, by any means, limited to counseling. Preaching and teaching are also open to the clergy, and they are of positive value in sexual matters. The pulpit itself remains a useful asset in sex education. Sermons can be utilized to communicate theological and pastoral elements of sexual values. Courses in the church school open the way for sex education of children and youth. Adult forums and Bible classes provide time and space for careful teaching about sexuality. Considerable sex therapy can be of this enrichment variety, which informs people about their sexuality and enables them to understand values about themselves as sexual beings. It can be hoped that such an educational program will head off the need for some later therapeutic work on problems.

In the ongoing work of ministry, the pastor can continue to aid the people's theological understanding of sexuality, for we recall from the order of creation that it was God the Creator who established us as sexual beings and then pronounced that result good.

21

James Alexander in Functional Family Therapy

Learning to become a family therapist is analogous to learning to drive a car. At first we jerkily attend to everything— often overcorrecting one process while ignoring another—with the result at best being an awkward movement in our intended direction. But after practice, we learn that many tasks become automatic and can be filtered out, allowing us to focus on other important matters.

James F. Alexander

Somewhere along the line in James Alexander's therapeutic practice, he became convinced that there is a vast distance between what counselees say they desire and what they really want. He noted repeatedly that they appeared to seek payoffs from their behavior, which he labeled "functional outcomes." It changed his whole approach.

Although he had begun his work, as so many others did, with a psychodynamic orientation, James F. Alexander then moved toward an emphasis on function and systems in family therapy. His work is an unusual, pragmatic integration of behavioral modification, communication theory, and systemic theory. The director of clinical training in the Department of Psychology at the University of Utah, Dr. Alexander not only teaches on that faculty but also conducts his own private practice in family therapy. He is the author of seminal articles in scholarly journals and of several books dealing with functional family therapy.

Functional Family Therapy

What distinguishes *functional* family therapy from other schools of therapy is its search for functional payoffs. The meaning of distress symptoms is interpreted in terms of the functional result they produce and the personal interactions they affect. The issue is put directly: What satisfaction does one gain from such behavior? Trained to consider all interpersonal functions as powerful, the functional family therapist does not expect such functions to be changed by external controls. Instead, the therapist must identify what ongoing processes or problem behaviors have led to the particular functions characteristic of family members, and then work to change them.

For example, it is not uncommon for a spouse to request more intimacy. The functional family therapist, however, assumes that if a wife actually wanted the functional outcome of closeness, she would have designed an interpersonal process to obtain it. The clinical problem is that people's requests for changes in the functions of family life are frequently inconsistent with their own behavior. Thus the woman who states that she wants intimacy may actually exhibit aloofness from the husband who attempts to offer it. Does she really desire distance? The objective is to learn what family members actually want, as opposed to what they *say* they want. The way to that objective is by evaluation of the functional outcomes (or payoffs) produced by their behaviors.

The functional family therapist assesses both the amount and kind of information revealed in the counselee's behavior. The method of assessment involves three elements: 1. An appraisal of the family's functioning, including its members' interdependent behavior patterns. 2. An evaluation of how family processes lead to relational functions for each member of the family. 3. The identification of what change (behavioral, cognitive, or emotional) will be necessary to bring about some solution to the family's problems.

It is up to this therapist to ask what functional payoffs are involved for each family member, or "where everyone is when the dust settles." Payoffs are variable. A mother may have her need for intimacy met through nurturing a fifteen-year-old son. She may need to be redirected toward filling these needs through relations with her husband. The husband may alter his behavior by accommodating her needs (and his own) by terminating an extramarital affair. The functional family therapist, Alexander notes, will assume that these interpersonal functions have been payoffs, and that any change in family behaviors will have to be consistent with the functions.

In this light, behavior-change technologies become a problem of "fitting." Rather than make the assumption that it is necessary to change people for optimal family functioning, the therapist assesses how symptoms are embedded within relationships as a vehicle to create interpersonal functions as payoffs.

> The functional family therapist should . . . attempt to psychologically place himself/herself in the role of a relational recipient of family members' behavior. The therapist can hopefully begin to evaluate what function (either distance or intimacy) is produced by engaging family members. The therapist might then appreciate firsthand the relational purposiveness created by relationships within the family.[1]

Trained to look for bits of information that reveal relational processes in family life, the functional family therapist must then identify how these processes lead to purposive functions. The constraints or aids that initiate family change must be identified simultaneously, if therapy is to proceed. Meanwhile, the therapist must assess the meaning of these behaviors and even monitor this assessment itself, lest mistaken suppositions take over. Such eval-

uation will alert a therapist to missing information and to a plan
for uncovering it.

Characteristics of the Functional Family Therapist

The quality of the relationship between the therapist and the
family is the best indicator of effectiveness in this form of therapy. Research by Alexander has ascertained that a family therapist's nonblaming demeanor will alleviate tension with humor,
and the use of self-disclosure with humor and warmth promotes
an optimal therapeutic relationship.

In addition, Alexander will integrate family behavior with its
effects, through complementary responses. Alexander illustrates
this with the Dad who complains, "My son's always goofing off,"
and the therapist who responds, "When he's goofing off, you feel
disappointed in him." The purpose of this is to sensitize family
members to particulars of family life they might prefer to ignore
and not communicate to one another. When parents explode
with an unspecific global accusation of "He's a rotten kid!"
Alexander will respond specifically: "You both feel frustrated
when he doesn't act in ways you'd like him to, such as going to
school."

Alexander's use of warmth and humor serves to defuse anxiety-
ridden and hostile reactions of families under stress. A counselee's challenging, "What makes you think you can help us?" is
countered with, "At this point, I'm not sure, but I hope I'll be
able to find out soon, so we'll all feel better." To a couple in bit-
ter, loud argument, he once asked, "Do you folks issue crash helmets?"

Taking issue with a onetime prohibition in psychotherapy,
Alexander advocates self-disclosure by the therapist. Useful for
both its content and process, self-disclosure permits an appropriate identification with people and their experience: "I've had the
problem of not being heard, too, and it makes me pretty frustrated. Can you all see how it might be for him?"

Functional family therapy utilizes structuring skills as a means of teaching families how to relate effectively. For example, *directiveness* is one; it includes giving instructions, prompting persons to speak, and making corrections when necessary. The therapist's *self-confidence* is another. To appear hesitant or unprepared is to cramp the therapy. Leading with confidence inspires confidence in the family and aids their coming to grips with the problems they present. Another of these structuring skills is *clarity*, for it is important that families hear and understand the critical elements of change. Alexander is concerned that therapists who are vague and nonspecific, provide too much information, or are disorganized create obstacles rather than bridges for change.

Methods in Functional Family Therapy

One startling method used in this form of family therapy is deliberate confusion. The functional family therapist's task, Alexander asserts, is to confuse the family members by leading them to question their view of the family and their problem. This confusion, or reattribution, is accomplished through utilizing the style and content in the family case. Its purpose is to foster a new way of considering the family and its dynamics. At the process level, the therapist asks each family member for information, thus affirming that this is a relational issue and that everyone has influence in the system. At the stylistic level, it means asking questions in a nonthreatening and nonjudgmental way. "What happened after that?" is a better question than "Was it then that you stalked out in anger?" At the content level, family members gain information about themselves and their interactions through careful questioning and reinterpretation of what they have been saying and what it might mean.

Alexander believes, however, that the most powerful tool for change in the family is the art of relabeling. By this means a rigid or authoritarian father can be portrayed as an active leader, and disrespectful teenagers can be described as struggling with their issues of autonomy. Relabeling, he believes, has a way of rebalancing behavior and revising family reactions to one another.

Alexander cogently notes that relabeling in itself has some fragil-
ity, as people will not maintain attributions that are unsupported
by data from their own environment. Functional family therapists must make sure that family members can maintain their
more benign alternative attributions through sustained behavioral
change, or else the game is lost.

In any event, what works for one case may not in another. The
therapist will need a range of interventions. In this school of therapy, the single most important skill for the therapist to develop is
being able to view behavior in its context. The most important
question is, "What is the result of these family interactions from
a relational standpoint?" In other words, what was their function
within the family? These questions can lead to insights into issues
that a family cannot or will not express.

An Alexandrian example is the family in which a mother
squabbles with her daughter, resulting in hysteria, leading to the
father being pulled out of his workshop into the role of disciplinarian. The function of that argument has been to force a distancing father into contact. This is but one of many reminders
Alexander uses to emphasize that therapists must look beyond
the apparent problem and focus on all the relationships, in order
to ascertain what is happening. It is the function of behavior,
rather than the motives people verbalize, that offers the key.

The example of the squabbling family has what Alexander has
dubbed a payoff. The squabble and its attendant aftermath paid
off in forcing the father into unwanted contact, at least briefly.
The payoff here was of the contact-closeness variety. There is one
other such category: the distance-independence state. Such behaviors are not to be ascribed to sickness, to faulty learning, or to
immorality. Rather they represent the rules families use to meet
their interpersonal functions (their payoffs).

Assessment Procedures

In treatment of troubled families, the functional family therapist assesses the payoffs, then moves on to some decision about
what has to change in their interrelationships.

Sometimes that assessment involves open discussion of the implications for the family if the symptoms were removed. Would the marriage be able to stand the shock if the husband were to get well? Could a mother adjust to the change if her truant son were to return to school? This way the therapist forces the family to deal directly with the symptom. Sometimes this technique takes the wily form of warning the family that they may not be able to handle the consequences if their problem is solved.

Techniques in Family Therapy

Contingency contracting, a technique functional family therapy shares with behavior therapy in general, is the process of striking a bargain in which both sides gain something that they want. The provisos of a good contingency contract include:
- It must be reasonable and realistic
- It must be open to change, if necessary
- It must be capable of being monitored.

Contingency contracting is more effective when a problem is specific, when the problem is stressful enough for persons to take hold at once, and when there is a *quid pro quo* arrangement that appears valuable enough to the participants. A common contractual arrangement between mother and child is one in which the child agrees to keep her room tidy and the mother permits a later bedtime and longer television privilege. Therapists can work through a few such contracts, but after a while, families can learn to make their own alone.

Tasks assigned by the therapist play a valuable part in functional therapy. A task can be designed that:
- Gives an immediate sense of relief
- Offers mutual payoffs to family members
- Can be understood well enough for all members of the family to explain it before they leave the interview
- Is simple enough to insure success
- Can be followed and credited by the therapist when completed.

A typical task assignment is the directive to practice a communication exercise at home during the week and report back at the
following session. Homework will encompass a number of varieties; it will be advantageous to assign some in the very first session. Alexander meets again with a family some three or four days
after the first session, to keep track of their interaction. It is unwise, he is certain, to allow them to settle into a homeostatic condition of unhappiness. Because the second session comes soon, a
short and simple homework assignment is given, not only so it
can be accomplished, but also to remind the family that there is a
plan and an orderly procedure to this therapy. They may be asked
to write down certain ideas, count certain behaviors (arguments,
late arrivals, dishes well done without a reminder). The initial
homework assignment is a simple demonstration that there are
new ways that they can relate to one another.

Education works as an effective intervention in the middle
stages of therapy. The therapist locates areas of ignorance, maladaptive habits, or skill deficits, and then suggests to the family
members that they can do something constructive about these.
Such educational ventures augment and strengthen the therapy.
Both therapy and education, after all, have change as their primary objective.

It would be odd if a family did not resist these interventions of
relabeling, directives, assignments, contracts, et al. Resistance can
be expected when the therapist begins to help one member of the
family change without providing for reciprocal adjustments in the
others, to maintain their own functions. But functional therapists
are ready with responses for resistance. Maintaining their nonblaming attitude and without defensiveness or impatience, they
can use such responses as "Sam, what is the effect on you when
Nell expresses such hopelessness as she is doing just now?" Even
better is Alexander's formula: "No, you're right. Just as your son
has never been a father, you've never been a mother, and so on.
None of us has ever really experienced what the other has, and
that's why we're working so hard to help each other understand."[2]

When it comes to the close of a session, Alexander and his co-horts believe each person should be able to leave with feelings such as these:

• The therapist sided with me as much as with the others.

• The therapist helped me see how my behavior relates to everyone else's behavior.

• I feel that if we continue with the program I will be safer, happier, and better able to get what I want.

• The therapist made it clear to me that I am not to blame. Even though I contributed to the problem, I am as much a victim as anyone else.

• The therapist helped me see how everyone else is also a victim and a participant. I now see the rest of my family in a different light.

• The therapist helped me to see that our problem isn't what I thought it was. I now see that our problem resulted from not knowing how to resolve differences.[3]

Functional Family Theory

We have seen how functional family therapy is applied. We now turn to some underlying principles on which this therapy is based.

Functional family theory is a synthesis of behavioral, interpersonal, and systemic orientations. Proponents aver that this therapy is more than a juxtaposition of such approaches brought together in an arbitrary, eclectic selection. They believe the integration of these various models will generate new theoretical and clinical methods.

In functional family theory, processes are seen to occur in circular and reciprocal fashion. It is the occurrence of a relational context that creates the meaning of behavior, rather than any individual focus. The assumption here is that behavior is relevant only as it is related to other behavior in an interpersonal situation. The nuclear family, naturally enough, is the finest context for evaluating phenomena in interpersonal behavior. Behaviorists have researched this area for some time, have found significant regularities in family processes, and have observed that these processes distinguish certain types of families. They have confirmed that people do not have to be able to articulate a general rule, or appreciate the complexity of their behavior, in order to attain functional outcomes. Indeed families, without understanding why or how they produce them, can alter functional behaviors.

Alexander proves to be no admirer of Christian ethics. As he sees it, timeworn traditional theories and models in psychology draw upon both Judeo-Christian theologies and Western culture, because they insist that individuals are largely responsible for their own behavior. To him, this is unrealistic. The result of this combination of religion, culture, and psychology has been a one-on-one treatment in psychotherapy, individual labeling and diagnoses, and "talking cures." Such forms of therapy moralistically have branded acts and persons as "good" or "bad."

By contrast, the meaning of behavior for the functional family therapist is derived from appreciation and examination of relational contexts. Behavior is not seen to be inherently good or bad, or even normal or sick, in functional theory. Acts of individuals are seen as meaningless in themselves, according to this amoral and iconoclastic philosophy.

A Pastoral View of Functional Family Therapy

James Alexander gives us pause when we read his iconoclastic resumé of Judeo-Christian ethics. His critique of individual responsibility for personal conduct is so closely tied to his attack on one-to-one psychotherapy that this appears to be the major reason for his stand against theological ethics. To him, such an ethical system has been too easily used to justify conventional psychoanalytic approaches in treatment.

This, however, is a divisible question. It is altogether feasible to understand that an individual can have responsibility for his own personal conduct and also be involved as part of a systemic influence upon human behavior. Christian theologians have long held that we are called to account for our personal choices, even while gathered up into the wider phenomenon of original sin, a condition William Temple once described as being "born into an infected world."

Similarly, the question is divisible in another way: It is altogether feasible to hold in tension both this theological conviction about individual and corporate guilt with a treatment modality that grows out of systems theory. As a matter of fact, pastoral therapists would not find it unusual to counsel with a church member who suffers from a sense of deep personal guilt and still do their greater part of that counseling within the family system. These two elements dovetail handily in family therapy.

But a defense of moral theology in the face of Alexander's critique ought not to blind us to a certain validity inherent in his charge of a central moralistic bent in our tradition. Although moralistic tenets are more the outgrowth of idiosyncratic applications, and often in violation of sound doctrine, none can deny that moralisms have been liberally slathered upon the faithful by homileticians, confessors, and old scolds. The awful truth is that we can be frightfully judgmental of the acts of others and should not dismiss too handily Alexander's accusation. Judgmentalism makes for bad theology and bad therapy.

Techniques in Family Therapy

From the stock of techniques Alexander advocates and uses in functional family therapy, three appear particularly suited to pastoral use. The first of these is bargaining, that *quid pro quo* deal that allows family members to gain something of value from each other in a no-lose agreement. Such contingency contracting can appeal to: competitive adults insistent on getting all that is coming to them; adolescents in their developmental ambivalence about autonomy versus receiving their fair share; children whose dependency needs impel them to seek justice for themselves in a world wherein everyone else is bigger. These contractual arrangements can work neatly between wife and husband or between child and parent, to the end that all profit from the arrangement, a new peace is brought into the relationship, and an interpersonal skill has been learned. It is not to be supposed that *quid pro quo* contracts actually overcome systemic disease, but they do make a difference.

Another technique, quite compatible with contracting, is education for change. The pastoral counselor, like functional family therapists, can use instruction to aid persons in their adjustments. Not only does this didactic approach enable persons to obtain previously unknown data and thereby find some consolation (like the mother who learns that other two-year-olds are also rebellious), but it gives an inferential permission to feel normal and to reorganize one's ways with fresh knowledge. Because teaching comes naturally with the skills of ministry, it is one intervention that clergy can easily combine with other interventions.

A third technique, simple to design yet powerful in effect, is the assignment of homework tasks within pastoral family therapy. Such tasks deliver what Alexander labels as a payoff. An assignment to a nitpicking father that helps him turn even one act a day from negativism to a positive relationship with his scapegoated daughter will accomplish not only relief in that particular, but a rippling effect into other interactions, as well.

It is in this construct called payoffs that functional family therapy makes its unusual contribution to pastoral counseling. As we learn to ask what function is served by a certain behavior or transaction within the home, we grow in our skill of assessment and begin to assemble appropriate interventions. It is far better for us to inquire what function is served by behaviors than to phrase a query that begins with the bald question, "Why?" Why questions place people on the defensive and send them down a less helpful path, looking for motivation instead of function. We do come to understand behaviors better when we study their end result and consider, without personal prejudice, what payoffs people are seeking when they choose to conduct their social transactions as they do.

In all this and more, Alexander leaves us with the conviction that we can make use of ourselves and our therapeutic skills to help our people with their family relationships. A saving grace in all this is his warm, serious appeal to humor as a therapeutic device of merit. Perhaps we can also face a squabbling pair engrossed in their mutual anger and blithely ask, as he did, "Do you folks issue crash helmets?"

Postscript

Because the clergy traditionally serve as society's primary counselors, the court of first resort for countless persons under stress, they have to be ever ready with resourcefulness for the cure of souls. Because today's personal relationships can become so convoluted, and marriage and family living so complex, the pastor, the priest, and the rabbi are obligated to be better prepared for this counseling ministry than ever before. Because more is expected from the clergy (being theologians) than straight social casework, when they meet with the troubled, they must also know where to link their pastoral care and counseling with spiritual direction.

Far from alone in serving pained and wounded persons, the clergy constitute one of the numerous helping professions. From colleagues in psychotherapy, and particularly specialists in family therapy, our spiritual leaders have learned much and have much yet to learn. Drawing upon such therapeutic experience, all ministers might well appropriate such lessons and methods as can be derived from theory and incorporated into pastoral care. As they adapt those techniques from family therapy that work for them, integrate them, and make them part of how they use themselves, clergy grow in self-understanding and in service to God and humankind. For this purpose they were called into their vocation.

Notes

Introduction
1. Gerald Gurin, Joseph Veroff, and Sheila Feld, *Americans View Their Mental Health* (New York: Basic Books, 1960), 307.
2. Roy W. Fairchild and J. C. Wynn, *Families in the Church: A Protestant Survey* (New York: Association Press, 1961), 181.
3. Richard Kulka, Joseph Veroff, and Elizabeth Donvan, "Social Class and the Use of Professional Help for Personal Problems," *Journal of Health and Social Behavior* 20 (March, 1979), 48.
4. Group for the Advancement of Psychiatry, *Treatment of Families in Conflict* (New York: Jason Aronson, Science House, 1970), 3.
5. Henri Nouwen, *Creative Ministry* (New York: Doubleday & Co., 1971), 65.
6. Charles Stewart, *The Minister as Family Counselor* (Nashville: Abingdon Press, 1979), 84.
7. J. C. Wynn, *Family Therapy in Pastoral Ministry* (New York: Harper & Row, 1982).

Chapter 1
1. Lynn Hoffman, *Foundations of Family Therapy: A Conceptual Framework for Systems Change* (New York: Basic Books, 1981), 221.
2. Donald A. Bloch, "Foreword," ibid., iv.
3. Virginia Satir, "Conjoint Family Therapy," *The Psychotherapies of Marital Disharmony*, ed. Bernard L. Greene (New York: Macmillan Publishing Co., Free Press, 1965), 121.
4. Ibid., 132.

5. Ibid., 129.
6. Virginia M. Satir, *Conjoint Family Therapy* (Palo Alto: Science & Behavior Books, 1964), chapter 12.
7. Virginia Satir, *Peoplemaking* (Palo Alto: Science & Behavior Books, 1972), 87.
8. Ibid., 75.
9. Satir, *Conjoint Family Therapy*, 117.

Chapter 2
1. Carl Whitaker, "We Became Family Therapists," *The Book of Family Therapy*, ed. Andrew Ferber, Marilyn Mendelsohn, and Augustus Napier (New York: Jason Aronson, Science House, 1972), 98.
2. Augustus Y. Napier and Carl A. Whitaker, *The Family Crucible* (New York: Harper & Row, 1978), 79.
3. Carl Whitaker, "A Family Is a Four Dimensional Relationship," and "The Hindrance of Theory in Clinical Work," in *Family Therapy: Theory and Practice*, ed. Philip J. Guerin (New York: Gardner Press, 1976), 183.
4. Ibid., 186.
5. Milton M. Berger, ed., *Beyond the Double Bind* (New York: Brunner, Mazel, 1978), 241.
6. Whitaker, "A Family Is a Four Dimensional Relationship," 162.
7. Augustus Napier and Carl Whitaker, "Problems of the Beginning Therapist," in *Techniques of Family Therapy: A Primer*, ed. Donald A. Bloch (Orlando: Academic Press, Grune & Stratton, 1973), 109.

Chapter 3
1. Ronald F. Levant, *Family Therapy: A Comprehensive Overview* (Englewood Cliffs, N.J.: Prentice-Hall, 1984), 180.
2. Carl R. Rogers, *On Becoming a Person: A Therapist's View of Psychotherapy* (New York: Houghton Mifflin Co., 1961), 16 *passim*.
3. Carl R. Rogers, *Client-Centered Therapy* (New York: Houghton Mifflin Co., 1951), 223.

4. Carl R. Rogers, *On Becoming a Person* (Boston: Houghton Mifflin Co., 1961), 51.

5. Howard Clinebell, *Basic Types of Pastoral Counseling* (Nashville: Abingdon Press, 1966), 275.

Chapter 4

1. Ross V. Speck and Carolyn Attneave, *Family Networks* (New York: Pantheon Books, 1973), 16.

2. Ibid., 13.

3. Ibid., 44.

4. Ibid., 6.

5. Ibid., xxii.

6. Carolyn Attneave, "Social Networks as a Unit of Intervention," in *Family Therapy: Theory and Practice*, ed. Philip J. Guerin (New York: Gardner Press, 1976), 228.

Chapter 5

1. Andrew Ferber, Marilyn Mendelsohn, and Augustus Napier, *The Book of Family Therapy* (New York: Jason Aronson, Science House, 1972), 32.

2. Jay Haley, *Problem-Solving Therapy* (San Francisco: Jossey-Bass, 1976), 72–73.

3. *See* Jay Haley, *Changing Families* (New York: Grune & Stratton 1977), 65–68.

4. Ibid., 66.

5. Vincent D. Foley, *An Introduction to Family Therapy* (Orlando: Academic Press, Grune & Stratton, 1974), 86.

6. Jay Haley, "Family Therapy," in *Progress in Group and Family Therapy*, ed. Clifford Sager and Helen S. Kaplan (Orlando: Academic Press, Grune & Stratton, 1972), 261–270.

7. Haley, *Problem-Solving Therapy*, 129.

8. Ibid., 112–113.

9. Philip J. Guerin, ed., *Family Therapy: Theory and Practice* (New York: Gardner Press, 1976), 417.

10. Jay Haley, *Strategies of Psychotherapy* (Orlando: Academic Press, Grune & Stratton, 1963), 144.

11. Haley, "Family Therapy," 261.

Chapter 6

1. Janet Malcolm, "A Reporter at Large: Behind the One-Way Mirror," *The New Yorker*, May 15, 1978.
2. Salvador Minuchin and H. Charles Fishman, *Family Therapy Techniques* (Cambridge, Mass.: Harvard University Press, 1981), 2.
3. Ibid., 29.
4. Malcolm, "A Reporter at Large."
5. Minuchin and Fishman, *Family Therapy Techniques*, 148.
6. Ibid., 166.
7. Ibid., 71.
8. Salvador Minuchin, *Families and Family Therapy* (Cambridge, Mass.: Harvard University Press, 1974), 121.
9. Minuchin and Fishman, *Family Therapy Techniques*, 1–2, 289.

Chapter 7

1. M. Duncan Stanton, "Strategic Approaches to Family Therapy," in *Handbook of Family Therapy*, ed. Alan S. Gurman and David P. Kniskern (New York: Brunner, Mazel, 1981), 370.
2. Gerald H. Zuk, *Family Therapy: A Triadic Based Approach*, rev. ed. (New York: Human Sciences Press, 1981), 81.
3. Gerald H. Zuk, "A Further Study of Laughter in Family Therapy," *Family Process* 3 (1964): 77–89.
4. Zuk, *Family Therapy*, 16.
5. Gerald H. Zuk, *Process and Practice in Family Therapy*, 2nd ed. (New York: Human Sciences Press, 1985), 15.
6. *See* Charles P. Barnard, "Family Therapy as a Theory of Roles and Values," in *Handbook of Family and Marital Therapy*, ed. Benjamin B. Wolman and George Stricker (New York: Plenum Publishing Corp., 1983), 213–230.

Chapter 8

1. Richard Fisch, Paul Watzlawick, John H. Weakland, and Arthur M. Bodin, "On Becoming Family Therapists," in *The Book of Family Therapy*, ed. Andrew Ferber, Marilyn Mendelsohn, and Augustus Napier (New York: Jason Aronson, Science House, 1972), 32.

2. Ibid., 133.
3. Arthur M. Bodin, "The Interactional View: Family Therapy Approaches of the Mental Research Institute," in *Handbook of Family Therapy*, ed. Alan S. Gurman and David P. Kniskern (New York: Brunner, Mazel, 1981), 297.
4. Ibid., 298.
5. Lynn Hoffman, *Foundations of Family Therapy: A Conceptual Framework for Systems Change* (New York: Basic Books, 1981), 203.
6. Ronald F. Levant, *Family Therapy: A Comprehensive View* (Englewood Cliffs, N. J.: Prentice-Hall, 1984), 135.
7. *See* Paul Watzlawick, John Weakland, and Richard Fisch, *Change: Principles, Problem Formation and Problem Resolution* (New York: W. W. Norton and Co., 1974), 87.
8. Hoffman, *Foundations of Family Therapy*, 199.
9. Ibid., 200.
10. Gregory Bateson, Don D. Jackson, Jay Haley, and John Weakland, "Toward a Theory of Schizophrenia," *Beyond the Double Bind*, ed. Milton M. Berger (New York: Brunner, Mazel, 1978).
11. Barbara Okun and Louis J. Rappaport, *Working With Families: An Introduction to Family Therapy* (North Scituate, Mass.: Duxbury Press, 1980), 42.
12. *See* J. C. Wynn, *Family Therapy in Pastoral Ministry* (New York: Harper & Row, 1982), 127.

Chapter 9
1. Bunny S. Duhl and Frederick J. Duhl, "Integrative Family Therapy," in *The Handbook of Family Therapy*, ed. Alan Gurman and David P. Kniskern (New York: Brunner, Mazel, 1981), 497.
2. Ibid.
3. Ibid., 506.
4. Ibid.
5. Ibid., 495.

Chapter 10
1. Murray Bowen, *Family Therapy in Clinical Practice* (New York: Jason Aronson, 1978), 545.

2. Murray Bowen, "Theory in the Practice of Psychotherapy" and "The Family's Reaction to Death," in *Family Therapy: Theory and Practice*, ed. Philip J. Guerin (New York: Gardner Press, 1976), 65.

3. Ibid., 77.

4. *See* Murray Bowen, *Family Therapy in Clinical Practice* (New York: Jason Aronson, 1978), chapter 21.

Chapter 11

1. James L. Framo, *Explorations in Marital and Family Therapy: Selected Papers of James L. Framo, Ph.D.* (New York: Springer Pub. Co., 1982), 167.

2. Ibid., 179.

3. James L. Framo, "The Integration of Marital Therapy With Sessions With Family of Origin," in *Handbook of Family Therapy*, ed. Alan S. Gurman and David P. Kniskern (New York: Brunner, Mazel, 1981), 145.

4. *See* James L. Framo, "Symptoms From a Family Transactional Viewpoint," in *Progress in Group and Family Therapy*, ed. Clifford Sager and Helen S. Kaplan (New York: Brunner, Mazel, 1972), 271.

5. James L. Framo, ed., *Interaction: A Dialog Between Family Researchers and Family Therapists* (Los Angeles: Singer Press, 1972), 280.

6. Framo, "Symptoms From a Family Transactional Viewpoint," 289.

7. *See* Richard B. Wilke, *The Pastor and Marriage Group Counseling* (Nashville: Abingdon Press, 1974), 53–71

Chapter 12

1. Ben Ard, "Interview With Boszormenyi-Nagy," *Family Therapy News*, March-April, 1984.

2. Ibid.

3. Ivan Boszormenyi-Nagy and David N. Ulrich, "Contextual Family Therapy," in *Handbook of Family Therapy*, ed. Alan S. Gurman and David P. Kniskern (New York: Brunner, Mazel, 1981), 167.

4. *See* David Cooper, *The Death of the Family* (New York: Pantheon Books, 1971).

Chapter 13

1. Norman L. Paul and B. B. Paul, *A Marital Puzzle: Transactional Analysis in Marriage Counseling* (New York: W. W. Norton and Co., 1975), 22.
2. Ibid., 14.
3. A. C. Robin Skynner, *Systems of Family and Marital Psychotherapy* (New York: Brunner, Mazel, 1976), 162.
4. John Macquarrie, *In Search of Humanity: A Theological and Philosophical Approach* (New York: Crossroad Pub. Co., 1983), 242.

Chapter 14

1. Vincent Foley, *Introduction to Family Therapy* (Orlando: Academic Press, Grune & Stratton, 1974), 57.
2. Philip J. Guerin, ed., *Family Therapy: Theory and Practice* (New York: Gardner Press, 1976), 74.
3. Charles Kramer, *Becoming a Family Therapist* (New York: Human Sciences Press, 1980), 43.
4. Nathan Ackerman, *The Psychodynamics of Family Life* (New York: Basic Books, 1958), 36.
5. Ibid., 15.
6. Nathan W. Ackerman, *Treating the Troubled Family* (New York: Basic Books, 1966), viii.

Chapter 15

1. John E. Bell, *Family Therapy* (New York: Jason Aronson, 1975), 103ff.
2. Andrew Ferber, Marilyn Mendelsohn, and Augustus Napier, *The Book of Family Therapy* (New York: Jason Aronson, Science House, 1972), 181.
3. Ibid., 182.
4. Bell, *Family Therapy*, 126.
5. Ibid., 123.
6. Ibid., 144.
7. Ibid., 125.
8. John E. Bell, "A Theoretical Framework for Family Group Therapy," in *Family Therapy: Theory and Practice*, ed. Philip J. Guerin (New York: Gardner Press, 1976), 141.

9. Bell, *Family Therapy*, 196–197.
10. Ibid., 191, 194.
11. Ibid., 229.
12. Ibid., vi.

Chapter 16
1. Lyman C. Wynne, "Some Indications and Contraindications for Exploratory Family Therapy," in *Intensive Family Therapy: Theoretical and Practical Aspects*, ed. Ivan Boszormenyi-Nagy and James Framo (New York: Harper & Row, 1965), 294.
2. Lyman C. Wynne, "What Family Therapists Do," in *The Book of Family Therapy*, ed. Andrew Ferber, Marilyn Mendelsohn, and Augustus Napier (New York: Jason Aronson, Science Books, 1972), 221.
3. Ibid., 311.
4. Ibid., 295–296.
5. Wynne, "Some Indications and Contraindications," 294.

Chapter 17
1. Charles H. Kramer, *Becoming a Family Therapist* (New York: Human Sciences Press, 1980), 176.
2. Ibid., 251.
3. Ibid., 91.
4. *See* Alan S. Gurman and David P. Kniskern, "Research on Marital and Family Therapy: Progress, Perspective and Prospect," in *Handbook of Psychotherapy and Behavioral Change: An Empirical Analysis*, ed. S. L. Garfield and A. E. Bergin (New York: John Wiley and Sons, 1978), 742.
5. Kramer, *Becoming a Family Therapist*, 21.

Chapter 18
1. James Woefel, "Listening to B. F. Skinner," *Christian Century*, November 30, 1977.
2. Gerald R. Patterson, *Families: Applications of Social Learning to Family Life* (Champaign, Ill.: Research Press Co., 1971), 61.
3. David Knox, *Marriage Happiness: A Behavioral Approach to Counseling* (Champaign, Ill.: Research Press Co, 1972), 25.

4. Robert Liberman, "Behavioral Approaches to Family and Couple Therapy," in *Family Therapy: An Introduction to Theory and Technique,* ed. Gerald D. Erickson and Terrence P. Hogan (Monterey, Calif.: Brooks/Cole Pub. Co., 1972), 123.

5. Gregory Bateson, Don D. Jackson, Jay Haley, and John Weakland, "Toward a Theory of Schizophrenia," in *Beyond the Double Bind,* ed. Milton M. Berger (New York: Brunner, Mazel, 1978), 20.

6. Charles H. Kramer, *Becoming a Family Therapist* (New York: Human Sciences Press, 1980), 143.

Chapter 19

1. Richard B. Stuart, *Helping Couples Change: A Social Learning Approach to Marital Therapy* (New York: Guilford Press, 1980), xii.

2. Ibid., 193.

3. Ibid.

4. Ibid., 207.

5. Ibid., 43.

6. Ibid., 68–69.

7. Ibid., 214.

Chapter 20

1. Helen S. Kaplan, *The New Sex Therapy* (New York: Brunner, Mazel, 1974), 305.

2. Virginia Adams, "Sex Therapies in Perspective," *Psychology Today,* August, 1980.

Chapter 21

1. Cole Barton and James F. Alexander, "Functional Family Therapy," in *The Handbook of Family Therapy,* ed. Alan S. Gurman and David P. Kniskern (New York: Brunner, Mazel, 1981), 418.

2. James Alexander and Bruce V. Parsons, *Functional Family Therapy* (Monterey, Calif.: Brooks/Cole Pub. Co., 1982), 63.

3. Ibid., 49.

Recommended Reading

These titles, not included in the Notes, are listed for those who seek additional references.

John E. Bell. *The Family in the Hospital: Lessons From Developing Countries.* Bethesda, Md.: National Institutes of Health, 1969.

Milton M. Berger. *Beyond the Double Bind.* New York: Brunner, Mazel, 1978.

Donald Bloch and Robert Simon, eds. *The Strength of Family Therapy: Selected Papers of Nathan W. Ackerman.* New York: Brunner, Mazel, 1982.

Ivan Boszormenyi-Nagy and James L. Framo. *Intensive Family Therapy.* New York: Hoeber Medical Division, Harper & Row, 1965.

Ivan Boszormenyi-Nagy and Geraldine Spark. *Invisible Loyalties: Reciprocity in Intergenerational Family Therapy.* New York: Harper & Row, 1973.

David Cooper. *The Death of the Family.* New York: Pantheon Books, 1971.

Bunny S. Duhl. *From the Inside Out and Other Metaphors.* New York: Brunner, Mazel, 1983.

Gerald D. Erickson and Terrence P. Hogan, eds. *Family Therapy: An Introduction to Theory and Technique.* Monterey, Calif.: Brooks, Cole, 1981.

Richard Fisch, John Weakland, and Lynn Segal. *The Tactics of Change: Doing Therapy Briefly.* San Francisco: Jossey-Bass, 1982.

Jay Haley. *Leaving Home: The Therapy of Disturbed Young People.* New York: McGraw-Hill, 1980.

Jay Haley, *Uncommon Therapy.* New York: W. W. Norton, 1973.

Helen S. Kaplan. *Disorders of Sexual Desire.* New York: Simon & Schuster, 1979.

Helen S. Kaplan. *The Illustrated Manual of Sex Therapy.* New York: Quadrangle, New York Times, 1975.

Charles Kramer. *Becoming a Family Therapist.* New York: Human Sciences Press, 1980.

Jeanette R. Kramer. *Family Interfaces: Transgenerational Patterns.* New York: Brunner, Mazel, 1985.

Jerry M. Lewis. *To Be a Therapist: The Teaching and Learning.* New York: Brunner, Mazel, 1978.

David Mace and Vera Mace. *Marriage Enrichment in the Church.* Nashville: Broadman Press, 1968.

Cloé Madanes. *Behind the One-Way Mirror.* San Francisco: Jossey-Bass, 1984.

Cloé Madanes. *Strategic Family Therapy.* San Francisco: Jossey-Bass, 1981.

William W. Masters and Virginia Johnson. *Human Sexual Inadequacy.* Boston: Little, Brown & Co., 1970.

Salvador Minuchin, et al. *Families of the Slums.* New York: Basic Books, 1967.

Salvador Minuchin. *Kaleidescope.* Cambridge, Mass.: Harvard University Press, 1984.

Michael Nichols. *Family Therapy: Concepts and Methods.* New York: Gardner Press, 1984.

David Roberts. *Psychotherapy and a Christian View of Man.* Philadelphia: Westminster Press, 1950.

Carl R. Rogers. *Carl Rogers on Encounter Groups.* New York: Harper & Row, 1970.

Carl R. Rogers. *On Becoming Partners: Marriage and Its Alternatives.* New York: Delacorte Press, 1972.

Virginia Satir, James Stachowiak, and Harvey Taschman. *Helping Families to Change.* Northvale, N. J.: Jason Aronson, Inc., 1975.

B. F. Skinner. *Beyond Freedom and Dignity.* New York: Alfred A. Knopf, 1971.

B. F. Skinner. *Particulars of My Life.* New York: Macmillan, 1978.

B. F. Skinner. *Walden Two.* New York: Macmillan, 1948.

Robert F. Stahmann and William J. Hiebert, eds. *Counseling in Marital and Sexual Problems.* 3rd ed. Lexington, Mass.: D. C. Heath & Co., 1984.

Richard B. Stuart. *Remarriage: Deciding to Do It and Making It Last.* New York: W. W. Norton, 1982.

Helmut Thielicke. *The Ethics of Sex.* New York: Harper & Row, 1964.

Paul Watzlawick and John Weakland. *The Interactional View.* New York: W. W. Norton, 1974.

L. H. Wolberg and M. L. Aronson, eds. *Group and Family Therapy.* New York: Brunner, Mazel, 1981.

Lyman C. Wynne. *Disturbed Families: A Psychiatrist Closely Examines the Families of Schizophrenics.* Philadelphia: SmithKline, 1979.

Lyman C. Wynne, Timothy Weber, and Susan McDaniel, eds. *System Consultation: A New Perspective for Family Therapy.* New York: Guilford Press, 1986.

Gerald H. Zuk and Ivan Boszormenyi-Nagy, eds. *Family Therapy and Disturbed Families.* Palo Alto, Calif.: Science & Behavior Books.

Index